THE GRAPHIC DESIGNER'S
GUIDE TO CLIENTS

HOW TO MAKE CLIENTS HAPPY AND DO GREAT WORK

ELLEN SHAPIRO

ALLWORTH PRESS
NEW YORK

Do you have a good "clients and designers" story? Or a
comment about this book? Ellen Shapiro invites your comments:
ellen@visualanguage.net.

07 06 05 04 03   5 4 3 2 1

Published by Allworth Press
An imprint of Allworth Communications, Inc.
10 East 23rd Street, New York, NY 10010

Copublished with the Graphic Artists Guild

Cover design by James Victore Inc.
Interior page design by Derek Bacchus

Page composition/typography by Susan Ramundo

Library of Congress Cataloging-in-Publication Data
Shapiro, Ellen
    The graphic designer's guide to clients : how to make clients
happy and do great work / Ellen Shapiro.
        p.   cm.
    ISBN 1-58115-276-0
    1. Commercial art—United States—Marketing.   2. Design
services—United States—Marketing.   I. Title.
    NC1001.6.S48   2003
    745.4'068'8—dc21   2003008986

Printed in Canada

This book is dedicated

my students: former, present,

and future. May you continue

to prove — as the designers

included in this book have

done — that making clients

happy and doing great

work are not mutually

exclusive activities.

CONTENTS

PART I

WHAT I'VE LEARNED ABOUT CLIENTS

PART II

CORPORATE CLIENTS

PART III

RETAIL AND ENTERTAINMENT CLIENTS

PART IV

INSTITUTIONAL CLIENTS

ACKNOWLEDGMENTS

MY THANKS TO

Tad Crawford of Allworth Press for his vision
and professionalism.

James Victore for his great cover design and
Derek Bacchus for designing the book so beautifully.

Communication Arts editor and publisher Patrick
Coyne and managing editor Anne Telford for their
continuing support.

My assistant, Andrea Baerenwald, for transcribing,
word processing, scanning, and everything else.

The designers all around the country who, by
graciously allowing me to interview them and their
clients, made this book possible.

PREFACE

For more than a decade I've been talking to the clients
and designers who've been responsible for some
of the best designed and most effective visual
communications—branding, Web sites, annual reports,
retail environments, books, catalogs, packaging,
product design, posters, ad campaigns.

How do successful business people and creative
professionals find each other, work together, make
decisions, and evaluate the effectiveness of their work?
What are their secrets? How do they resolve conflicts?
How do they do great work that achieves its objectives
and makes everyone happy?

The purpose of this book is to show you how they
do it—and how you can, too.

Author's Note

My first book, *Clients and Designers*, published by
Watson-Guptill in 1990, led to a long-term assignment
from *Communication Arts* magazine: two "Clients
and Designers" pieces each year. Of the seventeen
interview chapters in this book, eleven appeared in
CA from 1991 to 2000, and were recently updated to
reflect client-company ownership changes and relevant
events. The interviews in chapters 9, 10, and 20
appeared, in a different format, in the *Clients and
Designers* book.

PART **I**

WHAT I'VE LEARNED ABOUT CLIENTS

Financial matters aside, we graphic designers
need clients to give our work purpose and structure.
If we didn't have clients, we wouldn't all be making
fine art. We'd be out and about looking for clients.

1 | THE **CLIENT**—ELUSIVE, DIFFICULT, COVETED

Graphic designers are fairly predictable. We usually want the same things. The opportunity to do good work is at the top of most of our lists.

Yes, there are differences and debates. Over the last decade there have been philosophical rifts about legibility versus memorability; classicism versus New Wave. But graphic designers are usually in agreement on what constitutes great design. We love to admire the latest expressions of creativity, beauty, wit, insight, and technological wizardry. How did the designer do it?

All of us want to do something of that quality and impact, too. Not just for ourselves, or to be admired by our peers.

But for our clients.

A SERVICE BUSINESS

In the last century the art world, as it had functioned since the Middle Ages, was transformed. There are no more patrons who dictate appropriate subject matter and style. The artist now makes art to please him or herself. This paradigm shift has not only changed painting, drawing, sculpture, and photography, it has changed architecture and even cooking. Celebrity chefs have become independent *artistes*. (If you don't like how a dish looks and tastes, choose a different restaurant. Or perhaps something is wrong with you, with your unsophisticated taste buds and lack of appreciation.)

Are graphic designers the last remaining vestiges of the old paradigm? Maybe so. Whatever we produce has to please our patrons, the clients. If it

doesn't, they'll ask us to change it. In the worst cases, they won't pay for it—
and then hire someone else.

Like it or not, we work in a service business.

The purpose of graphic design is not to express our feelings about the world
(which doesn't mean we shouldn't believe in what we're doing). Our work isn't
created for exhibition in museums and galleries. It is used, to give just a few
examples, to "brand" a product or service, to tell the story of a company's year,
to give people a positive experience, to unite them behind a cause, to entertain, to inform, to announce an event, to raise money, to recruit, to sell.

NOT JUST ANY CLIENTS. GREAT CLIENTS

If we didn't have clients, we wouldn't all be painting and sculpting and creating nouvelle cuisine. We'd be out and about looking for clients. With a great
client, the process is a partnership. We don't feel like artists for hire. There is
no servitude. There is joy and excitement in the process. We work hand in
hand with an individual of vision to bring success to his or her organization.

Los Angeles designer April Greiman, whose work often blurs the boundaries between fine art and graphic design, says that she needs clients to give
her projects structure and purpose. "When you work with a visionary," she says
(see chapter 19), "there is always a conceptual collaboration and from that you
grow tremendously." Pentagram partner and 2001 AIGA medallist Paula Scher
also calls her best clients great collaborators. "The best collaborator in my
career has been George C. Wolfe of the Public Theater," she has said. "He
allows me to do fantastic work because he has a vision."

A great client has a vision, a great story, and a great budget. Okay, maybe
not a great budget, but an adequate budget, or at least an understanding of
what it takes to get things done.

WHY AREN'T THEY ALL GREAT CLIENTS?

If all clients were like George C. Wolfe, we would all be doing work as awe-
inspiring as Paula's Public Theater posters. Right?

So what's the matter with the rest of them?

After all, you and I have the talent and the skill to produce work of that
caliber, don't we? The only thing that comes between us and all that great
work, all the awards and recognition, is the client.

At first I was going to say, let's skip the horror stories. But, alas, there are
too few great clients.

There are few great *anythings* in this world. Just look around. Millions more
people shop at Wal-Mart than at that cool boutique you just discovered. Most
companies cater to a least-common-denominator mentality. Their marketing

managers are folks with jobs to do, office politics to worry about, budgets and sales quotas to meet. Groundbreaking design might not be the number-one priority on their agendas, as you've perhaps learned the hard way. One almost-great client said to me, while choosing a safe, plain-vanilla design over two much more interesting options (and, I guess, noticing the look on my face): "Ellen is seeing all her design awards fly out the window." A perceptive guy. He put the tastes of his future investors, or at least what he envisioned they would respond to, first. Some clients have less noble motivations. A few are far from tactful or respectful.

Yes, there have been the legendary Olivettis, IBMs, Container Corporations of America, Knolls, and Herman Millers. There have been the legendary CEOs like Thomas Watson, Jr., of IBM, who were, in fact, patrons of the arts — at least of the "commercial" arts of product design and packaging design, exhibition design, and advertising.

Contemporary design patrons include some of the same august corporations, as well as companies like Nike, Apple, Nickelodeon, and many entrepreneurs, publishers, arts organizations, and, of course, paper companies, who in their quest to induce designers to specify their premium printing papers commission top designers to create pieces that other designers will admire and want to emulate. Sometimes a small business, like a bakery or toy store or garage band, becomes a great client, offering a designer creative freedom and the opportunity to do fun, interesting work.

The number of organizations that are committed to design as an integral part of their corporate mission or culture is slowly increasing, and that's encouraging.

CAN *YOUR* CLIENTS BE GREAT CLIENTS?

Helping you make that happen is the purpose of this book. With the right tools, ranging from suggested questions to ask potential clients to examples provided by some of the most successful design firm principals and their clients — CEOs, managers, and marketers — you can help your clients become, if not great clients, at least clients with whom you can produce successful, satisfying work.

"Knowledge is expanding at an exponential rate," maintains Jon Esser, interim director of the School of Art+Design at Purchase College, State University of New York, where I teach. "There is good reason for designers to be optimistic. Clients are content providers, and content providers are increasingly in need of images, graphics, and text that excite and compel the reader or user. The overwhelming flow of information must be given shape, and designers are content navigation enablers. Another byproduct of the information explosion is the differentiation of markets," he maintains. "Marketing is no longer of the mass-media, one-size-fits-all variety. Custom solutions are sought around narrowly defined parameters. If the old metaphor was 'know your client,' the new one is 'know your client's niche markets.' That means more opportunities for more designers."

"The constant need to win market share will motivate clients to take more risks," he continues. "They will no longer define their needs as, 'Make us look just like our competition.' They are taking a bolder position: 'Make us look better than our competition.' That means more satisfying work for more designers."

More opportunities for more designers. More satisfying work. The potential is there. *If* you take the right approaches to meeting clients, establishing relationships with them, and keeping them happy.

CLIENTS ARE MUCH LESS PREDICTABLE THAN DESIGNERS. OR ARE THEY?

I can pretty much predict that Trixie, our German shepherd dog, will bark when a deer comes into the yard; she'll go ballistic when another dog and owner walk down "her" street; when company comes she'll hide under the coffee table, then emerge to be petted. Our former German shepherd, who had a different temperament, behaved much the same way. A guide to German shepherd dogs could be relatively easy to write.

But a guide to clients? I can't predict what my own clients will do from one day to the next. Much less yours, whom I've never met.

Or can't I? If your clients are of the old-school variety (and that doesn't mean they're old; they could be young and inexperienced), they'll demand an unreasonable amount of work in a ridiculous amount of time, for a fee that's much too low. They'll keep you waiting for half an hour . . . but if you arrive four minutes late, they'll be sitting around the conference table looking at their watches. They'll never have anything organized; won't take enough time to thoroughly explain their needs; will wait weeks before responding to a proposal and then call and say, "We need the job on Friday." When there's a tiny typo, they'll immediately point it out. But when you come up with the perfect solution, they'll barely acknowledge it or try to change it. They'll nit-pick and haggle over every detail but ignore the big picture. They'll insist that you cram enough copy for a well-paced twenty-four pages into half that many and then make you use a photo that ruins the whole thing. No amount of arguing and pleading and rational demonstrations of superior alternatives will cause them to change their minds. Then they'll try to get an agreement that stipulates they will own all the rights in perpetuity.

Okay, maybe I'm exaggerating. But it all goes with the territory of being a client.

After all, they are the ones paying the bills.

THE COMPETITION IS EVER-GROWING

If you don't agree to their requirements, they might take their business somewhere else. (That might not be a bad thing. It will free you up to do work for clients whose requirements you do agree to.) There will always be someone else willing to do the job. Clients' file drawers are filled with promise-filled pitch letters and clever promotional pieces and gifts. There are sites like Elance.com, kind of an eBay for clients in which competitors publicly bid to do the most work for the least money.

Every year, estimates Ed Gold, co-director of the communication design department at the University of Baltimore and author of *The New Business of Graphic Design* (Watson-Guptill, 1995), 10,000 to 12,000 students graduate from the approximately 2,000 design programs in U.S. art schools, community colleges, colleges, and universities. And he's not counting the hundreds of desktop publishing programs that award certificates to many more thousands of people. Every year, new business plans are written and new partnerships and firms are formed. Experienced designers from countries like England, Switzerland, Poland, Argentina, Japan, China, Korea, and Israel continue to emigrate to the United States. Public relations and marketing firms and printing companies "cross-sell" design services to their existing clients. Big agencies add more and more design "boutiques" to their mix of offerings, and they're often willing to lowball graphic design services or even provide free work in order to get or hold on to lucrative advertising and PR accounts.

"Fortunately," says Allen Kay, chairman of the New York ad agency Korey Kay & Partners, "there's no Home Depot for do-it-yourself advertisers." There are, though, plenty of Home Depots for do-it-yourself designers. They're called Kinko's, Staples, CompUSA, MacWarehouse, Paper Direct. Every year, more and more in-house art departments are formed, and more and more potential clients, heeding the claims of software makers, are trying to figure out how to do it themselves.

Our mission is to keep convincing clients to use us. We have the education, the experience, the talent, the insights. We can see things they can't, come up with solutions they could never conceive of, use the power of images and words to make their business dreams come true.

Then why can they be so difficult?

MANY GOOD CLIENTS ARE DIFFICULT, FOR GOOD REASONS

Good clients who are difficult can be the best kind to have. They challenge you to do your finest work. They don't want anything mundane. They don't want an imitation or something they've seen a million times before. They know that in order to sell their products or services they have to have a unique selling proposition, one that is visualized by unique, effective design solutions. They seek out designers who have distinctive voices and who can give voice to their visions.

Martin Zimmerman of LFC Capital offers the most articulate explanation of this that I've ever heard (chapter 9). "Why would I want an imitation of what my competitor already has?" he asks. Zimmerman gives designers creative freedom within the structure of carefully articulated business objectives. "The whole idea is to create a feeling of success and sophistication," he explains. "We want to be known as a creative-type financing source, where people can get new concepts for existing problems. There are lots of problems out there, but there are not too many fresh ideas on how to solve them."

It's much harder to create an original solution that satisfies requirements like Zimmerman's than it is to follow explicit directions, to do a formula design, or to lay out a client's text and pictures.

Sandra Ruch, who for many years was responsible at Mobil Corporation for its brilliant Masterpiece Theater posters, prided herself on being demanding. "I could be very blunt and say, 'This doesn't work,'" she said, describing her working relationship with Ivan Chermayeff and other top designers and illustrators. "There were times when it took us four or five months before we came up with the right image. Four or five months of working it over and over. Ivan went back to the drawing board many times when he didn't come up with something that we all felt equally was what we wanted, and so did Seymour Chwast. There's nothing wrong with that."

When the client is knowledgeable — and fair — the designer rises to the occasion.

BAD CLIENTS ARE DIFFICULT, TOO. HOW TO TELL THE DIFFERENCE

"We do our best work for the clients who understand the most about design," asserts Marcia Lausen, principal of Chicago's Studio/lab. "They are the ones who trust us. We have done good work for difficult clients," she adds, "and those difficulties usually result from misunderstandings about the design process and product, and/or issues of trust. To do good work for difficult clients means an extraordinary investment of time and effort spent on education and confidence-building. These are things that you can't bill for (can you imagine a proposal with these line items?), but they are keenly important."

My personal definition of a bad client is someone who wants a globe.

A few years ago I worked with the marketing director of a Silicon Alley upstart that characterized itself as a company of young, nimble, quick problem solvers. The marketing director told me she had sole responsibility for design decisions (how wrong they often are about this). "These are great," she said upon previewing comps of an identity based on collages of photographic images. My assistant and I had worked hard on them and thought they were pretty cool, too. I don't remember exactly what her boss, the company president, said a few days later when I presented them in his office. But I do remember (a) feeling like I'd been punched in the stomach and (b) suggesting that if he thought the concept was so out of sync with his vision of the company, we should start over and revisit Phase I. "We'll think about it," he said in a tone of voice that meant "You're out" just as clearly as Michael Corleone said it to his father's consigliore, Tom Hagen, in *The Godfather*. Several months later I visited the company Web site. The new solution: a globe. And not even a nice one at that.

A bad client is someone who claims to delegate responsibility, but really doesn't, or then takes it away. Over the years I have seen the authority pulled out from under many, many women (and a few men) inside corporations, law firms, accounting firms, nonprofit organizations. It's a sad commentary on American business. A bad client notices that other companies that are making money have globe logos (or swooshes, or elliptical orbits)—and wants one, too. A bad client bosses designers, as well as his or her underlings, around. A bad client thinks the software does all the work . . . so it should be easy to throw together a dozen more layout options overnight. A bad client's assistants have fonts and scanners and can put stuff together as well as you. Or if not quite as well, for a lot less money. And he or she thinks that it will be good enough.

IT'S EASIER TO SELL GOOD DESIGN TO A COMPANY THAT ALREADY BUYS IT

Early on in this business I met Arthur Michaels, a salesman for one of the top-flight New York printing companies. An erudite, literary type who always wore a suit and bowtie, Arthur was fond of saying, "It's much easier to sell good printing to a company that already buys good printing." Why? His answer: "If they've only bought bad printing they'll never understand the difference or want to pay for good printing." I've thought about that principle a lot over the years.

"Educating the client" is an essential part of our work, but designers bandy the phrase around as if somehow we could teach all the Philistines (and every other heathen tribe) the difference between good design and bad. Once enlightened, they would never buy bad design again. From us. Or from anybody else.

Every person who has ever sold anything knows that not all potential buyers are qualified. When evaluating each potential new business relationship, ask yourself:

- Will this client be a good fit for me and my business?
- What might this engagement lead to? (no idle promises or fantasies, but a realistic assessment)

- Will it provide the opportunity to do work of the highest quality of which I am capable?
- If not, what is its potential value?

Making an unwise choice can set you up for long-term frustration. The same time and effort (or less) that is put into courting and nurturing an unqualified client can be spent establishing a relationship with an organization that in one way or another is, or can be, committed to good design. Ah, you say, the IBMs and Knolls of the world already have designers coming out of their ears. They won't even return my call. My advice is, keep trying. Not necessarily them, but other organizations that, at least in some small way—whether it's a previous project, an ad campaign, the design of their products, the way their Web site works, or the way their offices look—demonstrate that someone there cares at least a little bit about design.

REMEMBER, IT'S SUPPOSED TO BE FUN. AND IT IS.

Sure, we could have chosen to open restaurants or antique shops (and sell stuff made by other people!). We could be leading tours of Macchu Pichu or designing dresses or interiors. Maybe we would make more money and have less angst if we did something else. But we chose graphic design because we love type and images. We love print media and ink on paper as well as electronic media and moving images. We love to change minds and influence people and add joy and interest to the environment. We want people to be better informed, have an easier time finding their way around, and be visually delighted. Why else? There's a whole bunch of reasons, each as individual as every one of us.

Mostly, I cherish the opportunities graphic design gives me to keep learning. I've learned over the years about how bone fractures are healed with electromagnetic signals, how offbeat independent films are distributed; how premium credit cards are marketed, how executive MBA students are recruited, tax-exempt revenue bonds are issued, and maritime law is practiced. I've had the privilege of working with Internet game developers; with development professionals at Israel's leading technology university and at the American Baptist Church; and with psychologists, scientists, financiers, management consultants, and academics. I've gotten to visit (as well as write about and art direct photography at) some of the world's finest hotels and resorts, at medical centers where cancer is cured, and at plants where network computers are manufactured.

I've been able to contribute to the state of the art of visually identifying and marketing my clients' organizations. I've helped motivate kids not to start smoking, and created my own products that use graphic design to help kids learn to read. And I'm not all that special. It's what graphic designers *do*.

Graphic design is more than fun. It's a life's work that can make a difference.

HOW TO **MEET CLIENTS**

Jonas Klein, design manager at IBM for many years, encouraged designers that he didn't know—strangers—to contact him. He advised that they phone first to introduce themselves, then send a package of printed samples. He wanted to see work that was relevant to IBM's business. If the right project came up, he would give the designer a call. "Most of us traditionally answered our own telephones," he said. "And I'm talking about senior executives."

Try doing that today. There is no way to get the phone number of any IBM design manager. Or even an e-mail address. A recorded message explains the "central procurement process for vendors."

CLIENTS ARE PEOPLE WHO KNOW HOW TO MAKE THEMSELVES SCARCE

Voicemail has made telephoning a lost art. I recently received a direct-mail invitation to a $1,200 seminar: "Voicemail Messages that Get Answered." Hmmm. Nothing can feel more humiliating than cold calling and leaving messages. CEOs and managers do not want you to bother them. And even if you get through? It sometimes doesn't work much better. Laura Yamner, who's been responsible for high-profile projects at American Express, Condé Nast Traveler, and Goldman Sachs, is a typical client who hates getting cold calls. "If I talked to everyone who called trying to sell services I would never get any work done," she says.

She has a point. After all, you are someone's target market, too. What would your day be like if you took all those calls from printers and other vendors?

The clients we'd love to have, as we all know, claim that they are happy with their current suppliers, aren't changing firms, aren't reviewing portfolios, aren't taking calls, and don't open unsolicited mail.

IF MEN ARE AT BALL GAMES AND WOMEN ARE IN YOGA CLASSES, WHERE ARE THE CLIENTS?

If they're not answering their phones or opening their mail, how will you find them?

It depends on the state, region, city, and industry. Clients belong to certain organizations, like chambers of commerce, associations of business communicators, societies of public relations professionals. They are listed in industry directories. They attend networking events, trade shows, and conferences (and, of course, some do open mail and pick up the phone; successful sales calls are made every day). Speaking at conferences is a tried-and-true way to market services. It's important to get on the roster of conferences that clients attend, not that designers attend. And to attend such potentially fruitful events as holiday parties at other clients' offices. Especially if they're service firms entertaining their own clients.

Cultural events can be good sources of like-minded clients. The client list of New York design firm Jelly Associates—which includes the Aldrich Museum of Contemporary Art, the Art Directors Club of New York, USA Records, Abrams Publishers, Chronicle Books, HBO, and Swissair—is pretty impressive for two young women who got their MFAs from the School of Visual Arts just three years ago. Partners Amy Unikewicz and Miriam Bossard have perfected the art of networking with fellow class members, faculty, friends, and former employers. Says Bossard, "Museum events and art gallery openings are great places to meet people who are on the same creative wavelength."

Designers meet clients in all kinds of other unexpected places. Not only on the proverbial golf course and tennis court, but at airport lounges (flying first-class does have its advantages, I hear), college reunions, and pancake breakfasts. New York parents have been quoted as saying they choose their children's private schools based on whether the other parents might be good client material (that's who they'll be hanging with at birthday parties and play dates for the next six or seven years).

A stranger sitting next to me on the Metroliner joined my firm's client list last year. He was talking on his cell phone, and the conversation seemed to be about closing a financing deal for a new company. It sounded intriguing, and he probably hadn't hired Pentagram—yet. Well, I thought, I can sit here and keep reading my *Vanity Fair*. Or I can try to turn him into a client. I had two hours and forty-seven minutes. What was there to lose? The worst thing that could happen? He could get up and flee to another seat or car.

"So," I smiled at him, "it sounds like you're in the XYZ business." We chatted for a while. He handed me a card that looked like it was put together at the local copy shop. "That's a great company name," I said. "You could use a great logo to enhance your message." I told him a little bit about my firm. When the train pulled into Penn Station, we shook hands and I gave him my card. A few days later, I sent a letter (a real, typed letter: "It was a pleasure meeting you . . .") with samples of relevant work. A few weeks later I got an e-mail: "How much would you charge for a logo?" (Notice that money, alas, is always the first question.)

I can't say that things would go as well with every stranger on a train. But a big part of being a design firm principal is seizing every chance to cultivate client relationships.

DO THOSE CLEVER SELF-PROMOTIONS WORK?

Last year I was assigned a magazine article on those 3-D holiday promotions designers love to send. You know, elaborately packaged goodies with rice-paper wrappings and raffia bows. I had created a few myself, some of which even got published in magazines and books, and which clients seemed to appreciate. But when it came to getting new work, a more direct approach, like spending a week on the phone calling clients to get referrals—instead of affixing hand-lettered labels to jars of barbecue rub—seemed to be a more effective use of time and resources.

I was ready to write an exposé. I was going to do for handmade designer gifts what Jessica Mitford's *Poison Penmanship* had done for the American funeral industry and for Famous Writers' School. I started calling up designers whose promotions had appeared in design annuals and books like *The Best Seasonal Promotions* (North Light, 1997) to get the lowdown on how these things eat up huge chunks of time and money while enlarging the designer's ego more than the client list.

But, according to the designers I interviewed, boy, was I wrong. "I've gotten calls as much as five years after a promotion was received," reported New York design firm principal Mary Pisarkiewicz, who told me that a client she hadn't heard from in years called to say, "I want to work with you again" after getting a clever holiday gift. Other designers' responses included: "These things keep your name in front of clients"; "They're great showcases for design and production techniques"; "They maintain our client base"; "They have a re-energizing effect on creativity"; "They give you the opportunity to have fun, to create something meaningful"; and "They always pay off."

Not everyone agrees that this approach will work. "They're all lying," claims one of the country's most successful designers. I won't go as far as to concur with him; I'll only say that gifts are a meaningful thank-you for clients you already work with and like. Just don't count on them to bring in new business for you as effectively as they did for Pisarkiewicz. If it happens, it's like getting a bonus.

TARGETED AND TIMELY MIGHT BE EVEN MORE USEFUL

One of the most useful things I've done over the years is keep a database in FileMaker Pro: a database of clients and potential clients, vendors, and colleagues. In addition to being an invaluable way to access contact data, it helps generate specialized marketing letters by industry, by state, by zip code, and by last contact date (why not re-introduce yourself to that company you sent a proposal to two years ago?). It takes effort to keep it current, but that often-backed-up disk is the first thing I'd grab in case of fire (in addition, of course, to my personally autographed Stefan Sagmeister "Made You Look" launch party poster with a picture of a German shepherd dog).

Anyway, instead of bottling edibles and doodads, I'd rather spend my time creating targeted mailings. Several weeks after September 11, 2001, when it still looked like the world might end, I was inspired by Paul McCartney's performance at the Concert for New York City. It was amazing: one of the "all you need is love" Beatles was singing about fighting for the right to live in freedom. People change, circumstances change, I reasoned. I had offered twenty hours of my firm's services, gratis, to those clients who had been displaced by the terrorist acts, but maybe certain other clients needed a gentle kick in the pants. So I created a four-page, 8½ × 11, black-and-white mailer. The cover said simply: "If not now, when?" Inside, the copy read like this:

At The Concert for New York City, Paul McCartney mesmerized and changed the thinking of a few million people with a simple idea: "I will fight for the right to live in freedom."

He wore a T-shirt and played the guitar. He didn't need glittery costumes, flashing lights, and elaborate choreography. In fact, those things would have hindered his message.

All the best communication ideas are like that: simple and human, strong, and powerful.

Since September 11, the media has saturated us with doom-and-gloom messages about the economy. We've become understandably cautious. But think about this: every building outside the Ground Zero site is still standing tall.

Don't let your product, your brand or your organization fall, or falter, in a psychic domino effect. Now is the time to act.

You don't need a big agency, flashing lights, and elaborate production techniques. You do need a strong, smart idea. Get your message out there. Motivate people. Touch their hearts. Take sales to the next level. Keep momentum going for your cause.

Call us. We can help you make it happen.

I illustrated the mailer with six pieces of my strongest work. It took me seven hours to write and design and cost about $750 for duplicating and postage. It generated several good pieces of business and quite a few phone calls and e-mails. I'd like to think that at least a few people will keep it and remember me for strong, simple solutions.

Earlier in my career I had a big success with a mailing to all the public corporations in the New York area that were listed in *Inc.* magazine's "top 100 fastest growing U.S. companies" issue. The brochure's cover read, "Finally, annual reports that make growing companies look like a billion." The inside spread was illustrated with nicely faked covers and spreads of annual reports for fictitious companies. That promotion led to half a dozen meetings and annual reports for three companies on *Inc.*'s list.

WHAT APPROACH BEST DISTINGUISHES YOU?

What industries do you want to target? What, actually, do you want to say (other than, "I do good design")? What will people in your target market respond to?

It might not be the same thing that graphic designers—or judges of design competitions—respond to. Pretend you have three minutes on the *Today* show. Three minutes to make your case to all the people you'd most like to work for. You've been coached by the best image and public-speaking consultants in the business. What, exactly, will you say when Katie Couric asks, "Why should a client hire you and not somebody else?" Build a mailer around that concept. Keep it simple and inexpensive. Then test it with a few members of your target audience. Ask, "How would you respond to this?" and "What could I do to generate a better response?"

And when it's successful, consider not publicizing it in the design magazines. Designers can be a bit too eager to show off their clever ideas to their peers (read: competitors). If you do so, your concept may not be your own any more. Other people may start doing it better than you. My quality-annual-reports-for-small-companies idea (in those days everyone went after Mobil, Philip Morris, and United Technologies) was overtaken by powerful competitors pretty quickly. (But at least we've come a long way in another respect: oil companies, cigarette makers, and munitions and defense companies aren't quite so popular among designers any more.)

DO THOSE STORIES IN THE PRESS REALLY WORK?

You open a design magazine, and there's an eight-page color feature about you and your work. It's one of life's peak moments. For a few weeks you'll get congratulatory calls and e-mails from colleagues and friends, and lots of résumés. You hope that the article will also bring inquiries from potential new clients. Maybe. But don't count on it. "I'm delighted to have been profiled in *CA*," says Richard Poulin, partner in New York's Poulin + Morris. "But our clients— architects and real estate developers—don't read graphic design magazines."

Few clients do. What do they read? Industry and business magazines, the newspapers. Publications which—unless you've designed something revolutionary that changes people's lives—are much less likely to run a story about design. The "Form and Function" column in the *Wall Street Journal*, for example, will report on design of bicycles for the handicapped and design innovations in software and hardware—but not on what the editor has told me he deems "marketing fluff."

There *is* news in what we do: signage and wayfinding systems that help people get around; packaging that doesn't just make goods look appealing but informs people of the benefits of what's inside; information graphics that make content accessible. The more design work is presented as solutions to environmental, social, economic, or other problems, the more newsworthy it will be to the business and general press.

If you believe you have a story, send samples of the relevant work with a letter to the managing editors of most appropriate magazines. Using a news release format is not really necessary, and may seem contrived. You can find the right people to contact in *Writer's Market*, an annual directory that lists every publication and what the editors are looking for (and not looking for). Poulin + Morris's work for medical centers, banks, and universities has been the subject of half a dozen multi-page color articles in *Sign Business*, a trade magazine with a circulation of 18,000 "management-level decision makers." The firm's work for Sony was featured on the cover of *Identity*, a magazine that showcases corporate graphics and signage. Stories like that build business.

Design stories are often part of a trend or cultural phenomena: what people are wearing, playing, eating, reading, buying. If you're not the whole story, perhaps you can be part of a story. Editors and writers often have an idea based on something they've seen, a trend they've noticed, and are looking for examples to illustrate it.

Because of this, a few graphic designers have become minor celebrities, and, like other celebrities, are in the news more often than we regular folks. When Milton Glaser's "I ❤ NY more than ever" logo with a burnt bottom edge was rejected by the New York State Department of Commerce after 9/11, it made international headlines. A Google search turns up 338 articles on the subject from newspapers and magazines around the world. The late Tibor Kalman, a fearless wit, was beloved by editors, who covered almost everything he did, from moving to Italy to edit Benetton's *Colors* magazine, to how his children's bedrooms were designed, to his last moments in the Caribbean before his untimely death from cancer (subject of a piece in the *New York Times Magazine*).

Some designers spend $2,000 to $5,000 or more a month on a retainer for public relations services. A PR professional knows the editors, how to frame an article, and how to act quickly if a story relates to breaking news ("New Florida Ballot Design Prevents Voting Error"). In a recent Small Business Special Report in *Crain's New York Business*, a story on Susan Karlin, principal of Suka & Friends design in New York's SoHo, described how she relied on cold calling to rebuild her business after the dot-com meltdown. "Pitched" by her PR professional, the story reported that Karlin's marketing campaign yielded two new clients, including a major Japanese automaker—and it brought her several more inquiries. "Three days after it ran I got a call from a major university with the opportunity to bid on a project," she said.

If you are profiled in a design magazine or if your opinion is part of a trend story, get reprints and send them to your clients and prospects. Let them know about your status in the design world, even if they don't subscribe to the magazines.

WHAT ABOUT DESIGN AWARDS?

Awards are important. To launch a firm. To keep your name in front of your peers. For self-esteem. To reward employees who contributed to important projects.

However, I have never met a client who admitted that he or she looked through an awards annual or went to an awards dinner. But then, maybe I've met the wrong clients. April Greiman says she keeps a high profile by working with organizations in the business of design—fashion, entertainment, design stores, furniture, and high-tech. "Design clients are great," she says. "They do pay attention to the magazines and are very aware of who's doing the best things."

There are even a few clients for whom being on the crest of the trends is apparently so important they'll count the number of awards in an annual and zero in on the biggest winner. In the eighties, when a much-awarded designer from Texas joined the New York office of an international firm, a top Midwest designer was upset, almost angry. "Why does this matter so much to you?" I asked. He answered that his firm had been winning the most awards in every major competition. When the Texas designer joins the international firm, he pouted, *they* will get the most awards and thus have the advantage. Looking back, I think he was right. However, it wasn't the number of awards *per se* that attracted so many more top clients to his competitor, it was the overall excellence of the newly merged firm's work.

Whether or not you do the kind of work that will attract the attention of the kind of clients who count awards, awards will always put your name in front of thousands of other designers. And being known by other designers can lead to getting clients. Ed Gold, who's interviewed more than three hundred designers around the country, asserts, "Word of mouth begins with design awards. Win awards, and your peers spread your name around in mysterious ways you don't even know about."

Awards have built the reputations of some of the most prestigious films and of agencies like Fallon McElligott, whose strategy was to let big-time awards for ads for small local businesses and nonprofit organizations (chapter 20) catapult the firm to national and international fame.

Should you spend the time and money entering competitions? It all depends on the region, the industry, who your clients are—and who you want them to be.

NO MATTER WHAT, REFERRALS WILL BE YOUR NUMBER-ONE SOURCE OF NEW BUSINESS

If you do good work, the word gets around. Both to colleagues within the organization and at other companies.

Most design firm principals report that the vast majority of new business comes from referrals from existing, satisfied clients. For example, Poulin + Morris are well known in the tightly-knit architecture and real estate communities because developers and building owners swap war stories about who's done outstanding work for them (and who to keep away from). So do company presidents, chairmen, and marketing directors. In chapter 9, financial services CEO Marty Zimmerman describes his quest to find the right designer: he called fellow CEO Gordon Siegel of Crate & Barrel and asked, "Gordon, who do you use for design? Who's terrific?"

That's how it usually works. One recommendation from a respected colleague can be worth more than scores of self-promotions, PR releases, and design awards. "The kind of work that you do attracts clients. Period," asserts architect Michael Rotondi, founder of the Southern California Institute of Architecture (chapter 19). "Those who do not grasp this simple relationship continue to wonder how to get better projects. If you do cheap, crummy work you attract cheap, crummy clients. If you do great work you attract great clients," he asserts.

Referrals can come from public relations firms and ad agencies. A big job to you may not be worth doing for them. Especially in smaller local markets, it's wise to make sure that the account executives and creative directors at the largest regional agencies know about you.

Referrals can also come from other designers. Klein Bikes (chapter 6) was referred to Liska + Associates by fellow Chicago designer Rick Valicenti, who already had a bike account and didn't want a conflict of interest. Valicenti thought that Liska's pristine, highly organized style would be a good fit for the client. Explains Steve Liska: "No one's sitting around with a big design job in their out box. Clients are very cautious right now. It's hard for them to get a decision from above. But word of mouth is still the most important way we get new business."

Reputations build referrals. When I came to New York in 1972 to work for the late Herb Lubalin, he had the deserved reputation of being the very best with type. Lubalin, Smith, Carnase's eclectic clients ranged from cosmetics companies to publishers to industrial corporations, all of whom wanted letter-heads and packages, ads and book jackets adorned with beautiful letterforms, ligatures, and swashes. Some of the studio's biggest projects at the time were logos for a big-three automaker, annual reports for a Fortune 100 oil exploration company, a poster campaign for a series of filmed plays, design of a multivolume sports encyclopedia, and lots of shampoo bottles for Loréal Paris.

I'm not sure a reputation for doing beautiful things with type would be enough to have a client list like that today. More of an industry specialization and results-orientation is usually needed. What works now is a reputation something like this: XYZ design firm manages corporate identities that unite disparate brands; knows how to communicate with extreme-sports aficionados; creates ads and promotions that can sell out an entertainment event.

GOOD NEWS SPREADS QUICKLY

Today, five years after the phenomenal success of its then-groundbreaking cam-paign for the musical *Rent*, Drew Hodges's company, Spot Design, creates the posters and campaigns for half the shows on Broadway (chapter 17). Hodges's expertise, knowledge of which has spread quickly from one entertainment mogul to the next, helps sell eight thousand tickets per week per show.

A referral can also come from a client's colleague or acquaintance in a differ-ent kind of organization, but one with a similar need. Liska + Associates got one of its most important clients, Expand Beyond (makers of IT management software) through a referral from a client in a different industry. Says Steve Liska: "Expand Beyond's founders called and said, 'We heard you're really good at helping people get businesses going.' We did everything for them—product naming, identity, print literature, ads, their Web site, the interface design with icons—in a month." A reputation built on that kind of expertise builds repeat business and more referrals.

Over the years, my firm may have gotten more new business from clients changing jobs than anything else. Remember the ditty you sang as a child, as a round at camp: "Make new friends and keep the old. One is silver and the other is gold." Being a rainmaker can sometimes involve fortuitous showers of new business that come when reorganizations and downsizings send talented people to other companies.

A WEB SITE IS AN IMPORTANT MARKETING TOOL

Study the Web sites of the design firms featured in this book. They're clean, organized, and a bit provocative. By that I mean they don't show and tell everything. They give a deliciously brief taste of the firm's work and capabilities. Then it's up to the interested party to make the next move, to pick up the phone or send an e-mail.

Steve Liska reports that a surprisingly large amount of new business comes from his firm's comprehensive, easy-to-navigate site. "People do Google and Yahoo searches for designers," he points out.

Spending the time it takes to design an effective site is a good investment. If you haven't done so already, it will force you into organizing your work, editing, creating simple, powerful images. You've got to decide which pieces to show that capture the essence of what you've done and are capable of doing. Captions must summarize your contribution in a sentence or two. The best sites have a smooth, effortless navigation system that guides you through a portfolio of a dozen to twenty projects; a bio or firm profile, a client list, a few "releases" of the latest news, and a "contact us" page. Clean, minimalist sites, not junky ones tarted up with spinning logos and animations, are the trademark of top design firms. The jury is still out on whether clients are impressed or annoyed by Flash animations set to music. If you must have an animation, be sure to include a "skip intro" button.

Boston design firm principal Michael Weymouth (chapter 10) says that when the highly animated Weymouth.com was launched it was ranked by a European magazine as one of the ten hot Web sites in the world. "It is my opinion, though, that 'hot' does not get you much work," he says, "so our new site—programmed so a new background photo rotates in every night—is more utilitarian. All we expect is that people will think highly enough of it to put us on their design review list." And then he adds, almost unnecessarily, "But if we had an ugly, dysfunctional site, we would not get that phone call."

Before you launch your site, test it. Upload the files to an FTP site and send your friends and relatives there. Let them look at it on Macs and PCs, large monitors and small, Netscape and Internet Explorer. Let them tell you what's wrong with the navigation, the fonts, the images and the spelling—before it's out there in the world.

When it's ready to launch, your e-mail sign-off can invite current and prospective clients to visit. So can a low-key e-mail campaign—to people you already know or know of. It's not spam when it's a personal "hello" note from you to a former or current or potential client. They might even enjoy hearing from you.

For those who don't know you—and might want to—do everything you can to help them find you. Meta tags and keywords should include your city, country, state, and words like "graphic design," "logo design," "Web page design," "brochure design," or whatever it is you want to sell. I want search engines to direct everyone looking for graphic design and/or writing in my area to *www.visualanguage.net*. It's not easy to make that happen—these days you have to pay for placement—but we keep trying.

WHY NOT JUST PICK UP THE PHONE?

For many people, cold calling is terrifying. Why open yourself up to rejection? Other people learn to enjoy it and make it part of their routine. "I'm never too busy to make ten calls a day," says Sue Karlin, whose successful cold-call techniques were the subject of an article in *Crain's*.

In his columns as editor of the late, lamented *Critique* magazine and in speeches at conferences, Marty Neumeier, now principal of Neutron, LLC, a San Francisco brand consultancy, excoriates designers for wasting time doing "indirect" things that he says don't work—like designing fancy capabilities brochures for themselves—instead of just picking up the phone and asking for an appointment.

"Marty, I have several questions," I asked recently. "One, people are fed up with cold calls. They're angry and doing something about it. I've read that legislation has been introduced in Congress to ban telemarketing calls. Two, how do you determine whom to call? Three, what do you say when you get the prospect on the phone? That can be a paralyzing moment. And four, why do you think brochures are such a waste of time?"

Neumeier is one of the smartest and most experienced people around when it comes to these things. "If that legislation passes, it'll be great because it will clear the field," he says. "There's a huge difference between telemarketing and legitimate introductory phone calls. Sure, there's voicemail, and companies have a million ways to screen you, like saying that they don't give out that information. I take that as a challenge," he asserts. "I go to the company's site and find out who's who. I call and ask for that person. I keep trying until I catch him or her. One secret is 'super Thursday.' We've found that you can get through to people on Thursday better than any other day of the week.

"And when you get through, have your story ready," he advises. Here is the story Neumeier tells cold-call prospects:

"You don't know me, but I think we may have some common ground. I've picked you because your company matches the profile of organizations we want to work with. I'm calling to set up a time for a presentation. It doesn't have to be right away. I want to show you some research I've done on your industry."

Before founding *Critique*, Neumeier made his mark by designing software packages for companies like Symantec and Macromedia. In those days, his firm's presentation was a slide show called "22 Ways to Sell More Software." He affirms: "Design means nothing to clients. Sales mean a lot. Talk about how your work increases sales."

HAVE A FOCUS

How can you get their attention? Get that meeting? Turn the meeting into real work? What if you've never done anything like design packages that make software jump off the shelves into consumers' shopping carts? "Have a focus, a specialty," advises Neumeier. "The last thing anyone needs is another generalist. Build your pitch around what you have done or can do that is unique."

"Find a niche," echoes Newport, Rhode Island, designer Tyler Smith, who made his mark in the men's fashion industry (chapter 16). "Focus on a vertical niche," he advises. "Whether it's men's wear like me, or design for restaurants or travel companies. Then you'll have a fighting chance." Here are some suggestions:

- "We are the only firm in Philadelphia that does annual reports for pet care companies"; "We are the only firm in Houston that does real estate brochures." (*hah!*)
- "We offer a mix or services that meets your needs: design and writing." (*Or* "design and photography.")

Or even:

- "We're in your neighborhood."

Austin, Texas, designer Marc English got a big client when the proprietor of a local riding-equipment shop let her fingers do the walking to the nearest firm listed in the Yellow Pages under "graphic designers." Finding his work too high-end for her needs, she referred English to her parent company, a Dallas aviation firm. "We created their identity from scratch and now we're working on marketing materials and advertising," English reports.

"We're in your neighborhood" is not such a farfetched selling point, even in an era when your work can be on a client's desktop anywhere in the world in seconds.

You Might Not Need That Brochure

If you do get through to the right person, the likely response is, "Send me something."

Doesn't every design firm need a brochure, if only for that? No, many top salespeople advise, the phrase "send me something" is just a way of blowing you off. If you're smart, you won't send anything. You'll ask for the opportunity to meet the prospect in person. You'll bring real, printed samples that the potential client can flip through, feel, and read. If you do interactive work, you'll bring a laptop presentation.

If there's anything I've learned from interviewing clients, it's that they want to see a real piece. They want to experience it from beginning to end. No client has ever told me that they were ever impressed by a design firm's brochure or were even interested in seeing one. Covers and spreads reproduced in capabilities brochures hide a multitude of sins, they say. They want solid evidence of what you've done for other organizations in their industry or for organizations in other industries who were faced with a similar business problem.

"The point is getting to talking about the project as soon as possible," stresses Neumeier. "Having a brochure about yourself doesn't give you an advantage. Everybody has one. Clients don't even know how to look at them," he says. "If you produced three real estate brochures that helped other clients make money, take them to the meeting. They will help you make a successful pitch."

Getting Started (Here's When Volunteer Work Is a Good Idea)

What if you're just starting out? You've been working for a design firm or in-house for a few years and think you're ready to strike out on your own. The problem is, you haven't actually been totally responsible for designing a piece you could claim helped any organization accomplish anything. Everything in your portfolio is still school assignments or stuff you assisted on . . . and maybe you don't even like the stuff anymore — but, hey, that job paid the rent. What to do?

Right now, I'm keeping my eyes open for a deserving nonprofit organization with a terrible logo. It won't be too hard to find. It might be a homeless shelter or a substance abuse treatment center. Redesigning the logo will be given as an assignment in my senior seminar class at Purchase College. The client will be contacted and informed that the organization can get a new, student-designed logo—if they provide a short, honest critique of each of about twenty logos, and, should one of them be chosen, pay the student an honorarium of at least $350. I will lead the students through the identity process, from defining "image characteristics" based on the client profile through creating and presenting an effective symbolic mark.

This assignment ensures that each graduate has at least one designer-client experience and "real"-appearing assignment in his or her portfolio. It was developed in response to the continuous lament: "Everybody is looking for experience. How can I get it?"

Creating an opportunity where none existed is a smart way to get it.

If you are lacking in experience (but not in talent or drive), take the initiative. Create work for yourself. Don't wait for it to come to you.

SHOW WHAT YOU CAN DO

Somebody you know or your parents or friends know runs a business or a nonprofit organization that could use your services. Show them a mix of your best school assignments and fantasy projects you create to show what you can do. Listen, really listen, to what they need. Offer your work at an irresistible price. Show what you can do with type and royalty-free images and black-and-white photocopies. Be like Fallon McElligott: do a knockout newspaper ad for the laundromat or barbershop or a compelling poster for the food bank or day-care center. If it's a religious or charitable organization or other cause you believe in, volunteer your services. Take Fallon group head Dean Hanson's smart advice (chapter 20): "That strategy has worked since the beginning of the industry. I've never met a good creative that didn't follow this route to some degree."

When I was a senior design major at UCLA, I couldn't afford a sofa, so I made giant floor pillows for my West L.A. apartment. People liked them so much that I created a little home-based business, for which I designed flyers and small-space black-and-white ads. I would take customers to stores, help them choose fabrics and trim, then stitch up pillows and cushions and bolsters. I soon got tired of having shredded foam everywhere and stopped advertising. But the "real" flyers and ads in my portfolio helped me land my first real job as art director at UCLA's Alumni and Development Center.

It also helped that I had taken the time on my own to master some of the techniques that weren't taught in school—and still aren't. When I wasn't sewing (or attending peace marches) I studied type books, ink swatch books, and paper sample books. By the time I graduated I knew the difference between Franklin Gothic and News Gothic, between Strathmore Grandee and Curtis Tweedweave. When I got hired, my future boss, who was looking for a recent graduate who could art direct a twenty-four-page alumni monthly, said, "You were the only person who knew anything about type." Maybe it was those pillow flyers that sold him.

WHAT ABOUT SALESPEOPLE?

It's every designer's fantasy. You can stay at your drawing board (computer, whatever) all day long, *creating*, while an experienced, persuasive yet sensitive account executive-salesperson scopes out all the big projects at major corporations and brings in the bacon. He or she knows exactly how to research the opportunities, set up meetings, show work, write proposals, price, close sales, and manage projects. If you find the right person, your firm will grow and prosper like gangbusters. It just takes a little patience and an initial investment.

I've tried it—several times—and can only, sadly, report that it didn't work. To make a very long story short, salespeople (at least those I carefully interviewed and had high hopes for) are expensive, spend a lot of your money, and don't bring in enough work or even the right kind of work.

In fact, much of the research for my entire first book, *Clients and Designers* (Watson-Guptill, 1990) was a subtle attempt to find out why hiring a new-business person didn't work. The straight answer: clients want to meet *you*. They will accept account executives at large agencies and branding firms. They hire smaller design firms precisely because they want to work directly with "creatives." In fact, they feel insulted if the person whose name is on the door doesn't personally come in to meet them. Taking the time to meet a qualified new prospect doesn't mean that you look too hungry for work. It means that you care. "What you have to do back at the office perhaps can be delegated to someone else," says Kathleen Zann, former manager of marketing communications for James River Corporation. "But I insist on meeting the principal."

New York multimedia phenomenon Hillman Curtis, author of *MTIV (Making the Invisible Visible): Process, Inspiration and Practice for the New Media Designer* (New Riders, 2002) is not too busy to go out and meet prospects himself. He says he gets clients on board at initial meetings by discussing "themes" that express the essence of what the client is trying to accomplish. He brings a laptop presentation with examples of past successes, which could include a style guide and a motion spot. "What I focus on is the client's current site or ad campaign," he says. "I talk about their identity, their story, their brand, and suggest ways we might support them, about thematic directions we might take." No one else could do this for him.

A salesperson can only "present." You can provide a taste of what it's like to work with you — something only you can do.

BE UPBEAT, NO MATTER WHAT

There have been outstanding years for this business. And horrible ones. My firm and many others survived the devastating stock market crash of 1987. And the recession that followed it. Many of us rode through the dot-com boom (when it seemed as if the MBAs and techies were getting a lot of the big-paying business we didn't know how to sell). Then we rode through the dot-com crash (when some of the interactive-design companies that had done so spectacularly went bankrupt, along with their clients). We were just entering a slow, hopeful recovery when September 11, 2001, happened. Right now, the war in Iraq is paralyzing marketing budgets.

If there's any immutable truth about business, it's that things are always changing. Ten years ago we couldn't have predicted that every organization in the world would need a Web site, and would need a design firm to develop and launch it. Who knows what will happen next?

Attitude has a lot to do with getting business. Even in a down market, project a positive attitude. Get out there. Take credit for your successes. Let them think your calendar is full. After all, it might be, tomorrow.

ONCE YOU'VE MET THEM, HOW TO GET CLIENTS TO **GIVE YOU WORK***

*(AND HOW TO GET PAID FOR THAT WORK)

If this book had been written twenty-five years ago, or even ten years ago, the word "money" would rarely appear. One did not mention money when discussing the august design firms of the 1960s, '70s, and '80s. When a client engaged the services of a designer, the "deliverables" were quality and originality. In design classes at UCLA, when we learned about the work of Charles Eames and Alexander Girard and Buckminster Fuller (or about the graphic designers who headed the offices in town where we wanted to work: Saul Bass, Robert Miles Runyan, Jim Cross), it was understood that clients were looking to capture a unique talent and vision.

Today, a client's first question is usually, "How much will it cost?" And it's not just for informational purposes. It's to see if you're willing to do it at a low price—or to begin a competitive bidding or bargaining session. A guide to clients, by definition, has to be a guide to positioning and pricing your work so you will *have* clients.

YOU HAVE TO PROVIDE SOMETHING THEY CAN'T DO IN-HOUSE

Quite simply, in order for you to get business, clients have to like you. They have to believe in you. And believe you can do something that they can't do—or shouldn't spend their time doing.

More and more, in the quest to save money, clients devise in-house "solutions" that involve buying and learning new software, even assembling things like promotional kits themselves. A wise design consultant might suggest that the clients' time would be better spent growing their companies, marketing products, contacting and cultivating donors — fulfilling their core missions. Nevertheless, most larger organizations have the staff for in-house layout and production. To justify hiring you, they have to believe you can do something that no one else can.

"Today, we've got to do the hard stuff," says Peter Farago, principal of Farago + Partners, a New York advertising and branding agency. "Clients will only pay for what they can't do themselves." Farago, whose clients call him one of the smartest and most creative people they've ever met (even after they've changed agencies — see chapter 12), says that these days everybody can (or thinks they can) design a page, lay out an ad, set type, get a picture from an online stock photo agency. What can't they do? Create interactive experiences that will keep users coming back to a Web site. Build Internet communities. Brand every aspect of a consumer's experience.

"We've got to keep doing the same things we've always done," says Farago. "Tell stories. Tell the client's stories. But in new ways, with new tools."

How Important Is Price?

If you offer a service they can do in-house, price is usually the biggest consideration. Or, put another way, the usual reason not to use in-house people is price: "If outsourcing is cheaper, let's go with a vendor," clients reason. If you provide a commodity item, like page layout, you can find yourself working cheap. And being treated like a vendor. Or worse, like a lackey (meaning you're expected to sit at your computer and make corrections all day).

On sites like Elance.com, price is the overriding consideration. At any given time, dozens of potential clients are soliciting bids for identity and stationery and Web design projects. Today, a career coach, a pain management center, a custom woodworking company, and a golf club manufacturer, among others, are looking for logo designers. Designers pay for the privilege of bidding, and there are ten or more bids for each, ranging from (gulp) about $195 to $375. You can view the designers' portfolios and read testimonials from other satisfied clients. You can read the designers' pitch letters:

> Hello! I will work to design your corporate identity for you until you are 100% SATISFIED! I will create several versions of a logo for you to choose from, all ORIGINAL art with UNLIMITED REVISIONS based on your specifications and input.

Once upon a time, designers might have been able to convince upstart entrepreneurs — say, the custom woodworker — that spending at least several thousand dollars for a logo was a wise business investment. Not any more. Why should clients do anything more than visit Elance.com and sit back until they're 100 percent satisfied? All in the anonymous, faceless, instant universe of the Internet. No temperamental artists to deal with, who'll want to argue or might leave the office in tears if a design is rejected.

The late, legendary Paul Rand reportedly charged Steven Jobs $100,000 for the NEXT logo. And he gave Jobs one solution, neatly explained in a little hand-bound book that graphically demonstrated how he arrived at the solution. One of Woody Pirtle's clients told me how lucky his $4 billion company was to get him and Pentagram. Obviously, to some clients, low price is not the goal. They have other considerations. Architect Michael Rotondi, former director of the Southern California Institute of Architecture, says of April Greiman: "You go near her and it's like you plug yourself into a wall socket. It feels good. You just want to keep doing it" (chapter 19). He might have said the same thing if they were not living together.

What about the rest of us, who are not a Paul Rand or Woody Pirtle or April Greiman? And for whom the rates paid by Elance customers are not an option, if we want to stay in business and pay the bills?

ASK FOR THE MONEY!

Superstar attorney Gerry Spence, author of *How to Argue and Win Every Time* (St. Martin's Press, 1995), writes, "Everywhere I go, lawyers ask, 'How do you get those big-money verdicts?' I reply that I simply ask for the money. I tell the jury what I want. It seems that the more we want something, the more hesitant we are to ask for it."

You've gotta ask for the money in this business, too. Okay, it's not the big money personal injury lawyers ask for. But why not at least enough to keep the business running and make a little profit? Why are we so reluctant to do it? We love what we do. We are still amazed sometimes that people pay us. We will do almost anything for the opportunity. And then we get angry and feel exploited when we realize we've made a bad deal.

My son Alex spent a summer in New Orleans soliciting memberships and donations door-to-door for the Sierra Club. They taught him to ask for the money. He and other college students went there for the food, jazz, and beer, but learned lessons about life and doing business, doled out in daily two-hour role-playing sessions. Before the students knocked on the first door of the day, the trainers corrected their mistakes from the day before and made sure they had the pitch down cold: "It's great to know you feel the same way we do about big oil companies polluting the Gulf of Mexico," they were coached to say. "We really appreciate your $25 membership in the Sierra Club. But, you know, if you gave $50 or $75, we could accomplish so much more."

You're already there. You have a willing, sympathetic customer. Seven people have slammed the door in your face. This one believes in your cause. He or she is on your side. The checkbook is out. The pen is poised. Ask for the money! What's there to lose?

But in design, if you ask for too much, they could go somewhere else. They very likely will, in fact, if your fee is too high. It's not like getting the $25 instead of the $50. It could mean getting all the way there, to the proposal stage, and getting nothing.

FIRST, FIND OUT WHAT THEY WANT

Before you ask for the money, you have to know what they want and how much they are willing to spend. This isn't always easy. But remember what Gerry Spence advises: "Tell them what you want."

"I want to do this job for you."

"I will do a good job."

"Here's how much I need: $10,000." Or "$50,000."

Ah, but the client wants to spend $5,000. Or $25,000. The budget is more or less set. And they haven't told you because it's a competitive bidding situation.

Here's a typical (losing) scenario: You meet a potential new client team. You show your work. You seem to hit it off. They seem interested, too. Great! You find out as much as you can about what the company is trying to accomplish. They describe their aspirations and goals. You can visualize the solution in your head. It will be beautiful! You can already see it on the pages of the design magazines. It's not only a splendid design idea, it will make them billions of dollars. A win-win situation. You offer to write a proposal and have it delivered the next week. They agree. You leave the meeting aglow. You spend three days on what you think is a dazzling proposal. Then you never hear from them again. Or, if they are unusually etiquette-conscious, you get a letter: "While we appreciate your most interesting proposal, we have decided to utilize the services of another vendor."

What happened?

You forgot to ask how much they had to spend. I know it's tough. I know they don't want to tell you. But don't operate on hopes, wishes, fantasies. Get as much real information as possible. Here are some questions to try (before wasting days of your life):

"Do you want to work with me?"

Maybe the answer is no, as they discovered upon meeting you, for one of a dozen reasons. But they politely agreed to the proposal. Why not? Company policy requires three proposals. Why not get one from you, since you offered?

"Is this a competitive bidding situation?"

Find out.

"Who else are you talking to?"

Maybe they'll tell you.

"What do I have to do to get this job?"

You really want the answer to that one.

"Are you looking for the best price, or are there other considerations?"

Face it. Almost everyone is looking for a good price, as long as their other considerations are met. Maybe they want a larger firm, a smaller firm, someone with more experience in their industry, or even someone with less experience in their industry (to avoid any perceived conflict of interest).

SET YOUR LIMITS

It's important to set your threshold and not go below it, no matter how much the economy has tanked or how seductive the client and project seem. If $2,750 is the lowest price you can charge for a logo design, stick to it. It's a matter of self-esteem, as well as what accountants call the "opportunity cost." The time you spend slaving on the $500 logo can be much better spent looking for the client who will pay ten times that much. You want a client who will come back for more of the right kind of work, not for more too-cheap work. You want the client's colleagues and friends to know about you: that you do great work, not that you charge low prices. You want them to believe that your fees are fair and reasonable, given the effort you expend on their behalf and the value you bring to the table.

Thus, it's just as important for you to qualify the client as it is for the client to ensure that you meet his or her organization's qualifications.

Keep asking questions:

"How much do you want to spend?"

"We don't know. We're waiting to see some bids."

"Will you go for the lowest bid?

If the answer is really yes, now might be the time to shake hands and leave, even if it hurts. There will always be a lower bid.

What is your range?

This is probably the most important question. Let them know, gently and tactfully, if you are out of their range. If they are impressed by you and your work, maybe there will be a higher range on the next project.

Buying graphic design is a little like buying cars. There are $600 cars in the classified pages of *Pennysaver*, and there are $60,000 cars on the floor of the Jaguar showroom. Which one does the client want? Many startups will be happy with the *Pennysaver* means of transport. They think it will get them where they want to go for the time being. No amount or arguing by you, or demonstrations of the superiority of the dazzling S-Type-R, will change their minds. The question is, will you, a competent designer in their area, a little hungry in this economy (as most of us are), perchance give them a Jag product for a *Pennysaver* price? It happens all the time. If they play their cards right, maybe they'll get it.

Not long ago I neglected to ask the "What are you looking for?" question of a somewhat glamorous New York nonprofit organization that called about a direct-mail campaign. I spent several days on a "brilliant" proposal, which I presented in person. I never heard from them again. Why? I didn't ask that key question and make sure I got an honest answer. They were looking for a pro bono agency that would work for free, ostensibly in order to get samples for their book. They kept their cards hidden, as smart players do. Right now, there might be half a dozen brilliant proposals on the director's desk, chock-full of ideas they can get their nationally known, pro bono agency to execute for free.

Are you shocked? Please. The papers are packed with news about the illegal and unethical activities of corporations. Today's business section, for example, features stories about the scandals enveloping Adelphia, Arthur Anderson, Dynegy, Enron, Global Crossing, Merrill Lynch, and Tyco. A client list of woe. In the name of profitability, these organizations have been convicted or accused of manipulating accounting procedures to show profits when there were losses; creating elaborate ruses to avoid paying taxes or to boost the value of their stock; falsely stating profits to lure or mislead investors and gain lucrative investment banking or accounting fees. And then hiding the truth and the evidence of their wrongdoing. And let's not forget companies like the toy and clothing and tobacco makers that exploit third-world labor and/or market products that cause illnesses and injuries.

And you expect them to be 100 percent forthright and honest and fair with you, one of their *graphic designers*?

MAKE SURE YOU'RE GETTING PAID BEFORE YOU START

"Before I begin working" are the key words. The biggest disappointments I've had in this business, the most emotional moments, happened when I thought I was working for a client (and should have been getting paid) and the client thought (or said they thought) I was merely marketing services, a part of the "free" process of generating new business.

There are a lot of tactics used to get you to start working before they commit to pay you. And even more tactics for backing out of the "promise" afterwards with a sincere-sounding explanation that circumstances have changed beyond their control:

"Don't worry. The contract is in legal, but we need to see something by next week."

"I'm sure you'll be the one, but I need you to meet another group of managers. Can you just bring along something to show them what you have in mind?"

"If you just do it this time, there will be a lot more work down the road."
"In addition to this proposal I need something visual I can show my boss."
"I'm leaving for Mexico City tomorrow and need to take it with me. We'll sign your
agreement when I get back."

Boys in high school didn't have nearly as many successful pickup lines. Clients know how to seduce us. We should be the ones seducing them.

And it's not limited to graphic designers. A management consultant recently profiled on the front page of *Crain's New York Business* said that her biggest problem was making sure she didn't end up spending three hours in a Starbucks telling a potential client everything she had learned over her entire education and career. "I tell new clients I provide one hour of complimentary consultation," she said. "After that, my time is billed."

We're in The Zone the minute we hear about an assignment. We live and breathe design 24/7. We want to transmit that excitement to the client. It's so tempting to include just one little comp in the proposal, to sketch an idea at the meeting table. It can be even more tempting when a potential client dangles the promise of a big, exciting, juicy new job in front of you—if you agree to provide a few free ideas first.

AS GRANDMA USED TO SAY, THEY'LL NEVER BUY IT IF YOU GIVE IT AWAY

Working on spec is one of the most controversial issues in the business. Sure, big agencies invest many thousands of dollars in speculative presentations to get new business. But (a) they have research departments; (b) they often get paid for the presentation; and (c) millions of dollars in fees and commissions are usually at stake. Whether design clients are capitalizing on this "industry practice" or are just curious or greedy, they will sometimes ask design firms— who might be paid $5,000 to $50,000 for the entire job—to undertake a similar speculative process.

Don't do it. Just say no.

I am telling you this from personal experience, and from many other designers' personal experiences, as reported in magazine articles, letters to editors, conferences, workshops, and anguished late-night phone calls. It just doesn't work. Even if you "win"—i.e., get the job, which is questionable— it won't work out. Why? Quite simply, the client knows you can be pushed around. If you do this much for free now, you will do that much more for free later. Everything that happens in the relationship will be a problem. Besides, the most likely reason the client cooked up the spec competition in the first place was to get a bunch of free ideas to execute in-house. And by execute, I mean kill, butcher, exploit.

"Designers have to be very clear about how much of a solution they're will-ing to give before the client can make a decision," advises Robert Mouthrop, a marketing and communications specialist at leading financial service firms and nonprofits for more than twenty years. "You have to put a realistic price tag on yourself and your time," he says. "From the client's point of view, if you can get it for free, how much can it be worth?"

The American Institute of Graphic Arts (AIGA), the leading U.S. graphic design membership and advocacy organization, has developed standards to "reflect conduct that is in the best interest of the profession, clients, and the public," and has published a binder of monographs entitled *Design Business and Ethics.* The "AIGA Standards of Professional Practice" monograph states:

> A designer shall not undertake any speculative projects, either alone or in competition with other designers, for which compensation will only be received if a design is accepted or used. This applies not only to entire projects but also to preliminary schematic proposals.

This language was developed after lengthy debate and a skirmish with the U.S. Department of Justice, which objected to what it characterized as possi-ble restraint of trade. But restraining trade is not what this is about at all. It's about the value of professional services. It's about having the opportunity to gather all the information needed to develop an appropriate solution, not a superficial one.

According to AIGA executive director Ric Grefé, "Designers deserve the respect of their clients as trusted advisors on solving communication challenges with effect and creativity. The only way designers can achieve this respect is to share a common set of values that communicate the value of their work. Spec work undermines this ethic. The creative services that many advertising agen-cies give away in spec work is simply bargaining at the margin, not with their core intellectual property, like it is with ours. The only solution is for each designer to live up to the shared values and, together, educate the clients."

Even a proposal can be speculative, if too much is asked. On larger projects, we should be expected to write a proposal that includes a fee estimate for the professional services we provide. It's unfair for clients to expect a total project price with detailed line-item costs for photography, illustration, printing, and other production costs. Providing those numbers forces us to virtually design the job—before we've been given the opportunity to do the research that will lead to the right solution. Just say no to that, too. Indicate that you'll develop two or more approaches within the client's stated overall budget—after you receive the signed agreement and the retainer.

THAT DOESN'T MEAN MONEY IS ALWAYS THE OBJECT

None of us want to be too hard-nosed. Money isn't the only object. There are times when, with the right client, a lower-paying or even pro bono project can be a meaningful, satisfying opportunity, worth more than a big fee.

"All of us must be dreamers," notes Jon Esser of Purchase College's School of Art+Design. "But we must also remain responsive to material constraints. The client engages you because of your knowledge and creative abilities. If you don't produce solutions, you won't last long in the field. But if you can't derive satisfaction from your work, you won't last long, either."

One of my office's best-known projects, the "Channeling Children's Anger" logo (a scribble that transforms itself into a heart), designed by Terri Bogaards, was 100 percent pro bono, donated to the Institute of Mental Health Initiatives. We did it—as well as the stationery, invitations, posters, programs, and T-shirt—for love, and to help a worthy cause. In 2001, we received an "Ideas That Matter" grant from Sappi Paper, and wrote and designed two brochures and a poster for the International Dyslexia Association, 100 percent pro bono. The Sappi grant paid for the printing and distribution. We did this gladly, because parents and teachers in the nation's most disadvantaged school districts now have more information about how to help children learn to read.

If there's anything that members of the design and advertising community have in common, it's a willingness to donate their talents to worthy causes.

And when you're first starting out, even on the paying jobs, you can't and shouldn't charge what the big guys do. "It's never easy," says Jelly Associates partner Miriam Bossard when asked how her three-year-old firm determines fees. "We look at the client's budget and the value of the project to us; whether it will be good creatively and give us good experience." Adds her partner Amy Unikewicz, "Later on we might be able to be a little more demanding."

A CONTRACT IS ESSENTIAL

A contract or working agreement doesn't have to be long and complicated. It can be short and sweet. It can even be part of your proposal, a page that sets out the terms and conditions of the relationship that, in hiring you, the client has agreed to.

Contracts are covered in detail in many other, excellent books. Templates are provided in *Business and Legal Forms for Graphic Designers* by Tad Crawford and Eva Doman Bruck (Allworth Press, 2003), which includes a CD-ROM of forty-five customizable forms; Ed Gold's *The New Business of Graphic Design* (Watson-Guptill Publications, 1995), and *Graphic Artists Guild Handbook: Pricing and Ethical Guidelines* (10th Edition, Graphic Artists Guild, 2001). Use one of them. Or adapt it. Use something. A document that the client, in addition to a judge or an arbitrator, can easily grasp.

It's important that at least the following are covered: A description of the work you will provide. The fee. What items are not included in the fee, such as out-of-pocket expenses, and how they will be billed. How the client will pay, and when. Who owns the rights. Clauses like client's responsibility for errors and omissions and for getting copyright clearances are important, too.

At a HOW Design Conference I devoted a full session to walking attendees through a model contract for services. Most of the audience members managed to stay awake, and actually followed attentively through an explanation and discussion of each of fifteen paragraphs, one by one. The questions afterwards were revealing: "This is great, but how do I present it to my clients?" and "How do I get them to sign it?"

Many designers, apparently, are scared or embarrassed to be proffering something as crass as a contract. Suggestions like "send it to them" and "ask them" were met with resistance.

I then suggested standing in front of a mirror and repeating:

"I need you to sign this before I begin working."

It sounded like more than a few people were too shy to do that. I hope they're getting paid.

ENTERING INTO THE RELATIONSHIP—FOR REAL

Your contract doesn't need to cover every point that can possibly arise, and you probably shouldn't even try.

When my husband, an intellectual property attorney, had been practicing law for less than five years, he attempted to get a court order to enforce a client's licensing agreement. Because the other party had been breaching the agreement, Julius asked the judge to rewrite some of the original contract provisions so his client wouldn't get hurt again. The judge did so; but acknowledging Julius's relative lack of experience, he shared this bit of wisdom: "The greatest contract in the world can't take the place of the trust necessary in any successful relationship."

If someone doesn't trust that the other party will honor the contract, advises a much more experienced Julius, one ought not to enter into the agreement in the first place.

So, before you start drafting your agreement, pay attention to what your gut is telling you. If you have any concerns about a client's take on certain issues—such as whether he or she really intends to pay in thirty days—don't conclude that a "tight" agreement will solve the problem. The client will conveniently forget the provision or say that he or she thought it meant something else.

Sit down and talk again, and try to establish that trust.

KEEPING CLIENTS HAPPY (AND COMING BACK)

You can get this far and still lose. The contract can be signed and something can go wrong.

"They just didn't give us what we wanted," clients say.

"They got locked into one design idea, which we didn't think was right for us."

"After all that selling, they put junior people on the job."

"They didn't listen."

"The work was incomplete."

"It was late."

"There were too many surprises."

"They kept trying to sell us stuff that was too expensive."

"They didn't tell us what the changes would cost."

"There were problems with the printing and the finishing or fabrication."

Your bill gets paid (or a portion of it), and the client is already working with someone else.

BE PREPARED TO MEET ALL OF THEIR EXPECTATIONS

In my senior seminar class I use a teaching aid entitled, "What Design Directors and Firm Principals Do." It's a chart with five rows of boxes.

The top row is labeled "Preliminaries" and includes a box labeled, "Meet with client to discuss project, define audience, and communications objectives, budget, delivery date." Another box is: "Ask probing questions; write and deliver or present proposal; negotiate proposal terms; get retainer and signed agreement."

The second row is called "Concept Development" and includes "Research and determine specific, ideal content, format, look and feel, materials and production techniques that will accomplish client's goals." I tell the students that this is all about understanding the client's business; not just doing what you think looks cool or expresses your personal feelings, or might win an "A" or the admiration of other designers and awards-show judges.

The third and forth rows, "Design and Art Direction," includes "Select photographers, illustrators; give creative direction." The last row, "Production Supervision," includes boxes labeled, "Deliver errorless files to vendors," "Make sure the project gets fabricated correctly," and "Follow up on delivery."

"Where Do You Fit In?" asks the headline.

Many students are a bit stunned. For four years their efforts had been solely focused on the activities described in one or two boxes out of twenty-eight—creating designs with images and type, designs that pleased them and that expressed their feelings and opinions.

Clients expect more, I explain. You can't even begin designing until you understand the clients' organization, what they are trying to accomplish. Then, if you screw up one or more of these other areas, the client may go somewhere else anyway, even if your creative concepts are excellent. (That's one reason it's a good idea to start your career at a design firm where you can learn from experienced people, rather than as a freelancer.)

To keep clients happy—and keep them coming back for more—you have to meet or exceed expectations in all of these areas.

Even top, experienced firms have to keep learning how to do this, explains Studio/lab's Marcia Lausen. "Doing good work often requires an extraordinary investment of time and effort spent on client education and confidence-building. We always and willingly take on that extra effort. But there are a few times when we miss the mark," she adds, "because we haven't yet learned enough about the client's business or the specific needs of the project. Then an extra investment of time needs to come from the client side. We have longstanding clients who have been very patient with our learning curve."

TALK THE TALK

Students spend four or more years learning to talk about juxtapositions, imagery, irony. I surprise them when I suggest that they read the business press. Those pages are where you learn to talk client talk. A senior designer or firm principal should be almost as comfortable discussing return on investment and marketing strategies as Garamond versus Sabon, Flash versus Shockwave.

You were hired to make the right choices. You should be able to justify those choices if asked. And the answer should make business sense. It should not be about decoration. "Why did you choose this paper?" Answers like "Because it looks cool" or "I saw this really awesome promotion designed by so-and-so" will always be wrong. "Because it has the right color and texture to communicate the following characteristics of your organization" is more like it. And while you're at it, don't fall into the clichés associated with "flaky creatives." Don't miss deadlines. Show up on time—no, ten minutes early, for meetings. Be prepared. Look and act businesslike.

In addition to reading the design magazines, try to make *The Wall Street Journal* a habit, at least weekly. The writing is superb. You will gain many insights into how clients think and what they are looking for. The ads can teach you a lot about branding. Read the business pages of your local paper, too. And *Fortune, Business Week*, and *Fast Company* never hurt a designer, either.

BUT DON'T LAY IT ON TOO THICK

It's a long way from "because it looks cool" to "dynamic sensibility of vision" and "coherent yet multi-layered visual message." Where did all the designer jargon come from? Once upon a time, in order to communicate with high-level executives and charge higher fees, designers at big-time corporate identity firms must have taken a look at *The Harvard Business Review* or *Artforum* and said, "Ah ha, here's how to do it." Great visual communications masters like Herb Lubalin and Saul Bass, if they were still among us, might not be able to recognize the epidemic of verbiage that resulted. As just one example, I found the following in an article about a new institutional logo:

> The contemporary and dynamic geometric asymmetry of the color planes sit in contrast to the elegant academic tradition of the classic typeface. Distinct negative/positive relationships invite the viewer to complete the message by attributing form and meaning to negative space. This exchange makes the mark more memorable. The chosen colors . . . achieve a pleasant, yet energetic high-contract interaction that communicates clarity and determination.

Heaven help us. I mean, it's an okay logo. And sure, a successful solution needs a bit more documentation than "Because it looks cool." But let's not gag clients with pages of purple bureaucratese. Graphic design is a visual art. Most intelligent people can see if something works or not, looks good or not, right away. That's the whole point. The flowery rationale isn't going to be there when a future customer looks at the thing, scratches his head, and asks, "What the hell is that supposed to be?"

And, by the way, the correct grammar is: "*asymmetry* (singular) *sits*."
I don't mean to sound cantankerous, but when you write, make sure your
subjects and verbs agree. To write well, try to follow the advice of Strunk
and White in their classic *The Elements of Style* (Macmillan, 1897), a must for
every reference shelf:

> Write in a way that comes naturally. Omit needless words. Do not over-
> state. Do not explain too much. Do not inject opinion. Be clear.

PRESENTATIONS THAT SPEAK FOR THEMSELVES

The most successful designers know how to present work in a way that is not
only clear, that not only "sells," but that begins and continues a dialogue with
the client.

Ed Gold has identified what he calls "the ten common characteristics of
great designers."

After "talent" ("their work flat-out looks good"), Ed ranks "advocacy" as
the number-two necessary characteristic. "A designer who can't sell an idea
is probably not going to be very successful," he says, adding, "I'll go a step
further. A designer who can't sell an idea will never be a great designer." He
advises all designers to take courses in persuasion and presentation.

As you've probably experienced, there is nothing less inspiring than a portfolio presentation in which a job candidate recites in a monotone: "This is a
piece I did for so-and-so; this is a piece I did for so-and-so." It's equally
depressing to clients when designers start explaining how they used type or
images. The results are there right in front of their eyes.

As Hillman Curtis cautions in *MTIV*, "Never, never, never sell your design.
You should be able to lay out your comps in front of clients, and if you have
heard them, stayed true to their desires, and included them in your creative
process, the designs will speak for themselves. You can stay quiet, answer their
questions if necessary, and listen to their feedback. Take notes and bring it
closer on the next rev[ise]." Curtis writes that he always tells his designers that
if they find themselves saying things like, "We used Helvetica because it's simple yet strong," then they haven't done their jobs.

I have been preaching the same thing for years to students and to the
designers who've worked for me. You, the designer, won't be there when the
reader opens the brochure, turns the page, clicks on the home page, or sees
the logo or ad for the first time. Like the student portfolio, if it needs an
explanation, something's wrong. Verbal pyrotechnics and even reams of
support documentation can't transform an unsuccessful design into one
that works.

WHAT ABOUT LUNCHES, DINNERS, AND ALL THAT?

Taking clients to lunch used to be part of my routine. From The Four Seasons to Asia de Cuba, sushi bars to Indian buffets, I was out at least twice a week with clients and prospective clients. Not any more. No one has time. Me included. Expensive lunches might seem almost decadent in this environment. Before I decided to move my office out of New York City, I kept a diary of how I spent my days: At my computer ten hours a day, five days a week. Six of the ten talking on the phone and e-mailing stuff back and forth. A few client meetings a week—at their offices. A quick bite at a salad bar, sandwich place, or my desk. (Could do that from anywhere and save all that commuting time—and rent.)

Is there a place in business today for wining and dining? Some designers and clients say yes. Others no. "I might be more successful if I did more of that," muses Drew Hodges. "But it seems like nobody wants me to take them to lunch. Everyone's too busy."

Michael Mabry, identified in a 1997 national survey as "the most influential graphic designer in the United States," says he wouldn't even want to have lunch with most clients he's met over the years. "Clients should be people you want to go to dinner with. But it's very, very rare." Mabry, who moved his office from San Francisco to Emeryville, California, to be closer to home and his young daughter, has been somewhat pessimistic on the subject of clients for years. "Companies that I thought I liked disappointed me too much," he confesses. "Once you get into the inner workings, you see arrogance, lack of vision, fear of the CEO, unwillingness to try new things." He's recently found happiness, though, working for children's furnishings retailer and cataloguer The Land of Nod. He even likes to have lunch with the principals. "The company was founded by two friends," he explains. "It's a joy to work with them and go out with them. This has never happened before, but it's a real natural thing to spend time with them, to share a meal, to watch TV with their kids. In a perfect world that's what all client relationships would be like."

FOES OR FRIENDS?

True, in a perfect world, more clients and designers would be friends, rather than wary adversaries, each trying to hold onto his or her vision of the project while the other tries to "ruin" it.

In the Chicago suburb of Dundee, Illinois, SamataMason principal Pat Samata says that she and husband/partner Greg Samata and partner Dave Mason work hard to nurture client relationships that turn into friendships. "I can't tell you how many times I've said, 'This friend of mine, she's a client, she's also a friend,'" says Pat. Instead of traditional client entertainment based on wining, dining, and tickets to sports events, clients might be invited to supper at the Samata home, sharing a bottle of wine that Greg uncorks while the kids are running around the table. "We wouldn't want to work with anybody we wouldn't want for a friend," Pat adds, describing how the partners chose to resign the firm's highest billing account because the client was "chewing up the staff for breakfast." She explains, "Nobody wanted to pick up the phone. Life is too short for that." It's no surprise that SamataMason's mission statement and Web-site theme is "We do good work for good people."

Adds Marcia Lausen, "Design is a life-consuming business. I can't think of a good friend who is not a colleague or a client. The client who becomes a true friend is easy to talk to about difficult things, such as money issues or a return to the drawing board. And because we're friends, we do talk. If I need money, I can say how much and why. They know I wouldn't ask if I didn't have to, and will give a short, straight answer like, 'Okay, that sounds fair,' 'Sorry, I can't get it,' or 'I'll see what I can do.' Business is great when it's like that."

A new-client friendship can be tricky to handle at first. Should you extend that invitation to a Saturday-night dinner at your home or to your end-of-summer barbecue, or not? Will stepping over that line muddy the waters? Will knowing that the client has been in your kitchen, used your bathroom, or seen your three-year-old have a tantrum, make it more or less difficult for you to bring up such issues as the invoice is fifteen days overdue? You have to feel your way through every situation. Occasionally "very-good-friend" clients do give once-favored designers the brush-off after there is a business disagreement or "management decides to change vendors." Don't fool yourself; friendship is no guarantee you'll get all their work forever. And that can hurt. But many designers think it's worth it to attempt to become friends. Because, as Lausen says, design is a life-consuming business and we want our good clients to become part of our lives.

PAMPER THEM

Consultants to the graphic design business claim that the number-one secret of success is to make clients feel pampered. And that doesn't just mean wining and dining them when appropriate. It means making them feel like you're 100 percent there for them.

Business consultant Maria Piscopo writes in *Step Inside Graphics* magazine: "Clients are sometimes like children who need handholding. Indulging them without doing yourself a disservice promotes a relationship where they feel you are on their side." Adds Don Sparkman, a Washington, D.C., design firm president and the author of *Selling Graphic Design* (Allworth Press, 1999), "A certain amount of coddling encourages clients to become repeat customers. Clients want to feel that you are their special designer, even if they work with other designers."

Correct. Clients also want to feel like they are your special client—even like your *only* client, while you're engaged in their projects—even though they know that isn't true or even possible.

If it were only up to clients, you would always be at your desk when they call. They would get 100 percent of your undivided attention. You would never be in a hurry (except when doing something for them, of course). When the call is a request, the work would be finished and delivered, if not by 5:30 P.M. that day, by 9 A.M. the next morning. Every e-mail would be answered within five (no, make that two) minutes. If a meeting is requested for tomorrow, your calendar would be wide open. Overall, you'd put in twice as much effort and attention as anticipated and the bill would be 30 percent less than the estimate.

Realistic? Not exactly. But those designers who are able to create that illusion might be enjoying the greatest success.

Perhaps the interview in this book that comes closest to unlocking the secret is the one that explores the relationship between Pentagram partner Kit Hinrichs and the late Tom Wrubel, founder of The Nature Company (chapter 13). This client-designer partnership seemed to have it all. Hinrichs's identity, packaging, and catalogs for The Nature Company not only won a zillion design awards, they used the power of design to help build a single Berkeley store that sold field glasses and books about insects into a $90 million, international empire. The secret ingredient? Hinrichs and Wrubel drove around the Bay Area together and talked about life. Hinrichs was not a "vendor" or a "service provider," or even a "creative," but a trusted confidante and advisor. Nature Company merchandising and marketing manager Kathy Tierney has stated, "We won't have a meeting without him." Was that unique? Not for Hinrichs. "It's not unique to the Nature Company," he said. "Tom and I spent a lot of time together. I was on retainer as a consultant, and we used to drive around to the stores together and spend hours talking. You can always do better work if you know the top person well. And, sure, you can be dedicated to more than one client."

WHAT IF THE CLIENT REALLY NEEDS HELP?

Most clients are not like Tom Wrubel. Some, as you've probably learned, might not even know whether something is doable, printable, or even legal or advisable.

"Educating clients" is something we hear and talk about all the time. Accomplishing that successfully while keeping them happy is not easy. Most clients are pretty sure that they know what they're doing, and they resist being "educated," especially about basic stuff they don't know (the number of pages in a book has to be divisible by four), which would embarrass them, or stuff you think they should know (that it costs more than $250 a day to hire a photographer) that contradicts what their boss has asked them to do. Sometimes they don't appreciate the value of what they're getting. "An oxymoron is a grateful client," grouses agency chairman Allen Kay. His compatriot Peter Farago agrees, "Clients can be just like your children, resentful, unappreciative." Adds Kay: "If we still had all the clients we had over the years we'd be billing $2 billion."

But looking at things in a more positive light is the only way to keep sane —and to move forward. Les Daly, for thirty-three years vice president for public affairs at Northrop Corporation (chapter 11), advises that clients and designers are in a teamed situation, whether they like it or not, whether their experience levels are equal or not. Daly, who's worked with many leading design firms, says that designers who want to show clients the "right" way to do things should take it slowly.

"Let's look at the struggle of a designer with an average client who knows little or nothing except what he or she may be afraid to like," says Daly. "Decisions in a bureaucracy are more often made by fear than conviction. Respect that fear. Move in small steps. Take the client by the hand at every turn. This may not be the right moment or project for leaping to the edge. And get rid of attitude. Too many designers arrive excessively alert to any signal that their design integrity may be threatened. Remember you aren't in some kind of contest," he warns. "Ideally it's an opportunity—in the case of an annual report, a once-a-year opportunity—for the client and designer to both expand their experience, learn from each other and from the printer and photographer how to achieve the company's objectives and their own professional and artistic goals."

LET THEM KNOW IF THERE ARE CHANGES— AND HOW MUCH THOSE CHANGES WILL COST

If referrals are the number-one source of new business, not letting clients know the cost of changes may be the number-one source of lost business.

The chairman wants to see more ideas. More meetings are required. More pages are added to the book or to the site—more products, more copy, more pictures, new layouts. What is the assumption? That you love to work so much that it won't cost any more? This would never happen with a plumber ("Just fix the pipe in the *other* bathroom"), an auto mechanic, a dentist. Why should it happen with a graphic designer? Maybe the answer is because we've let it.

Let's not, any more.

Technology has made the issues more complex. You agree to a fee to design a magazine. The client sends all the pictures as color JPEGs, some of dubious quality. It's a black-and-white magazine. Forty pictures have to be changed to TIFF format, color information removed, sharpened, straightened; curves, brightness, and contrast adjusted. It's a time-consuming, but essential, process. Don't include all that work in your fee—in essence doing it for free—and be angry about it. Calculate a number that covers your costs, then send the client a memo. *Before* he or she gets the bill. Explain that the work is additional and was not anticipated in the proposal. If the client is a reasonable person, you will get a verbal okay and there will be no unpleasant surprises for either of you later.

You agree to a fee to design an annual report. At the last minute the chairman rewrites his letter, making it 2,000 words longer, and requests two more charts, all of which will add four pages to the book. Calculate a number that covers the increased costs, then send the client a memo.

Several years ago I moderated two panels for the AIGA New York Chapter: "Marketing Design Services from the Client Perspective" and "Effective Billing and Collecting." Both the panel of esteemed clients and the panel of esteemed designers agreed: there are always changes, and changes cost money. "Let us know how much. Let us know right away!" cried the clients, almost in unison. No client wants to be in the position of having to get the boss's approval on an invoice that's 30 percent higher than the estimate—even if the boss is the one who requested the changes. You might be under tremendous pressure to finish a job (it's especially crucial if that's the case), but still take five minutes to write and fax the memo.

Part of your role is to make your client into a hero. Heroes don't get bills that put them in difficult positions. That five minutes may save your relationship, and maybe even your client's reputation within his or her organization.

THREE WAYS TO LOSE A CLIENT

There are three almost-guaranteed ways (other than a too-high bill) to ensure that someone else gets to work with your client next time. Maybe, after the fact, you can cleverly talk your way out of them . . . but why put yourself in that position?

One: Something gets messed up in the printing. It's usually not the printing per se, but it's something the printer is responsible for, like the binding or laminating. You've signed off on the sheet, having sweated bullets to get the printer to do more than he wanted to (change a plate, change an ink color, run more ink). The pressman and your salesman argued against it, but you prevailed, confident that the sheet was perfect when you left. Then, when the client opens the cartons, you get the irate phone call: Some of the covers are crooked, a page is upside down on a few copies, the aqueous coating is bubbling. (I can count on the fingers of one hand the number of times this has happened to me, but that's still too many lost clients for one career.) Whether you are paying for the printing (and marking it up as compensation for your supervision services) or it's billed directly to the client, you've got to convince the printer to redo the job, whatever it takes, even if the printing company has to eat its costs. (And don't work with that printer again, no matter how many lunches they want to treat you to. Poor quality control is never an isolated incident.)

Two: There's a typo. Your basic misspelled word that nobody caught can turn a "great" job into a nightmare. Even in this age of spell-check (and Quark has a totally inadequate spell-check), it happens. It may be the client's legal responsibility, according to your agreement, to check proofs and sign off, but they hold you responsible anyway, and want you to pay for having the whole job redone. And, afterwards, they still won't use you again. Right now, I am really, really embarrassed that a client e-mailed me from a conference location to let me know that the ad I did for the program back cover has a typo. I replied that I'd make it up to her. But how, really? What to do? Have someone else, the most nit-picky person around, read *everything* before it goes out—with dictionary in hand, if necessary. Hiring a professional proofreader is the only thing that really works, and it's essential for all large projects.

Three: The client feels that the work has been "passed down" to a junior designer (who won't or can't do the job as well as or better than you). Clients want "principal attention." One of the first, and best, lessons I learned in this business was from Joyce Cole, former communications director at W. R. Grace & Co., where they gave design firms the opportunity to "try out" on a small project before trusting them with bigger and more significant ones. This was twenty years ago, and my firm was assigned the employee newsletter for the division that made plastic film for the meat-packing industry. Entertaining a belief that the subject matter (snapshots of shrink-wrapped pork butts coming off the assembly line) was beneath me, I gave the assignment to a junior designer, who did a not-great, but I thought good-enough, job. When I brought the comps in to Joyce, she looked at them, pulled her glasses down on her nose, looked at me, and said, "Ellen, *you* didn't do *these*, did you?" When I admitted I hadn't, she said, "Let me give you some advice. Don't let this happen again." I didn't. (I redid the newsletter design and we went on to produce several very significant projects together. In fact, Joyce, now the head of a custom knitwear company, is still a client.)

Clients hire *you* because they want *your* designs. I know it's a tough position to be in, but your clients' wishes are more important than your employees' feelings. Employees can redo the work—under your direction, learning from you, their mentor, how it should be done—but a lost client is most likely gone forever. As a boss, you have to make sure that everything that leaves your office is as good as if you'd done it yourself.

STAY IN CONTROL OF THE PROJECT

For all the designer self-promoting, sometimes we "forget" what experts we are. When it really counts—in a new business pitch or creative presentation— we are often too modest about our accomplishments and value. We do know more about the design process than the client. (If you don't, you should still be working for someone who does, and learning from him or her.) Yet, when it comes to how the project should be managed, we often let clients intimidate us. We let them tell us what to charge, how we should organize our working phases, how to make a presentation ("just e-mail us a PDF"), and what the results should be, aesthetically.

The client's job is to tell us what results are needed, *businesswise*, and to let us present the correct solution and methodology.

If you have achieved successes in the past, say so. Tell them. Ask them to follow your lead. You are the expert. That's why they hired you and are paying you. It's appropriate to say things like this:

"This is how the job needs to be managed if you want the results you are looking for. [describe exact steps]."

"I need all people who will have veto power to be present at the first meeting."

"It's worth it to wait a week until the chairman/president gets back to get his or her input before I start working/move to the next phase."

"If that doesn't happen, we may have to redo the phase and you will be charged for it" [works like a charm].

"I need you to do this for me [whatever it is] before we move on to the next phase."

"This [whatever calamity you foresee] has happened to me before and I want to ensure it doesn't happen with your organization."

"I won't be able to help you unless you do [X, Y, or Z]."

"If that's the situation, maybe you should find another designer."

"Maybe you should find another designer" is not a threat. It's a simple statement of fact. It can open a valuable discussion. You have certain expertise, insights, and talents to offer. If the client is not listening to you, perhaps another designer will be a better fit. On the other hand, that statement may bring to the client's attention the fact that they have chosen you and that it would be in their best interests to follow your lead.

But you had better know what you're doing.

For more ideas on how to position yourself and the entire profession, see the new AIGA strategy (*www.aiga.org*). Developed to "drive significantly deeper success in the profession of design," the strategy includes tools to help designers to more clearly advocate for the power of design and to articulate the value design can add to business at each step in the process.

What If the Client Hates Your Idea?

You and I are not the only ones who have this problem. Far from it.

Let's say that Stefan Sagmeister is one of the most admired graphic designers in the world. He can pick and choose his clients. As was widely reported, he spent 2001 as a "reflective" year without clients, but they kept calling and trying to get him to change his mind. (When the rest of us spend years or months without clients, it's usually not by choice.) And Sagmeister's clients are not your run-of-the-mill marketers or brand managers. They're often stars of music or media or fashion who've engaged a kindred spirit to help craft an image and transmit a message to the people who will have the most affinity with it. Nevertheless, Sagmeister still has to fight for his ideas. "I fight for things all the time," he says. "I cry and beg."

Let's say you show three concepts, in the order in which you think they work best to transmit the message. Naturally, the client picks number three, your least favorite. You don't hate it, but it's obviously not the caliber of numbers one and two. "The full-bleed photograph is much more dramatic in number two," you might venture, trying to sell your rationale. "I like number three," the client replies, in a tone of voice that clearly means: "I made my decision. Don't even think about crying and begging."

What would Sagmeister do in that situation? His answer: "It would never happen. As a rule, we show one thing. Our clients know from the beginning that the presentation will have one solution. Even if they are marketing people used to seeing three or five comps, I tell them that if we did that, the overall quality would be lower. After all, it's the job of the designer to pick the best solution." Sagmeister says that he only breaks the rule when the solution is something that would require a tricky manufacturing process that might be too difficult or expensive to pull off.

And what if the client doesn't like that one solution? "We talk about it," says Sagmeister. "I ask questions. Why don't they like it? What's bothering them. Our second presentation incorporates what they did like about the first one. There is almost never a problem then," he says. "Actually, crying and begging is a last resort."

Is one good idea enough? Or should you present a range? To some clients, one concept that hits the mark is enough. Others do need to see a range, and many designers want to explore the choices with the client. "This is a full-service agency," asserts Drew Hodges of Spot Design and Spotco. "I am not a personal visionary. My clients want to be choosy. They want to have a role in the choice. I always say, 'I think this is the one,' but I show at least half a dozen. There are always different ways to solve something."

One word of advice: Never, never show a design that you do not under any circumstances want the client to choose. For obvious reasons, that is always a mistake.

HOW IMPORTANT IS PERSONALITY?

Very. Sagmeister credits the late Tibor Kalman with showing him how to make clients fall in love with designs they thought they hated.

Make clients fall in love with designs they thought they hated.

Isn't that the secret we're all looking for? If we knew that, we'd all be rich and famous and ecstatically happy.

How, exactly, I asked, did Tibor accomplish that?

"He overwhelmed the clients," is Sagmeister's answer. "He had more personality than the minyan of ten marketing people in the room. He spent an incredible amount of energy making sure things got through the process and produced the way he wanted them. He built elaborate presentations. He was honest. With all the ass-kissing going on in this business, clients thought it was refreshingly honest when Tibor called them idiots. If a client was cheap he might lay a row of pennies or dollar bills from the front door to the conference room. And he was willing to fight, to pull the job. He would threaten: 'Okay, we'll stop working for you.'"

Is this the way Sagmeister operates? "No. Not at all," he asserts. "It makes no sense for me to emulate that. I have a different kind of personality."

I never fail to be amazed by Tibor stories. An up-and-coming entertainment client told me that Tibor thought that his company's logo should be a rowboat going upstream. I was not only struck by the offbeat brilliance of the idea, but by the reverent tones that the client used. Len Riggio, chairman of Barnes & Noble (chapter 12) changed ad agencies on the strength of Tibor's recommendation.

How can I project that kind of confidence, you are probably wondering right now? How can I get that kind of respect and attention? What should I say or do to make it happen? All of us wonder that all the time.

"These are very individual occurrences," says Milton Glaser. "They're based on personal chemistry." He admits that his then-radical ideas for Grand Union Supermarkets (chapter 14), such as European-market-style environments for selling fresh fish, cheese, and herbs, would have gone nowhere if it weren't for his friendship with the client, Sir James Goldsmith. "We liked each other," Glaser says simply.

Perhaps the real secret is taking the time to find the clients with whom the chemistry will happen for you.

GET REFERRALS TO THEIR FRIENDS AND COLLEAGUES

Okay, you've done everything right. The project is wildly successful. You've even gotten paid. Now what?

Keep in touch with your client and ask for referrals to his or her colleagues.

There is a fine line between keeping in touch and being a pest. Learn where that line is, and stay on the good side of it. Call once in a while just to say hello and find out what's going on at the organization. Send holiday greetings. Even birthday greetings, maybe. Make the assumption that the client is happy and that you will continue to be "their" designer. Ask for referrals, too. As attorney Gerry Spence has said (chapter 3), "It seems that the more we want something the more hesitant we are to ask for it." There's nothing wrong with calling every once in a while to ask:

"Is there anything else I can help you with?"

"Are there any projects coming up in the next six months or year?"

"Is there anything happening in other divisions of the company I should know about?"

"Can you introduce me to some of your colleagues in other departments?"

"Can you give me the names and numbers of people who might be interested in my work?"

If you've truly met the client's needs, it's likely you will be getting more work, both from the client and from his or her friends and colleagues, both inside and outside the organization. It may not happen immediately. But it will happen. The phone will ring. It will be the marketing director in another department or at another company. Ask:

"Where did you get my name?"

And don't be surprised when you hear it was from that client you made into a hero.

THE PEOPLE WHO
DO IT RIGHT

The clients and designers in this book are big names for a reason. The following seventeen chapters will show you why.

THE SECRETS OF SUCCESS ARE BETWEEN THE LINES

Over the years I've had the privilege of interviewing many of the top players in this business—the people who've made this elusive, collaborative client-designer partnership work the best. Up to now, you've read mostly about what I've experienced, sprinkled with experiences of other designers. From now on, you'll hear directly from some of the world's smartest clients (and their designers), in a question-and-answer format.

Q&As are honest and revealing. The writer doesn't provide a narrative or interject a point of view.

Why a focus on superstars of the business? Let me answer that by relating this anecdote: One of the first talks I gave, sort of a disaster, introduced my first book, *Clients and Designers.* The organizers of a conference invited me to talk about the book, and I took the request much too literally. I had slides shot of pages of the book, which was highly illustrated with color photography, and showed those slides, spread by spread. After a few minutes, one audience member got up and said, "If you're going to talk about a book, I want my money back!" If that weren't bad enough, another said, "I don't want to hear about those famous people! Tell me what I can do, not what Michael Vanderbyl or Ivan Chermayeff has done."

Actually, I shouldn't have gotten ruffled. It was true then, and still is now, that the way we learn is from the masters. Not only how to design (which is not what this book is about), but how to work with clients so that your designs will see the light of day.

"What they have done *is* what you can and should do!" I insisted that day —and still insist.

THEY ARE ALL GREAT DESIGNERS

According to Ed Gold, all great designers share ten common characteristics. Numbers one and two, as mentioned before, are *talent* ("their work just seems to look better; when we look at it we almost always say, 'Gee, I wish I'd done that'"), and *advocacy* or sales ability. Ed identifies the other characteristics as *curiosity, dissatisfaction* (which he defines as the determination to do things that haven't been done before), *perfectionism, energy, confidence* (the belief that they can design anything, in any medium), having the right balance of *idealism and realism, wit,* and the fact that they just *love their work.*

I hope you'll be inspired by the designers interviewed for this book, especially by their confidence. None of them can be pushed around. They expect clients to listen to them. And for the most part, they do. In the words of Mike Weymouth, "Clients who come to my firm tend to know they're going to get 'new and different,' and they actually listen to us, believe it or not. They ask us for our advice and, by and large, they take it." April Greiman characterizes herself as "shy," but she's not too shy to say this about her clients: "Having identified with my aesthetic, ideologically, they give me freedom. My clients have done their homework in terms of which designer they've chosen. I don't interfere with the way they manufacture their products or run their organizations. They don't question my aesthetic or interfere too much with my design."

These designers are the ones who have positioned themselves as experts worthy of clients' trust and respect. They haven't merely "positioned themselves." They *are* the experts.

THEY ARE ALL GREAT CLIENTS

In the next seventeen chapters you'll also be hearing from some of the world's most successful clients—CEOs and marketing and communications managers. All of whom, as you'll see, also share some common characteristics:

They have *vision*, a vision of their organizations and an understanding of how design can help bring about that vision.

They *trust* their designers. They give the designer the opportunity to do his or her job without interfering or micromanaging.

They can do this because of their *professionalism*; these are people who articulate their needs masterfully and present clear, intelligent design briefs. They push, when a design isn't working, in a way that inspires the designer to do better, not that ridicules or belittles.

Interestingly, great clients share many of the traits of great designers: *curiosity, dissatisfaction, perfectionism, energy, confidence, idealism, wit.* And they also *love their work.*

ARCHETYPES, NOT STEREOTYPES

Is it fair to label clients, as I've done in the chapter titles? To call them "The Visionary," "The "Financial Wizard," "The Tycoon," "The Scientist-Entrepreneur," and so forth?

Yes and no. They are all individuals, yet each represents an archetype of the most positive kind, one that is the most worthy of emulation.

I hope that by absorbing what each client—and each designer—has to say, by reading between the lines a bit, you will feel as if you are having a series of private meetings with some of the smartest people around.

ONLY A DIAMOND LASTS FOREVER. THIS IS BUSINESS

As anyone who reads the advertising columns in the newspapers knows, clients change agencies all the time. There are "incumbents." Agencies are "in review." Sometimes it's because sales are down. Sometimes it's a new management team. Sometimes a personality thing. The same thing happens to design firms. It just isn't reported in the papers because millions of dollars spent on public media aren't at stake.

Your best client today may not be there for you when you call three years from now. What happened? Did you do something wrong? Probably not. It's business. Companies are merged and acquired. Business strategies change.

Some of the legendary relationships chronicled herein—Grand Union and Milton Glaser, The Nature Company and Kit Hinrichs—did not last forever (as noted in the introductions to each chapter). While they lasted, though, a lot of extraordinary work got done. And it doesn't make what we can learn from them any less valid.

MAYBE NOT FOREVER, BUT FOR A REALLY LONG TIME

If there's anything I've tried to emphasize in this book, it's that doing good work for satisfied clients will lead to more work for them, their organizations, their colleagues, friends, and others who are impressed by your work—and who hear good things about you.

All of us want to make clients happy and do great work. I wish there were ten easy steps guaranteed to make that happen. Although every situation is different, here are the ten key things I've learned from these interviews:

1. Don't just start designing. Do research.
2. Don't reinvent yourself as a marketing consultant. But *do* use your clients' products, talk to their customers. Learn what makes them different and better.

3. Take things slowly. Don't come in to your first meeting and tell potential clients how to run their organizations. These relationships take months or years to develop.
4. Collaborate; involve the client in the process.
5. Dealing with big clients often means dealing with big egos. Many clients like to take credit for the creative work. Let them.
6. Develop your own working style. Some designers like to show one solution that they've determined is best. Others show a range of solutions. Do what works for you, and adapt it to the needs of each client.
7. Listen more than you talk.
8. Have the confidence to stick up for what you believe in.
9. Study the best work out there. Don't copy it, but figure out what makes it great. Then strive to produce work of that caliber for every one of your clients.
10. You don't get too many big opportunities in life. Take full advantage of those you get.

MOTIVATE YOURSELF WITH CHALLENGES

Last September, Jerry Seinfield presented what he called a bizarre challenge to himself. He wandered around New York's Upper West Side, people-watching, looking for seeds for a new standup comedy routine. Why was Seinfeld returning to comedy clubs, wondered *Times* reporter Rick Lyman, who accompanied him on his journey ("Going Hunting in Seinfeld Country," *New York Times*, September 15, 2002), when he could take his millions and live in St. Barts? "The reason, I guess," answered Seinfeld, "is that I really love standup. It's fun and it uses everything you have as a human being."

"It's a really crazy idea. It probably won't work, but that will be interesting, too," Seinfield continued, describing his quest to find new material among the denizens of upper Broadway. "You have to motivate yourself with challenges. That's how you know you're still alive. Once you start doing what you've already proven you can do, you're on the road to death."

Most graphic designers can relate to that. We will probably never make enough money to go to St. Bart's for more than two weeks. We aren't after the biggest laughs. But we do what we do because we really love it. And we are after the biggest reactions. No one wants to do dull, boring work just to pay the rent. With great clients, work is fun and it uses everything we have as human beings. Like Jerry, we are always ready for the next challenge. We never want to keep doing what we've already proven we can do. That's what keeps design —and us—alive and fresh.

PART II

CORPORATE CLIENTS

Some corporate clients make products, like bicycles, airplanes, and artificial hearts. Others provide services, like consulting and investment banking. Whether it's a literary novel or an ergonomic chair, the focus is equally on the design of the product and on the way it is packaged, launched, and advertised. Even those clients who are strictly business-to-business use print communications and the Web to keep customers informed, and coming back.

6

THE HARD-CORE
AFICIONADO

Klein Bikes *and* Liska + Associates

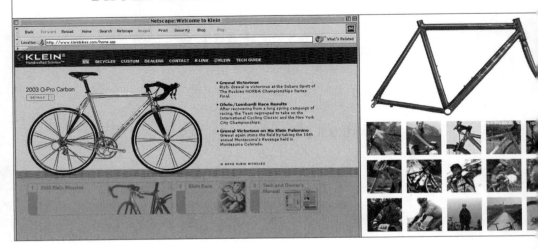

KLEIN BICYCLES, located in Waterloo, Wisconsin, is internationally recognized for its high-performance, handcrafted road and mountain bikes. Founded in 1975 in an MIT lab, the company holds twenty design patents and produces more than 20,000 bikes a year, which are sold in forty-five countries. *Connie Ryland* has been the brand manager for Klein since 1988. Prior to working at Klein, Ryland was an in-house marketing executive at San Francisco–based The Gap, and an assistant account executive for Foote, Cone and Belding, Chicago. She is a 1987 graduate of the University of Wisconsin at Madison in journalism and advertising.

LISKA + ASSOCIATES is a brand and communication design consultancy founded by *Steve Liska* in 1980. With thirteen people in its Chicago headquarters, the firm opened a New York City office in 1995. A frequent design judge and lecturer and chairman of the honorary membership group 27 Chicago Designers, Liska has taught in masters programs in design at The School of the Art Institute of Chicago, Kent State University, and Syracuse University. Lead designer on the Klein account is *Kim Fry*, design director in the Chicago office, who has responsibility for client contact, creative direction, and production supervision.

Clients need design firms that can help them do what they can't do in-house. For example, to build an online community that attracts customers and keeps them coming back. It's called "permission marketing," and it's what all brand managers want: a loyal cadre of aficionados who regularly visit their site, participate in interactive activities, engage in dialogue via e-mail, and ultimately buy their products. By applying the principles of information architecture to interactive design, Liska + Associates has proven that this can be done elegantly, without flashing banners. With Liska's help, "cult" racing and mountain-bike maker Klein Bicycles moved into the broader luxury sports and leisure product category, increasing sales while retaining its original customer base. Approximately 5,000 Klein owners belong to the K-link online community. The site, *www.kleinbikes.com*, gets more than 60,000 visits a month.

To find out more about how his firm helped make this happen, I met with Steve Liska at his New York office in a gallery building on West 26th Street. Design director Kim Fry later joined the conversation.

Steve, how did Klein become your client?

LISKA: It was a referral from fellow Chicago design firm principal Rick Valicenti. Four years ago, Klein's marketing and photography budget was almost bankrupted by a West Coast design firm. Connie Ryland needed to change firms, knew of Rick and his work for Gary Fisher Bicycles, another Trek-owned bike company, and so she asked him for a referral. Because of his relationship with Fisher, it would have been a conflict of interest for Rick to work for Klein, so he recommended us. Klein called us, saying, "We need a brochure, point-of-purchase materials, hangtags, a Web site. We don't have much money. And we're losing market share."

What was the first thing you did?

LISKA: We started riding their bikes. Connie gave one to Kim and one to me. Then we visited a lot of bike shops. We found out right away that the bicycle resale world is intimidating and esoteric. If you go into a bike shop and want to spend $300 or $400, a hard-core guy tries to sell you an obscure bike that costs ten times that much, because that's what he likes to ride and thinks is cool. Unless you know exactly what you want, you can be left feeling embarrassed that you even wanted a $300 bike in the first place, even if that may be what's best for you and how you ride.

Everyone at Klein is a hard-core biker, just like their customers. They're avid racers and triathletes. Marketing-wise, Klein had been talking to people like themselves, the biking elite, pros and fanatics. We concluded that in order to survive and be profitable, the company needed to change its strategy without alienating their current market. Klein bikes are high-level cult objects—exquisite, coveted, lightweight, beautiful, and the best engineered in the world. But there are not enough elite racers and mountain bikers to sustain the business. The technical specifications that Klein was so fanatical about had no meaning to the larger, broader audience they needed to attract in order to stay profitable. But we couldn't lose all the science because it is fundamental to Klein. They had never gone after the luxury-product market: People who have a Mercedes or a BMW or a $70,000 Lexus SUV in the garage, and the means and the desire to spend $3,500 for a mountain bike or $4,000 for a racing bike, maybe only to ride on weekends.

This kind of thinking is a level or two beyond what one usually thinks of as the role of a graphic design firm. You are acting as marketing consultants. Is that how you usually work?

LISKA: Yes, always. All effective design firms need to ground their work in strategy and goals, or otherwise they are merely decorators.

How did you present your conclusions and recommendations?

LISKA: First of all, it was hard to get them off their bikes. But we showed Klein the big picture and convinced them that a broader audience of consumers—once they were educated and empowered—could make smart decisions. We walked them through a total brand re-assessment: the attributes of the product, the audience, the challenges, the potential. The presentation showed them how we planned to reposition the way they visually presented the bikes, talked about the bikes, and explained their value. We said that our first step would be to educate consumers about the bikes' features and teach them how to decide which bike would best fit their riding style.

In addition to their former catalog, which was too big and expensive, Klein had a homegrown Web site. At the time, 1998, people were really getting into using the Web for research and reference, so a new site was an important part of the strategy. We wanted Klein to have a site that would speak to its new target audience and help educate them about Klein and its bikes. We showed how the marketing materials would be completely harmonious; that the site, the point-of-sale materials, the ads, and the catalog would all work together to tell the same story.

What was the reaction to the presentation?

LISKA: They were very unsure, worried. They said, "You're not bike people." At first, Connie was nervous and skeptical, too. But she was responsible for the success of the line. And she trusted us.

And they went ahead with the plan?

LISKA: Yes. It took about a year, with five people working on it, to complete it for Klein's domestic and international markets. There were an incredible number of materials to create, many of them translated into six languages. The selling messages had to be broad enough to include Klein's international and domestic audiences: what people in Italy are looking for, what the Japanese are looking for, what Seattle is looking for. We shot all new photography that could be re-purposed for every medium. When we were done designing the catalogs and Web site, we created dealer incentives, 3-D displays, demo kits, and sales training materials to support the Klein dealers. We wanted to make sure that the dealers had the tools needed to promote the brand and reach the new target audience, as well as to show their sales staff how all the new materials worked together. Then it took a while for the selling channels to actually implement the changes and make them happen.

Kim, what were your goals for the design?

FRY: Visually, all communication needed to reflect the product. It had to be sophisticated, streamlined, and educate the audience about the technical value. We wanted to combine this with lush, dramatic photography of the bikes, which would elicit a visceral response. On a basic level, the bikes are so frigging beautiful, we wanted to show that. But to appeal to the new market, the design also needed to be accessible and create an awareness that wasn't previously there.

The Web site is clean looking, but complex and detailed. The credits for some larger sites typically read like those for a TV show or major motion picture. How many people at your firm worked on it?

LISKA: Three. You don't need a big team. We are extremely focused.

Many graphic designers have problems with the lack of consistency in Web design. Once a site is up and running and the client takes over its maintenance, which can mean daily or even more frequent updates, the integrity of the design can go downhill pretty quickly.

LISKA: Connie not only wanted us to design the site, she wanted us to maintain it. Our role is to continue to help Klein maintain its best-of-class status. Everything always revolves around the Klein product—it's not about people sitting around talking about biking. It's about how great Klein bikes are and how they perform.

Kim, you are responsible for creative direction and staff and production supervision. Tell me about your role and how you function on this account.

FRY: Our office is very collaborative, so we all work together on the creative. On a daily basis, my role consists of communicating with the client and coordinating the budgets, production schedules, translations, photographers and photography, the printer and the designers who work on the project, which was a full-time job for several months. Connie and I have weekly status conference calls to review the projects, which is great, because there is a constant line of communication open that helps us anticipate and avoid problems.

These days, everyone talks about "building online communities." Most need consultants to provide this service, which can make or break a brand. How do you go about doing it?

LISKA: First of all, we don't force community. We're not trying to involve people in something they're essentially not interested in. We knew that hard-core Klein fanatics would visit the site anyway. The new audience we were trying to attract needed to know a lot more about the bikes. Our goal is to inform and educate, to provide lots of product information, so they would naturally want to keep returning to the site. We also tell the story behind the company. Gary Klein was literally a MIT rocket scientist who applied his knowledge to design some of the world's fastest, lightest bikes. We have a section on his "personal-fit" philosophy. The site makes you aware that there are things like fit philosophy that make a Klein superior to other bikes. We filled the site with consumer-focused features, accessible articles explaining the technologies behind Klein, and then started adding attractions like contests and premiums.

Contests and premiums? Your firm is known for design that's not junked up.

LISKA: A contest doesn't have to be a big, red, flashing banner. We make sure the look of everything mirrors the technologically advanced look of the product. Our position to the client is, "Trust us to design it the Klein way." When we do something like a free T-shirt offer, it always looks like it's coming from Klein.

Kim, to you, how does "the Klein way" translate into design decisions?

FRY: In the first weeks of the project we worked with Klein to set up parameters that define "the Klein way." Before any design decisions are made—then and now—we make sure they adhere to these brand standards. This directly affects the integrity. Decisions are never random, they're analytical. The design is fluid enough to evolve with the bikes, but the core attributes remain the same, so we stay true to them.

What makes this online community successful goes deeper than T-shirt contests, doesn't it?

LISKA: It's all about the ride. Klein bikes are experiential. Regardless of where you fall in the market category, when you begin riding, you become a missionary in search of converts. The bike becomes a part of you and you feel special. What we really did was create a site that helps people to express their love for their Kleins. Another innovation is K-link, an online club. It allows you to register your new bike online, or sign up if you're already a Klein owner. You can register for offers like free helmets and saddles. We post race results there, and we also link to dealer promotions. Klein communicates regularly with its K-link members by e-mail. A piece of technology sends product announcements and other information directly to members' mailboxes.

What was the initial result?

LISKA: Connie was overwhelmed with the number of people who signed up, from the moment it first launched.

One of the nicest features of the site is the language options: The first thing you see after "Welcome to Klein" is a row of boxes: "English, Deutsch, Français, Español, Nederlands, Japanese."

LISKA: Klein has a very strong, loyal international market. It was important for us to create a site that would speak to these customers in their own languages. A great, HTML-friendly translation company handles the translations. We send the whole Web-site file to Japan periodically so that they can update their version.

How much time do you spend working on the site now?

LISKA: I spend a whole day every two weeks or so on the account. In the process, I have also become a major fan, and so have the designers who have worked on Klein projects. I could totally wear myself out telling people how much I love my Klein bike. I ride every weekend.

LATER, I SPOKE WITH CONNIE RYLAND.

Steve said it was hard to get you-all off your bikes to make his initial presentation? Was he kidding, or is Klein really an organization of "hard-core bikers" who are not into stuff like marketing?

RYLAND: Klein employees sometimes spend up to two hours a day on their bikes, testing new frames and designs. But we are just as professional as the marketing managers at any other company.

I understand that your reaction to the Liska presentation or plan was "nervous and skeptical," in fact, that you thought it might have been just plain wrong. From your point of view, what was Steve's presentation like?

RYLAND: In the beginning we thought he overcomplicated things and that the layouts were over-engineered. We wanted to pull back and simplify things. We were always on board with the strategy. We were always the Lexus of bicycles. Nobody had to sell us on that. Liska affirmed where we were headed.

What was the assignment to Liska, exactly? Did you tell them what the "deliverables" should be, or did they tell you what you needed to do in order to accomplish your goals?

RYLAND: The assignment was to create an all-new Web site, to create a community online. We asked, "Can you do this in multiple languages?" They said, "We'll try." They did a good job. We have been very pleased with the number of hits. The site gets about 15,000 visits a week, confirming that the Web is a tool that speaks to our tech-savvy customer demographic.

From your point of view, what does creating a community online mean?

RYLAND: It means building customer loyalty. We do this by means of specific promotional offers designed to drive people into a store. For example, if someone buys a bike with a custom paint scheme, he or she can get a limited-edition wool jersey. If they buy a USA paint scheme, money will be donated to the September 11 Fund.

One of the hallmarks of Liska's work is the clean, pristine, organized design. Many e-commerce sites get pretty messed up with flashing banners, contests, etc. You did not bring the maintenance of the site in-house . . . because?

RYLAND: Liska does pretty much everything on the site. It's a grassroots effort. We drive the content, but they do the content updates. They are very good executionally and their customer service is exceptional, a combination that's not always easy to find.

To you, what are the benefits of K-link?

RYLAND: We've had K-link for a year and a half, and approximately five thousand people belong to the K-link online community. One of the most successful promotions was posting members' ideas for custom paint schemes. It was a virtual-marketing contest juried by our in-house product-design team, and it was a huge success, both from an exposure and marketing-spend perspective. It gave people a strong reason to come back and see if they were a finalist. We had more than seven hundred submissions from avid cyclists who are graphic designers, architects, and others comfortable with Adobe Illustrator, Photoshop, and other software. In fact, the winning entry came from a graphic designer in Minneapolis. Needless to say, we're doing it again.

What are some of your other favorite features of the site?

RYLAND: I love the way Liska made previewing the custom bike options really easy and clean and fast. The product rollovers—the way you roll over the list of the bike components (frame, wheel system)—and up pops a red circle showing its position on the picture and a description. That's really clever. And I like the way they were able to do that in all six languages. That takes a lot of coordination.

How are you working with Liska now? Any interesting projects on the horizon?

RYLAND: We are really focusing them on the Web. We want to keep the site growing. We are always interested in more and better ideas for driving traffic to the site.

What would you advise other designers who would like to work with companies like yours?

RYLAND: I would tell designers to make sure that your ego isn't out of line with your talent. There has to be the right balance between good, creative customer service and attention to detail. A lot of firms give you good creative but fall off on the other two.

What would you tell other entrepreneurial companies — not just bike companies — about design and choosing designers?

RYLAND: I would advise them to invite design firms — those firms who have been sending you things and that you are impressed by — to come in and make a pitch. A lot of the decision is based on personal chemistry and visual cues. Ask those you like to do a pitch assignment, with a financial incentive. You'll see right away whether they have what it takes to not only quickly understand your brand, but to take it in new directions. It's hard to find really good thinkers — look for this in the pitch. Look for those who think beyond the status quo. Also look for good copywriting: that's where the thinking really plays out, and grabs the consumer. Good copywriting is very, very hard to find.

THE **DESIGN ICON**

The Knoll Group *and* Chermayeff & Geismar

THE KNOLL GROUP was formed in 1990 when the Knoll International, ShawWalker, Reff, and Westinghouse Furniture Systems brands were bought by Westinghouse Electric. Beginning in the 1940s Knoll made its reputation with architect-designed furniture; today, its major product lines are office systems, ergonomic seating, and contract textiles, which are distributed through independently owned dealerships. Knoll's vice president of communications, *David Bright*, who worked with Chermayeff & Geismar on the branding and visual communications for the newly merged entity, received a degree in art history from Brown University and an MBA from New York University.

A principal of **CHERMAYEFF & GEISMAR INC.**, the twenty-five-member New York design firm he founded with Ivan Chermayeff in 1960, *Thomas H. Geismar* has been responsible for more than one hundred corporate identity programs, including Chase Manhattan Bank, Best Products, Rockefeller Center, PBS, Mobil Oil, and Xerox. After concurrently attending Rhode Island School of Design and Brown University, from which he received a BA, he earned an

MFA from Yale University School of Art and Architecture. A member of the Alliance Graphique Internationale, Geismar has served as a director of the American Institute of Graphic Arts. In 1979 he received the AIGA Gold Medal, shared with Ivan Chermayeff, and in 1995 he was awarded the Yale Arts Award Medal and the Presidential Design Award.

In 1940, Hans and Florence Knoll opened a design studio and shop on Madison Avenue that changed the face of commercial interior design. In the tradition of the Bauhaus, they commissioned renowned architects to design office furniture to complement Modernist architecture. And they commissioned graphic designers to mirror the spirit of the furniture and the company. Over the next thirty years, Knoll advertising and promotion created by Herbert Matter and later by Massimo Vignelli became synonymous with interiors designed by Florence Knoll and furniture designed by Saarinen, van der Rohe, Noguchi, Bertoia, Breuer, Diffrient, and many others. The ads, catalogs, and product brochures were breathtaking in their simplicity, use of color, and extraordinary studio photography. In 1972, an exhibition at the Louvre celebrated the company's achievements in product, showroom, interior, and graphic design. Several years ago, an intriguing Knoll look and spirit began to appear, including perfectly executed small-space newspaper ads that caught my attention with clever headlines ("Designer Recliner") and made me want to run right out and buy a Frank Gehry Power Play Club Chair for $1,653 and matching Off Side Ottoman for $518. What was up at Knoll? I had the opportunity to find out by speaking with Knoll's vice president of communications, David Bright, at the Knoll Design Center in a spectacularly converted warehouse on Wooster Street in Manhattan's SoHo district.

A new corporate identity often signifies change, a restructuring, or repositioning. What was the situation at the time Knoll began working with Chermayeff & Geismar?

BRIGHT: From a pure identity point of view it was a time of considerable chaos. There were four companies with four separate identities and corporate cultures, and we needed to fuse all those traditions, many of which were very strong, into a singular identity. Once the strategic decision was made to create a new business based on the best aspects of all these players and to capitalize on the recognition factor of the Knoll brand name to leverage all their attributes in the marketplace, we embarked on the new identity program. Our goal was to reinvent or redefine many of the elements and messages that had existed in the past—without denigrating any of the work that had been done previously, especially by Massimo Vignelli, who had been responsible for the worldwide Knoll design and communications positioning.

It's widely acknowledged that the work Vignelli had done for Knoll was world-class in scope and execution. One might ask, why go somewhere else?

BRIGHT: The company founded by Hans and Florence Knoll had transformed itself from one that was involved with object furniture for executive offices, corporate boardrooms, conference rooms, and high-end residences to one primarily focused on office systems and ergonomic seating. The first dramatic change happened in 1986 with the launch of the Morrison Office System, a successful entry into an area where Knoll had never been a player. We went from selling beautiful furniture to serving the broader needs of the workplace. In 1990, the scale of the company quadrupled in size overnight. Our graphic and communication demands became much greater, the markets in which we were operating were very different. Office system products such as ergonomic seating with adjustable features required technical and planning guides that had to rely on text more than on beautiful visual elements. We had a big job to do. It was an unparalleled opportunity to start at square one with identity issues, to strategically look at the situation, to decide how we were going to approach the problem, and then work out a written execution plan that would serve this company long-term. And there was the implementation of everything from business papers to truck graphics to plant signage to product literature formats.

In addition to Chermayeff & Geismar, did you approach other firms that specialize in corporate identity? Was there a request for proposals and a competitive bidding situation?

BRIGHT: We did not solicit bids, and we did not go through a protracted evaluation process. We initially contacted Tom Geismar based on a referral from David Boorstin, a writer and consultant who recommended Tom as an excellent person to work out business and executional issues. We hired Chermayeff & Geismar on the basis of that referral and on the historic strength of their work and their ability to interact with a diverse group of people. Their experience in varied sectors of the economy was appealing, and they had proven themselves over the years by completing broad-based programs for large corporations. A second aspect of this decision was pure personality. I found Tom to be pragmatic, sensitive, artistic, and concerned with the impact of his work on a client's business. Our senior managers were able to develop a good rapport with both Tom and Ivan. They're easygoing and have a non-confrontational style that is appealing to an organization going through lots of change.

What was working on this project like on a day-to-day basis?

BRIGHT: This was not a project in which we sent designers off with an assignment and asked them to come back and make a presentation. It was a process, and as the client we were embraced in it. Tom Geismar led the team, but all the partners at C&G have developed a practice that fosters collaboration and interaction. Ivan was involved in the presentations and the development of the work, especially the work that related to trade shows and showroom interiors. We worked very closely with designers Cathy Schaefer, Emanuela Frigerio, and Weston Bingham. The presentations were more or less conversations, and as a result of those conversations the work evolved. Maybe that's part of my personal style. I don't like hierarchical presentations; I can't work in the kind of mode where you first present to one group and you send it up to another group. We had discussions and presentations with all the people in the room who needed to make a decision; we would think about it for a while, come to consensus, and move on. And to establish a new identity in the marketplace we needed to move exceptionally quickly. In some cases our products had previously been sold by different sales forces in different showrooms.

So a dealer could now be selling a chair under the Knoll name that might have been formerly sold by ShawWalker or Reff?

BRIGHT: Correct. All of a sudden, we needed to have a singular brand identity, and we needed our salespeople to be out there right away selling hard against the competition. We compete in the general office market with Herman Miller, Steelcase, Haworth, Kimball, Allsteel, and a host of smaller manufacturers that are also represented by our dealerships. So one of our biggest challenges was to get our dealer community behind us, understanding the commitment the corporation was making to support the Knoll brand.

Are you saying that a collaborative process can lead to better solutions because it doesn't foster situations in which the designer presents something and the client says, "We can't do that"—the traditional battleground in which the client is trying to make changes and the designer is desperately trying to hold on to what he or she considers the integrity of the design?

BRIGHT: Absolutely. Those types of confrontations don't happen here because they are adjudicated at a different level. Since its early years, Knoll fostered the idea that graphic design is just as important as product design. We are totally involved in the design development process for our products and for the whole range of marketing materials we produce in-house. There's a common interest in design management and appreciation of design, especially as it relates to Modernism. One of the things I most respect about Tom Geismar is that he never comes in and says, "Here is the solution." He certainly has personal preferences and he may have a preconceived notion of how he thinks something should be, but one of his strengths is to reveal a range of ideas. Unlike principals of other corporate identity firms that are more research-focused, it's not his style to write lots of decks and create reams of documentation, but he operates strategically rather than from a visual execution point of view.

Some people might characterize this work — the colors, the imagery — as a bit of a departure for Knoll. What was the reaction in the field?

BRIGHT: The response has been extraordinary. It was overwhelmingly positive from our salespeople — the folks who use the tools in the field every day. And it was overwhelmingly positive from the dealers — the individuals who are on the front lines of our business — as well as from the architects and interior designers and corporate facilities managers who specify our products. Every time something from Knoll comes across their desks, it just pops off the table. The materials are charismatic in a way that's not off-putting or unapproachable by a broad range of people. There is a visual sense that is exactly right for this company.

Tell me about the ads with headlines like "Eero-Dynamic" and "Very Gehry" that appear in the Home Section of the New York Times.

BRIGHT: Those ads may be visually appealing, but they are strategically driven. There is a consumer end-benefit to every ad in the campaign, which is being done by our in-house graphics department. The message is that consumers can now buy furnishings at retail directly from Knoll at our Wooster Street location here in New York City. Traffic has increased. The ads are just one of the things we are doing in-house. We have fifteen people here who work on a range of projects, including press relations, direct marketing, graphic design, and advertising. People in many areas of our company are using the new identity guidelines to produce packaging, signage, newsletters, and corporate communications on a day-to-day basis. One series of pieces stemmed from

Knoll research relating to the workplace and the Americans with Disabilities Act. Cathy Schaefer at C&G developed these formats, and my colleague Bill Robinson was responsible for the project.

If another company would like to achieve identity standards and graphics of this quality, is there any rule of thumb you might offer as to what they should be prepared to spend?

BRIGHT: Although implementation costs can add up, the relative cost of good design and corporate identity is minuscule compared to the total investment a company makes in undertaking a merger, upgrading manufacturing technology, building plants and showrooms. I am constantly amazed by the responses of other corporate executives to The Knoll Group Identity Guidelines. They say things like "I've never seen anything done to this level of finish before" and "Wouldn't it be great if my company could take on this kind of program." My response is, in certain businesses you can't afford not to. If you believe your brand has a long-term value in the marketplace, building that brand among the people who work in the company and among the outside people with whom you do business is a key factor that will drive the success of the company.

There's also an investment here in quality photography, printing, paper, in good writing.

BRIGHT: Knoll historically has recognized the value of those components in marketing communications. This is a company that was founded on the idea that graphic design and communications go hand in hand with product design. It's just one of the special things about Knoll. There's never a need to rationalize or justify those investments.

You do need to explain one thing: near the entrance of this showroom Florence Knoll's picture is displayed with the caption, "Good design is good business." As you know, that quote has been much attributed to the late Thomas J. Watson, Jr. of IBM.

BRIGHT: If someone could tell us who said it first, it would solve one of the great corporate mysteries. Of course, IBM was an early client of Knoll, and Florence Knoll consulted on space planning and interior design.

So she may have designed Mr. Watson's office?

BRIGHT: Perhaps, and one day whispered, "Good design is good business" in his ear.

LATER, I SPOKE WITH TOM GEISMAR AT CHERMAYEFF & GEISMAR'S ART-FILLED OFFICES OVERLOOKING MADISON SQUARE PARK.

Do you consider your work for Knoll a departure for Chermayeff & Geismar?

GEISMAR: No. People aren't aware of the range of things that we do. I see the Knoll work as an expansion or further expression of that range. It's all part of a continuum. We have been purposely trying to reestablish the Knoll tradition and play up some of the things that were done in the fifties through the seventies that established the company as a leader in design. Knoll graphics have a great Modernist tradition going back to Herbert Matter and it just seemed appropriate to us that it should be carried forward. The difference is that computers have enabled us to do things with imagery that might not have been possible before. So there is more complexity. For example, in the opening pages of the capabilities brochure, we were trying to convey the basic attitude of Knoll, the idea of the intelligent workspace, so we looked for imagery that would suggest that, and it ended up as photographic collages.

Can you describe how the images were created and how they were reproduced?

GEISMAR: Actually, we started out looking at something quite different: symbolic fish and animals, but eventually we decided to combine images that are more closely related to Knoll's business. And as the collages developed they became more and more interesting as a visually exciting way to express the message of a company that sells design. The work you do is very much affected by your tools, and in this case the computer let us take specially shot and stock photographs and combine them. Then we manipulated the images on the system to change the natural colors to a range we selected. We also changed the percentages of intensity so certain layers became transparent.

How was the scope of the overall project described to you?

GEISMAR: Our original involvement was to look at the identity of the newly merged company, The Knoll Group, and its long-term business plan. We ultimately recommended that "The" and "Group" be dropped and that everything be marketed under "Knoll," which was so well known in the marketplace. We went through a whole study and came up with a new design for the Knoll logo. But in the end the decision was made to stay with the basic Knoll typography that had been in use since the late sixties. Our focus was on using the single word Knoll on everything. Colors were standardized. We developed a stationery system with interim guidelines, how to do the letterhead, and very basic guide-lines for the dealers. Dealers were encouraged to use the Knoll name but also shown how to use their own store names on stationery. We did the same with signage. There were a whole series of interim guidelines books, and a compila-tion of them became the identity manual. In a company like Knoll there aren't thousands of people around the world doing these things; there are a few peo-ple in a few offices, so it's not hard to communicate in a relatively compact manual that codifies everything in one convenient place.

How did you present your ideas to the client? Was the reception always as positive as David Bright indicates, or did you ever have to go back and change things?

GEISMAR: No, never (laughs). Knoll has always been a very demanding client, and it's also a company in flux. It's been an extremely difficult time economi-cally for the office furniture business. And there have been changes in direc-tion, changes in people—all the things that make life complicated. Even though we have had presentations with everyone from the chairman down, all along we worked closely with David and with Bill Robinson, and having those two contacts gave things stability. But, yes, things did go back and forth a number of times. The identity went into various directions, with agreements one way and then a shift. But these things are normal in these adverse times.

Young designers often wonder how firms like yours get projects like this—how you make proposals, how you price, how it all really works. There's kind of a fantasy that only five guys in the world really know how to do this—you're one of them—and that you work some kind of magic no one can quite figure out.

GEISMAR: I don't know any secrets! Identity is difficult. It takes a lot of experience and clear thinking, because you're dealing with long-term issues. Generally graphic design is ephemeral; you're creating things that are seen, used, and done away with. There's a certain charm to that. But identity is different; if it works it's going to be around for many years. At this office we've always taken pride in the fact that most of what we've done is still around and doesn't look dated. We're not interested in what's in fashion. In fact, we try to avoid being fashionable, and attempt to think through the implications of what we're doing and how it will physically work in all its uses and ramifications. So we go to great lengths to never simply present a mark or logo, but always to show it in context. As a way of evaluating it, we do mock-ups of the most-used and most-seen applications: the stationery, ads, trucks, brochures, and signs. And sometimes when we get to that point we realize that the thing doesn't work and either throw it away and start again or change it. If you don't go through that process you might fall in love with something and think it's really clever without ever objectively and properly evaluating it.

How different is what we're looking at today from the first presentation you made?

GEISMAR: It's only different in detail. In fact, the cover of the identity guidelines manual is one of the first things we showed: how we could break the logo into two parts and make it a little more decorative and abstract. There were certain concepts presented originally that have continued to form the basis of the ongoing program. One is to use the Knoll logo simply and boldly. You can see this on the trucks, on the catalog binders, on the signs. Another concept is to use Bodoni Book as the major typeface. It provides a nice contrast with the bold logo. It's elegant and it was already being used for Knoll product literature. Limiting the number of typefaces can often be a big help in terms of achieving a consistent look, and you can see the Bodoni Book used on everything from stationery to the small newspaper ads we developed. The third idea originally presented is to use overlapping and transparent imagery, in a variety of forms, to convey ideas and feelings. We've already talked about collaging photo images for the capabilities brochure. Photo and word images were combined for the visitation program, and for the interim guidelines brochure the grid format itself became the basis of the design. The fourth basic concept is to use bold colors.

I've heard that "Vignelli red" was the starting point of the color palette. How did you feel about that?

GEISMAR: That red is also our red. We always refer to it as O-R-O, which is the Color Aid designation of orange-red-orange, which we used before Pantone existed, when Color Aid was our only source of color chips. We used O-R-O all over the place, and it made us happy that Knoll's color was more or less the same. I personally love bright colors. It seems like Ivan and I are the only two people in existence who still do.

I wonder how many clients would automatically reject certain color combinations, saying things like "Purple with green, that's too weird" or "We can't have an orange cover." Do you have to sell things, to convince clients of their rightness, or do you believe that a correct solution sells itself?

GEISMAR: Again, I think "appropriate" is the key word. In the chair catalog we chose all the fabrics, all bright colors from Knoll's range of textiles. They have a lot of fabrics that are subdued, but it seemed to us that on the page color made the chairs stand out distinctly from one another and reinforced the whole identity. We might not photograph products the same way for another client, but it was appropriate for Knoll. In terms of "selling," we have a rationale for what we're doing, and explain it to the client. But the design itself has to be interesting and convincing.

There's a real contrast between the New Wave kind of sensibility in the visuals and the structured page layouts with classic typography on white paper. Where do you stand in the visual excitement versus legibility debate?

GEISMAR: Those things don't have to be mutually exclusive. Covers can suggest a brochure's contents in an evocative and attractive way, and the inside pages can be absolutely straightforward if they're intended to be used as functional tools. There is a tremendous amount of self-indulgent design being done right now. Sometimes it's interesting and well done, but claims are made for it that go far beyond reality. I always consider what a piece is trying to convey, who's going to read it, who's going to understand it. The graphic design problems that most of us face every day can be a struggle. But if people would stop looking at design magazines so much and think more about what it is they're trying to say, it would expand the potential of what they're creating. Here, we play ideas off each other and see if they work. We formed our office so that we could work in a collaborative way, and collaborating with each other and with our clients opens up more possibilities.

What's your reaction to the in-house work Knoll is doing?

GEISMAR: Very nice. They're doing some very nice things. It has always been our attitude that certain things should be absolutely prescribed, labels and binder covers, catalog pages, and so forth, so people don't have to spend too much time on them. There has to be a commonality so when you put everything together it won't look like a mess. But you don't want to restrict the creativity that goes into promotional pieces and posters, whether directed to the consumer or the sales people. You want to make those things lively and fun. They should be part of the interesting spirit of Knoll, and they are.

Although this client came about by referral, do you get into competitive bidding situations?

GEISMAR: All the time. In the case of Knoll, David Bright called me up and it was as simple as that, but it usually doesn't happen that way. This week we spent a lot of time writing a proposal for a very large project and I have to do another one today. They are all competitive, absolutely.

Do you feel that at some point in a design firm's history one ought to be able to say, "Our fee is $100,000, just to use a round number, and if you want to work with us, take it or leave it"?

GEISMAR: Well, I understand Paul Rand did something like that. But I don't think there is anyone else in the world who can get away with it. It would be great if that were the case. It is very much a competitive situation, and you're not judged just on your fee, it's your past work, your approach, and your fit for the particular problem.

Chermayeff & Geismar is known for going far beyond traditional graphic design services: interior design, exhibitions, art consulting, and so forth. Has that been the case with Knoll?

GEISMAR: We designed showroom environments for Neocon, always looking to make them special. For example, we took crude drawings of people and laser-cut them out of aluminum. At the Wooster Street showroom we did a series of wall graphics. At the IDCNY showroom they were trying to express environmental concerns, and we developed a large forest of abstract corrugated cardboard trees to convey the message. Our office works on many museum exhibits and we also do a lot of work with architects, such as special projects in environmental graphics. It's interesting, though, that people in corporations who are involved with identity and graphic design usually don't care about these other areas. We do. One of my partners is an architect by training, and Ivan comes from a family of architects, and we continue to do these diverse things because we enjoy them and they make our practice more interesting.

You don't see a competitive advantage to offering more services?

GEISMAR: I don't think so. But it does give us a slightly broader perspective on things, which is helpful. This week, in fact, we got involved in a strategic identity problem that is truly not a design problem, and are bidding against a lot of firms that specialize in that kind of thing. We showed our work the other day and one of the potential clients said, "Gee, that worries me. You guys are designers." I answered, "Yes, we are, but we also think about these things and know how to approach them."

Do you also get involved in the copy concepts? For example, here's a cover that reads, "Smell, touch, taste." Are these ideas, in which the copy is integrated with the visuals, generated by you, the client, or a writer?

GEISMAR: Actually, by a designer. This series, a visitor pack, was created for people who come to see the Knoll plants and tour the facilities, and includes nametags, menus for luncheons, notepads, and so forth. Weston Bingham developed the idea of combining the words and imagery, and we had a lot of discussion about which words would be most appropriate.

Do you think that companies generally undertake identities when the going gets rough, when customer or investor confidence is low?

GEISMAR: They might, but management soon learns that it's not as simple as that. Graphics don't make a company successful or unsuccessful. The products and the way they are sold and distributed are at the heart of every company. Many of us think of Knoll for the Mies chair and the Saarinen furniture and all those other classic pieces, but they represent a very small part of sales. The real thrust is in the office systems market, and Westinghouse intended to bring its technological and management expertise to play, to make manufacturing more efficient, to make pricing more competitive, to make distribution better. In order to work, the graphics have to reflect reality, which in Knoll's case they do.

Matthew Evans is chairman of **FABER & FABER LTD**., the United Kingdom–based publishing group founded by Geoffrey Faber, T. S. Eliot, and other authors in 1925. The company specializes in high-quality fiction, poetry, plays, and screenplays and nonfiction books about such subjects as architecture, current affairs, history, and music. Faber is known for publishing literary fiction by contemporary authors such as Milan Kundera and Mario Vargas Llosas, as well as the classics of Lawrence Durrell, James Joyce, and many others.

A partner in **PENTAGRAM** since 1974, *John McConnell* is a board member of Faber & Faber—an unusual role for a design consultant—and is responsible for overseeing the design of nearly three hundred book jackets a year. He has also created identity programs for companies including Clark's Shoes and Boots Chemists, and is currently working on Granada Hospitality, a chain of service stations along Britain's motorways. Co-author of *Living by Design* and *Ideas on Design*, he is editor of Pentagram Papers, a series of limited-edition books. In 1985 he received the London Design and Art Directors Award for outstanding contributions to design. Pentagram has offices in London, New York, San Francisco, Austin, Texas, and Hong Kong.

Increasingly, the book jacket has become an artist's canvas—the illustrator's as well as the designer's. An exhibition of the latest trends in typographic design and visual imagery is as close as the "contemporary fiction" shelves of your local bookstore. Each cover of the more than six thousand designed by Pentagram for Faber & Faber not only identifies the publisher (in the U.K., book jackets are more a tribute to the publisher than to the author) and captures the spirit of the book, it is a pocket-sized exhibition of contemporary illustration. That's not only due to the talents of Pentagram, it's the result of executive decisions by Matthew Evans, a chairman who is not afraid to buck tradition—or start new ones. His strategy doesn't sound too complicated: hire the best design firm you can and then let the designers do their job. Perhaps other firms could have developed an engaging logo and design concept. But could they, like Pentagram, keep the momentum going at the rate of nearly three hundred jackets a year for more than twenty years? I spoke about this with John McConnell in a skylit atrium of Pentagram's London offices, a converted stable in the residential neighborhood of Notting Hill.

Can you give us a capsule history of book design at Faber & Faber?

MCCONNELL: Faber is one of the few private publishers left, and they were one of the first to actually take on the responsibility of designing the interiors and covers of the book. Until the turn of the century the publishing house simply brought the manuscript to the printer. There were classic printers who produced beautiful work, but it came from a craft tradition. Faber was the first to appoint a design director and had a small in-house team that commissioned illustrators. They used some very, very fine people: Eric Gill, William Morris. It was really quite a remarkable tradition. But it was not looked after properly for a long period. When Matthew Evans became chairman and managing director, he looked for someone to take on that mantle, and they experimented with a couple of people, both of whom failed. I was the third person asked to take on the job. The department had been left alone for such a long time, they resented anyone coming in and suggesting change, and so the production department saw off the first two candidates.

Saw off?

MCCONNELL: Got rid of them, made them resign, made their lives so miserable they packed up and the programs they wanted never succeeded. So it was a fair challenge when we came on, in 1981. We said, okay, we'll try again. That is partly why they asked me to join the board. The other people had been employees.

What was the first thing you had to do?

MCCONNELL: There had been no budget for doing covers and doing design properly and there was no mechanism to manage it. There were no regular meetings. The first thing I had to do was find a way to manage these internal people, stop them, make sure nothing went wrong. Now, all the jackets are done up here, 250 to 300 a year, that sort of mark. I set up a manager and a number of staff in Faber who do the interiors of the books.

And in terms of the design?

MCCONNELL: In America and here in the U.K., too, the current publishing technique is to suggest that every book jacket should be different. I went against that and argued that there is real benefit in having a house style. I said, "There is value in this book looking like that book, or looking like a brother or sister of that book." Because, as a reader, if I have good experience with this book, I then can assume that I will have a fairly good chance of having a good experience with the next book. And therefore goodwill builds up for the publisher's product.

That point of view will probably strike Americans as very strange.

MCCONNELL: It is un-American, certainly more European. But I'm very un-American. And all the research said I was wrong. I'm sure if you were in a bookshop and I asked you, "What are you looking for?" you'd say that you were looking for a book on gardening or a novel or an author. But I think eventually you'd start to think about who it was published by. An analogy I like to make is that I quite like music, but I'm not a specialist, so if I go into a music shop, I tend to buy Deutsche Grammophon recordings, because after I know the composer and piece I want, I want to make sure I'm getting it done well. And I know that Deutsche Grammophon does it well. Penguin is a very famous brand here, and as a matter of fact people used to say, "I'm going to buy a Penguin." So the publisher is part of the purchase decision. The other terrific thing, of course, is if you get six books in a bookshop and they look like brothers and sisters, you appear to have a greater presence.

And within the house style, you introduced a range of variations.

MCCONNELL: I introduced a new look for each of the areas. A look for poetry, a style for fiction, and a style for nonfiction. What they had in common was the panel—a rectangular panel in which the author's name and book title appeared. We also put certain authors and illustrators together. Pierre LeTan did Garrison Keillor, so Keillor became absolutely associated with Pierre's drawings. It's nice because you can give an author a little personal style. We ran with that scheme for ten to fifteen years. Three years or so ago I revisited Faber and we instituted a whole new look.

I understand one reason for the new look was that other publishers followed suit to the first look you designed. Did they copy the designs outright?

MCCONNELL: You couldn't tell the books apart.

If Faber enjoyed the reputation you describe, do you think the motivation to copy was to fool people, to get them to think that their book was published by Faber & Faber?

MCCONNELL: No, I think they saw it as representing classy literature.

How would you describe the new look?

MCCONNELL: It stands out by reversal. Every sales director wants to know if they can have the title bigger. So I say, "The book is only six inches wide and you cannot get it any larger. I've blown it up as big as I can. I simply cannot get it any bigger." But what they really mean is, "Can you make my book stand out more in the shop?" Nothing stands out in American bookshops because they treat every book as a product in its own right and they're all screaming so loudly. They have their volume knobs turned up full blast. So when you look around, it's a blank-out, you see nothing. The trick is to go the other way.

And they listened to you . . .

MCCONNELL: By being quiet you actually get recognition. You have to remember that Faber & Faber has a very unique position. They are a specialist in high-quality fiction, not pulp romance fiction, so they don't need the gold inlaid lettering and the lovely lady fainting in the arms of the handsome man. Faber's books on the whole are more difficult to read properly, so the small type says, "I'm a more serious book." People are attracted to a tranquil look, and quiet, centered type is a very English tradition. The illustration tends to come fairly low down on the book, and that gives the type a lot of space to breathe.

The titles and author's names don't appear to be any larger than 18 point. And within each group they're all set in the same typeface. Was there any resistance to this extremely restrained approach?

MCCONNELL: There is inevitably resistance when you put change into any organization. But it wasn't immense, and the board were very brave and said, "No, we're going to back John." They supported me and finally the success started to happen and all the criticisms went away.

How much does being a partner in Pentagram help?

MCCONNELL: It helps. No question. And of course, so does bringing other commercial experiences to bear. Most people in the book publishing business are amazingly uncommercial.

Can you describe the process by which the jackets get designed?

MCCONNELL: When I first went into Faber, covers were designed in the corridor or they sort of just materialized out of ether. So I set up a meeting routine every fortnight [two weeks] in which the editor brings in a brief that describes the book, and that brief is discussed by the sales director, the overseas salesperson, some marketing staff, and myself. Then I make the necessary design and bring it back a fortnight later. The financial rewards for doing book jackets are not high, so you have to get very good at doing a lot of them very quickly. So every fortnight I pick up twenty briefs and drop off twenty designs. Some of the meetings are funny and some are tense; there are good days and bad days.

When you say, "Make the necessary design," does that mean one design or do they want to see a few alternatives?

MCCONNELL: I have always done only one. I don't believe in the business of, "Here are six designs," because I don't know how you could do more than one properly. That's not to say that they all get through every time.

When they don't get through, what kind of criticisms do you hear?

MCCONNELL: Usually it is, "You've missed the flavor of the book." In fiction, what you're trying to do is get a sense of the mood of the book and the atmosphere the book provokes. So the editor is much more likely to say, "You haven't gotten it yet," or, "It's more surreal or less surreal than that," than, "I don't like that yellow."

I've heard that you don't read any of the books.

MCCONNELL: I argue that, if you read a book, you get enthralled by it and therefore your emotions about it become too complex. You're trying to translate a five-hundred-page novel, which is an extremely elaborate, layered object, into one image. It gets dangerous if you get too close to it. People may resent me for this, but I find that by standing back, it's easier to get a sense of it. The editors at Faber are extremely good at explaining an idea, a feeling, what it's "sort of like." They might say, "Do you remember such-and-such a book we did three years ago? It's sort of like that." The beauty of dealing with fiction is that it helps not to be too literal. You want to come in slightly obliquely, to give sufficient room for the reader to interpret the imagery. And if you make it too direct, the author might get upset because somehow you've turned an idea into hard reality by making a picture of it. If you depict a character in the book, it's dangerous because they didn't see it that way in their mind's eye.

Over all these years you've done more than five thousand jackets — is it still exciting and fun?

MCCONNELL: Yes, absolutely.

I understand you are a director of the company. Isn't this an unusual role for a graphic designer?

MCCONNELL: I was a board director of Clark's Shoes in America, so I've done it a number of times. If you consider that the visual presentation is of commercial value, you really should have someone in authority managing it. All companies have personnel directors who manage people and financial directors who manage the money and probably a legal director. Why not a design director? Designers must get out of the position of being "typeface choosers" and must take the debate to senior management about the assets and value we can bring. If you think about it, they commission us to make their businesses better. The discussion is not about whether you should use Times Roman, but about how what we do can make an impact on how well the company does.

What do you think of the so-called anti-Modernist designers who are into illegibility or who treat typography as bits of concrete poetry?

MCCONNELL: I have a feeling that all of that is a backlash against clients who are more demanding and want you to work more for less money. It relates to the Victorian concept of the artist who starves for his art in his garret. The argument goes that being commercial is in poor taste; doing your own thing is the only thing worthwhile, and it's worth starving for. It's marvelously self-fulfilling because you could be producing the worst stuff in the world. No one's buying it, but at least you're starving so you must be doing something right. It's a lovely way out.

LATER THAT DAY, I MET WITH MR. EVANS IN FABER & FABER'S OFFICES IN BLOOMSBURY, NEAR THE BRITISH MUSEUM.

John explained the strategy he presented to you at the outset: if a reader enjoys a book by a publisher, he or she will seek a similar experience from other books in the publisher's list, which are identifiable because of a house style of design. Was this a radical idea for you to accept?

EVANS: In the sixties and seventies Grove Press followed that kind of thinking. The City Lights bookshop imprint had a certain pulling power. Actually it was a very easy idea for us to accept. Our books generally have a comparatively small audience, say, five to ten thousand people, so you can take that kind of approach. When you get into the mass market, which we get into with film—one screenplay sold 200,000 copies last year—we approach things a little differently.

How did you get started with Pentagram?

EVANS: In 1982 I went to Australia and suddenly saw how dowdy and dull the Faber book covers looked in comparison. I came back saying, "We must do something about this." It was a moment in Faber's history when a whole new generation had come into the firm. So it seemed a good idea to use design to reinforce the idea that the firm was pointing in a different, more modern direction. Somebody here knew a partner in Pentagram, we started discussions with them, and they decided it would be good for them, too. They seemed incredibly grand for us. They were doing a lot of work for Swiss banks and Arab banks and perhaps feeling that they'd lost touch with their real constituency, which was publishing. They all loved designing covers. The only reason we were able to afford Pentagram was because they wanted to do it and agreed to a rate we wouldn't have been comfortable with had they charged us full price. Once they came on board they set up a way of running design, which has worked quite well.

Which is?

EVANS: The first lesson we learned is that you can't design by committee. So when Pentagram made its presentation to Faber, which was an all-embracing presentation about our writing paper, the way our invoices looked coming off the computer, what our packing cases looked like in the warehouse, what our books looked like, the only reason we were able to force it through was because I said, "This is going to happen." If I had asked everybody here, "What do you think?" the whole thing would have been watered down. Fortunately, I had the power base to do that.

What was the reaction?

EVANS: At first the marketplace hated the sudden switch from basically typographical covers to this modern look. Ever since T. S. Eliot, Faber poetry has been looked on with great interest. If a new book appeared in a bookshop people said, "I must buy this because it will be interesting." All of a sudden, everybody wondered what on earth had happened to Faber. The sales reps hated it. The poets hated it. But we just kept going and gradually everybody's attitude changed. After a couple of years it was something that everybody liked.

From everybody hated to everybody liked? What do you think caused that kind of change in attitude?

EVANS: To look at a cover in isolation is very difficult. But soon things began to build up to a range of covers. So when you went into a bookshop, you began to see a whole row of books, which had a real impact. And because the covers were perceived to be so attractive by the retailers, they used Faber books almost as design statements themselves, and so the windows would be filled with our books; they thought the design was so attractive it added value to the store. At the Frankfurt Book Fair praise was heaped on the Faber stand. We started getting compliments from the design markets that are much stronger than Britain: Italy, Germany, Sweden.

Are you saying that the relationship between the public and a new design is something like an arranged marriage? It takes about two years for the partners to appreciate each other?

EVANS: Absolutely. It's hard to describe the impact now because we've been doing this for such a long time. But all of a sudden here was Faber demonstrating *design matters*.

And your competitors followed suit?

EVANS: Faber could not claim to be the first publisher to put titles in rectangular panels on covers. But certainly the idea was copied in the sense that a lot of publishers then went to design firms, some of which came up with a solution that wasn't a million miles away from the Pentagram work for Faber. There were one or two European publishers who just completely ripped off our look. I mean, it was like looking at a Faber catalog. That's when I asked John to take things in a new direction.

Can you tell me about your firm's design briefs?

EVANS: The way you run design in a place like this is interesting because editors tend to be quite articulate and quite difficult. John's idea was to have a meeting every other Wednesday in which the editors present a brief for their books. The idea of the brief is to describe the book, not to tell the designers how to design the book. After they describe the book, the editors can say, "I suggest this or that," but they can't say anything about the design, because that isn't their talent.

I understand that authors can be difficult, too, and can have veto power. What percentage of jackets are not approved?

EVANS: Chances are that if we like them, the author will as well. It's a very small percentage. That's because we have a very dictatorial way of doing things around here. Me supporting John. It was wonderful in the early days. It was very tough, there wasn't too much consensus, and there was a lot of tension. I think that a lot of good design came out of that tension.

We've all seen that the best design can happen when there's someone in a dictatorial position.

EVANS: Everybody has an idea on design, which they don't have on the content of the book, or on how to sell the book. I'm amazed by how people don't respect the designer's position, because by saying, "I think this or that color ought to be altered," what they're really saying is, "You don't know how to do your job."

Why do you think people believe anyone can be a designer, but not a writer?

EVANS: Design is all around us, and everyone has a view on it. Design is what sort of shoes you put on in the morning, what color tie. Everybody makes design decisions all the time, and nobody can evaluate how good they are at it. In moments of extreme anger, the sort of abuse that comes out of my mouth has to do with calling editors visually illiterate who say they want a color changed or something moved. You've got to be very tough. But we also get 125 unsolicited manuscripts a week, all of which except the tiniest fraction of a percent are dreadful, so a lot of people do think they can be a writer.

After all these thousands of jackets, does Pentagram bring in things that astonish and delight you?

EVANS: Yes, absolutely. Ours is a creative relationship, but it's also a sort of sausage-machine relationship because we have to have 250 to 300 new designs every year. A huge amount of their work is fantastic. This is the thing that keeps it all going and alive. There is a new partner in Pentagram from Germany, Justus Oehler, who will be looking after the account. When he took over a few months ago, he asked, "Do I have to follow John McConnell's footmarks?" and we said, "Absolutely not, you have to do your own thing because good design can't stand still. You've got to keep developing it." Justus is just starting to find his feet, and I think he's going to take us in a different direction.

Do you have any idea what that might be?

EVANS: No, it's entirely up to him, and so far his work has been greatly admired. He just commissioned a New York illustrator, David Miller, for Kundera. Kundera is one of the world's great writers, and he absolutely loves these covers.

9

THE FINANCIAL WIZARD

The Linc Group *and* Rick Valicenti

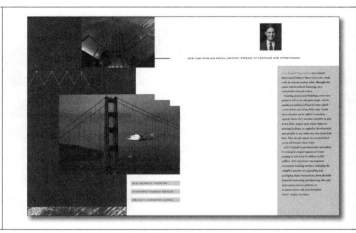

Martin E. Zimmerman is president of **LFC CAPITAL**, a Chicago-based boutique investment bank, which specializes in providing financing to healthcare providers and service companies. Previously he was chairman and CEO of LINC Capital, Inc., a financial services company that provided equipment leasing, accounts receivable financing, and rental financing to the healthcare industry. Zimmerman earned a B.S. in electrical engineering from MIT and an M.B.A. in finance from Columbia Graduate School of Business, where he was elected a Kennecott fellow and a McKinsey scholar. A contemporary art collector, he is a trustee of the Museum of Contemporary Art in Chicago, MIT's Council for the Arts, the Permanent Collection Committee of the Photography Department at the Art Institute, and a member of the Board of Overseers of Columbia Graduate School of Business.

RICK VALICENTI is founder of *The Thirst Universe*. A member of AGI (Alliance Graphique Internationale), Valicenti has served on the board of AIGA Chicago and as president of the Society of Typographic Arts (now the American Center for Design); has jurored the Presidential Design Awards—for Presidents George H. W. Bush and Bill Clinton—of the National

Endowment for the Arts; been nominated twice for the prestigious Chrysler Design Award; selected to *ID* magazine's forty top designers; and is the subject of a 356-page color monograph to be published by the Monacelli Press. Thirst's clients include Gilbert Paper, Herman Miller, Holly Hunt, The Chicago Architecture Foundation, and the Illinois Institute of Technology's College of Architecture. He worked on the projects for Linc in conjunction with Todd Lief, a Chicago marketing consultant and writer.

Marty Zimmerman is the consummate designer's client. Rick Valicenti calls him "brilliant." That's because he sees the big picture. He does not want a repetition of what his competitors are already doing. He is a guy who says, "In many companies, there tends to be a kind of committee approach to design. We are more forward-thinking." Zimmerman sought a designer who would never give him the plain-vanilla look favored by many financial services companies: the blue textured cover, the gold-stamped logo, the group shots of the partners. Instead, he chose someone who's known for pushing the edges of the envelope pretty hard. Zimmerman's ideas about proven concepts, industry expertise, and using experts perfectly illustrate how to respond when a client asks a difficult question—or asks you to design a repeat of what his competitors are doing. "Being able to translate someone else's success into something fresh and new to your industry is what separates really successful business people—who don't make many mistakes—from the people who do," he says.

What are your key objectives for your company's communications?

ZIMMERMAN: I want to influence people's thinking about us. Our printed communications are a means for closing a sale at the second level after we've been recommended at the first level. It's common in selling to hospitals, for example, that you sell to the person you're initially in touch with, usually a technical or financial officer. Then he goes to a committee and makes a recommendation—maybe of two alternatives—and the committee or the administrator who is his superior will make a decision. You can't get at that second level directly. You have to get at it through advertising or printed materials.

Are you competing against big-name investment banks?

ZIMMERMAN: We're competing against big-name commercial banks, big-name leasing companies, and in some cases, big-name investment banks. We call our business "lease investment banking" because it's more than leasing. But it's not typically long-term financing; it's typically medium-term. We're a smaller company competing with large institutional-type players. We have to be able to explain why it is an advantage for an institutional user to work with someone other than an institutional supplier.

Institutional suppliers, and by that I assume you mean banks, often request a design approach they think will appeal to their clients—a low-key, restrained look. Some people like to use the term "plain vanilla." What makes you more daring?

ZIMMERMAN: That's changing to some extent, but it's still largely true. In many companies, there tends to be a kind of committee approach to design. Our approach is more forward-thinking, more on the leading edge. We sell the firm with this concept: We're more specialized, we've got all the experience, but we're not as large; along with our smaller size comes flexibility and responsiveness and more attention by senior people. The whole idea is to have a serious approach to solving problems, but one that is more creative.

How much direction did you give Rick Valicenti?

ZIMMERMAN: Quite a bit. First of all, we voiced our philosophy. That took a series of meetings. We have content objectives that we need to accomplish with a given piece of collateral or advertising. A certain type of content or editorial approach suggests a certain type of design approach. But we don't want to be totally pinstriped, so I'll give a designer flexibility in terms of imagery. The whole idea is to create a feeling of success and sophistication. We want to be known as a creative-type financing source, where people can get new concepts for existing problems. There are lots of problems out there, but there are not too many fresh ideas on how to solve them. We're the guys people come to for the tough ones. With that reputation, I hope we'll be called on for the easier ones, too. So the idea is to get on everybody's bid list and have a shot at getting new business, not simply by virtue of a low price but by virtue of more value added.

You are the chairman of the company. I am impressed that you deal directly with designers.

ZIMMERMAN: I don't like to work through someone else. I want the designer to be there, and he appreciates it because he can defend himself. I might comment on what I think is wrong or right. Then he'll say, "Here's what I've been trying to do," or "Here's why I did it." And sometimes I'll step back. I don't dictate to designers—ever—particularly if a designer feels strongly about something. Most designers are sensible enough to know that their client has a sense of what he wants to communicate; that he wants something fresh, attractive, and interesting; and that he wants to avoid the dull, repetitious stuff that bores him and, ultimately, bores the reader.

Do you ever criticize a detail, such as "Why do we need this little red line right here?"

ZIMMERMAN: If I think something's extraneous, sometimes I'll ask why it's used, and sometimes I'll get an answer. I usually don't fight that kind of thing. I do pay a lot of attention to things like legibility of subheads—the layout from the point of view of the reading public. Sometimes designers will devise a layout that's simply hard to read because they use reverse type or type that's not bold enough. For example, in our brochure the subheads have been screened back too far. Small matter, but it's something that impacts legibility. Now, when we reprint, we're not going to change much, but we'll make those heads darker. Ordinarily, though, I wouldn't say anything about little red lines. I want the designer to feel that it's his or her design, and that it hasn't been all gouged up by the client. So I refrain from commenting on design issues that don't directly pertain to the communication of the copy.

What was the industry response to the brochures?

ZIMMERMAN: Quite positive, on the whole. Actually, our own people found them a little sophisticated at first, but they've gotten used to them. Have they changed the way our clients think about us? There's no doubt in my mind. They've been very, very important to us. Our ads have, too, and they reflect the sophistication of the brochures.

Do you view your brochures as an investment? Very often, to accomplish something this ambitious, designers have to do a huge selling job on the client, who might not be able to project the benefit of techniques like matte and gloss varnish to his business. Did you have to be sold?

ZIMMERMAN: Well, I certainly looked at the pros and cons of those decisions. Ultimately we look at something major like this brochure series as having at least a two-year life. We're dealing in an area where the difference of $5,000 or $10,000 can be made up for by just one sale. So if I can see something that might get me a sale over the course of one year or two years, it's much easier to justify. For example, I know that varnish, which is a significant extra cost, protects the piece and prevents fingerprinting. Since we hope each brochure will be seen and handled by several people, this is an important consideration.

Can you relate specific things like additional ink colors to making a sale? Or do you feel, instead, that high quality in general makes a subliminal sell to a prospective customer?

ZIMMERMAN: Both. We want to make sure that our stuff looks as good as that of any bank or investment bank. I mean, you decide how you want to spend your money! A six- or seven-color job was appropriate in this case because it was an omnibus corporate brochure. We made it go further by using the imagery in the individual operating company pieces. So we spent a lot of money on the images, but this cost was amortized over many different pieces. And sometimes we do produce one- or two-color pieces. And then it's especially important that the design is striking and enhances the message.

If other clients wanted to educate themselves about using the available marketing tools and talent to impact their businesses in a positive way, how would you suggest they go about it?

ZIMMERMAN: I think you learn a lot by interviewing the smartest, most successful practitioners around. I got my first designer by calling a housewares specialty retailer in Chicago, Crate & Barrel, that had—and still has—wonderful design. I knew Gordon Siegal a little bit, and I asked, "Gordon, who do you use for design? Who's terrific?" And he said, "Here's the guy." That's how I got started, and from there it was just constant interviewing, constant talking to people, and constant looking. Making sure that I kept up with some of the good stuff that's been done.

You ended up being in the forefront of it.

ZIMMERMAN: If you get lucky, you're able to do that.

I wouldn't attribute it to luck. You had a plan, and you followed it. I'd like to discuss another issue, which is the line between industry expertise and perceived conflict of interest. First, industry expertise. Would it matter to you if your designer had never done a brochure for a company in the leasing business?

ZIMMERMAN: It wouldn't matter a bit. In fact, I'd rather they had never done one. What concerns me is whether the designer had worked for companies that wanted to achieve the kinds of objectives we want to achieve. I'm concerned that the designer know the kind of look I identify with as an emerging growth-type company, trying to be leading edge in a conservative market. Being able to reflect that image is more important than knowing anything about the technical side of my business.

One designer I know submitted a proposal to one of the major airlines for a series of international tour brochures. Apparently, the airline was impressed with the presentation, but because the firm's portfolio didn't include another travel brochure exactly like what they were looking for, they chose another designer. What would you say to a client like that?

ZIMMERMAN: I would tell a client that if you find exactly what you are looking for in a designer's portfolio you are setting yourself up to get a repetition of what somebody else—your competitor—has already used! The advantage of using someone who has done effective work in a similar opportunity or problem area, for another industry, is that you can translate someone else's success into something fresh and new to your industry.

That's a perfect answer. If the designer had said that, the client might not have believed it.

ZIMMERMAN: That's what separates really successful business people—who don't make many mistakes—from the people who do. Let me explain. The way of avoiding mistakes is to take a proven concept and use it in another industry. To come up with a concept that's never been used anywhere is risky, because you don't know whether it will work at all. But it's a lot less risky, for example, to introduce McDonald's in Uruguay when you know it has worked in Brazil and all over the U.S. That's what we do to minimize risks. It's not always possible, but I've borrowed lots of ideas from computer leasing and from investment banking. I try to bring them into the context of health care finance and our other activities. Our corporate structure reflects the structure of one of the most successful computer manufacturers, an emerging growth company. Why? Because I've seen it work, and I'm close enough to what that company's done to know that it's a sensible corporate structure for us, even though I also know that there's no other corporate leasing company in the country that uses it. To me, it's been proven. I'm just applying it to a different industry.

When a prospective client says, "You've never done one for someone exactly like us before," I bet a lot of designers wish they could make an argument as articulate as yours. What should they say?

ZIMMERMAN: If a person knows they might not be able to respond persuasively, the easiest thing to do is to refer to an expert. Here are three ideas: One way—and this is not the solution for everyone—is to work with a marketing or communications consultant. Our consultant, Todd Lief, who works as the interface between us and our designer, was formerly a principal at a couple of major Chicago boutique agencies. Designers are constantly faced with marketing issues that are difficult for them to respond to, and they just don't have the credibility of people with a full-scale marketing background. So it's helpful for a designer to have someone like that on board. Then the designer can say, "Look, it's worked here, and our marketing expert recommends it for your situation. Why don't you discuss it with him?" The second thing the designer could do is tell the client directly that it's very effective to apply something that's been used in another industry. In reality the problem's the same, but it will give the client something fresh and not a rehash of what his competition has done. The last thing we want is something another leasing company has done! A third way to sell a concept is to ask the client in your initial conversation, "What company in another industry would you model yourself on?" It may be that someone would model his company on Federal Express. Then when you come back, you can make that comparison and say, "Federal Express has used this technique and this kind of a look to distinguish themselves, and we're suggesting that you use something a little bit like that, but updated." Comparative selling can work very well. It depends on the person you're trying to sell.

You suggest working with a marketing person. Many clients I've spoken to are opposed to the kind of marketing person who sells design services. But you are talking about a different role: Someone who is perceived as working on behalf of the client rather than selling for the designer.

ZIMMERMAN: Yes, exactly. The marketing person we work with is an independent professional. He's on our team, so to speak, as well as on the designer's team. Together, they provide many of the services of an agency. From Rick Valicenti's standpoint, I think, Todd not only writes the copy, he helps to translate our objectives and sharpen the focus of the materials. Because of that, Rick doesn't waste time going down creative blind alleys; the work is on target. How to market services is always a dilemma for the really good independent designer. An agency has its own people to market its services—the account managers, the senior guys, whatever, and design is provided within the context of the overall solution. But I think a more interesting issue is how an independent designer markets his services, and does he use a marketing person? It can work if the marketing person is not just a salesperson, but an adviser to the client.

Let's talk a bit about the flip side of "You've never done it before," and that's, "You've done too much of it." Many clients, especially in the service and financial sectors, are worried about conflict of interest. The same designer who didn't have specific tour brochure experience went to see a large accounting firm. His firm had done several projects for Big Six firms, and the reaction to the presentation was, "You work for other accounting firms. We can't possibly use you; the partners wouldn't go for that because of conflict of interest." He couldn't win! Here's what is seen as a potential problem by the client: "You talk to our competitors. You're going to let our secrets out."

ZIMMERMAN: It's a problem shared by agencies, a complicated issue. I don't really have an answer for that, because it's all in the individual's mind. Why do certain clients resign if the agency gets another client in the same industry?

How would you feel if your designer/consultant also worked for one of your competitors?

ZIMMERMAN: I probably wouldn't want it if it were the same direct market, with the same customers, with the same kind of product. If it were a different product, or a different market, I wouldn't have a problem.

My thought would be that a designer, having worked closely with several competing firms, could see their differences clearly and would be better positioned to give them different looks, different approaches. Does the concept of industry expertise have any value for you?

ZIMMERMAN: Yes, except I use a designer for ideas as well as for visuals. And I want to make sure that other people don't have access to those ideas. In terms of a product design or a stationery design, it really wouldn't be a problem. But I use a designer for considerably more, such as coming up with thoughts and observations as well as reflections on marketing communications. I don't want to get thoughts that are reflective of what someone else is doing.

RECENTLY, I FOLLOWED UP WITH RICK VALICENTI.

When you started working with Marty Zimmerman, did you know anything about the technical side of his business?

VALICENTI: No, and I probably still don't. But I know a lot about him. I was able to design ads and brochures about equipment investment banking because in that particular situation I had the luxury of working with Todd Lief, and he distilled the message in language I could understand and that Linc's audience, an enlightened and curious audience, could understand.

How would you describe Mr. Zimmerman as a client?

VALICENTI: Not only is he brilliant at acquiring companies and creating new business models, he is a contemporary art collector. He started his collection with artifacts of contemporary architecture—architects' drawings and models. He has a particular interest in Chicago architecture—Louis Sullivan terracottas and Frank Lloyd Wright drawings and glass. There was new art in his office every time I visited. It could be Jenny Holzer, Andre Serrano, Cindy Sherman. The walls were painted by Sol LeWitt. I would ask him, "Marty, how do you have the radar? When you're collecting it, it's unknown, and a year or two later it's at the forefront of the art world." It's his vision. He sees the world with clarity.

What took place during your initial conversations?

VALICENTI: The first thing he said to me was, "What I admire about your portfolio is that you conceal compromise." He told me that he knew that every process has its compromises. He had evidently interviewed several designers in which the compromises were evident in their work. You know, when you're looking at a portfolio and the designer says, "The client made me do this or that." He recognized that it takes a good designer to navigate the entire process and have the compromises be transparent at the end.

How did you work through the details, such as the little red lines or slightly too-hard-to-read subheads he described?

VALICENTI: Most of this work was done in the spray-mount era, halfway between the rubber-cement era and the Mac era. I would make page compositions with greeked type and photo collages using stock images or pictures we would shoot to show what we were proposing. I would bring in a number of these collages or mock-ups, variations on a theme. Right in his office I would move the pictures and the copy blocks around, and we would talk about them. That's a good way to get agreement from a busy person.

Are you working with Linc or LFC now?

VALICENTI: In the last several years, we've moved away from financial services and other corporate clients to design clients. By that I mean clients who are involved in *design* the process, *design* the noun. Our clients are architects, paper companies, companies who are bringing designed objects to market. It's the most challenging to work with that type of client. Inherently they understand a forward-thinking position. The discourse is more about design than about middle-management dramas.

You can pick and choose your clients so precisely in this economy?

VALICENTI: We have a bit of that luxury, but we've consolidated our space and are working a little leaner, with nine people. This has always been a teaching environment.

How do you define "teaching environment"?

VALICENTI: At least once every six weeks I visit a school—a design department at a college or university, or a graduate school—and I give a lecture or a workshop. We always have an intern at the office. Interns spend a year or two here, learning, and then it's time for them to leave the nest.

What do you teach about how to best work with clients?

VALICENTI: It's quite simple. There's one word that sums it up. That word is *relationship*. Good work only comes from a good relationship. And that means a relationship in which there can be a discourse. There's give and take. You build the relationship on that trust. It's not like you're presenting to Julius Caesar. Then when the client calls and says, "I'm in a pinch. I need something really good but I don't have the budget," you can give of yourself, agree to a reduced fee. Down the road he or she is going to remember.

And your definition of discourse?

VALICENTI: Being able to have a discourse means I am not seen as a vendor. I'm perceived as counsel. And I encourage everyone here to behave as counsel. That means being able to ask the client, "Are you sure?"

To the question, "Are you sure?" can't the client's answer be, "Yes, I'm sure. Now use that picture"? What about being more direct and telling the client, "No, don't use that picture"?

VALICENTI: "Are you sure?" encourages dialogue. It's less aggressive, less defensive than "Don't use that picture." I don't like to give outright advice. That's not how I want to be spoken to. Another line I use is, "I want to go on the record [as recommending such-and-such]." It's a classic line. It buys time. It challenges the client to think about the issue. The next morning he or she might call back and say, "I thought about that" or, "Let's talk about it." Then you have another opportunity to build on your successes.

10

THE SCIENTIST-ENTREPRENEUR

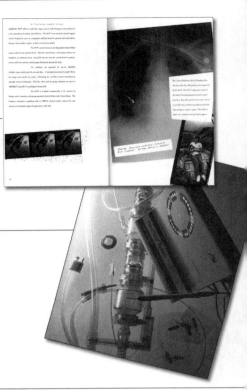

Abiomed, Inc.
and
Weymouth Design

Dr. David M. Lederman is chairman, president, and chief executive officer of **ABIOMED, INC.**, the Danvers, Massachusetts, medical device company he founded in 1981. With an initial public offering that raised $12 million, Abiomed became a public company in 1988, and since has led in the development of cardiac devices that benefit patients during or after surgery, after a heart attack, or while waiting for a donor heart for transplant. Dr. Lederman received his B.S. in engineering physics, and M.S. and a Ph.D. in aerospace engineering from Cornell University. He has written hundreds of scientific papers, been a principal investigator on numerous National Institutes of Health programs, and speaks at national and international forums on cardiac technology. Abiomed made the network and front-page news in 2001, when its permanent artificial heart was successfully implanted in a dying patient who lived for several months.

Photographer and graphic designer *Michael Weymouth* studied at New England School of Art and worked for ten years in the Boston design community prior to founding **WEYMOUTH DESIGN** in 1973. His firm produces more than twenty annual reports each year—mostly for

Boston-area high-technology companies—and also specializes in capabilities brochures, identity programs, multimedia presentations, and Web sites. His firm's design work and his photography have repeatedly been honored by the Mead Annual Report Show, *Print Casebooks*, *Communication Arts*, and *PhotoGraphis*.

While still in the R&D stage, years before it would have any FDA-approved products to sell, Abiomed invested in top-quality photography, design, printing. It makes sense; why not do things from the outset that communicate quality to shareholders and get noticed by the investment community and the media? Dr. David Lederman, a leader in developing cardiac support technology, also proved himself a leader in how to find and work with a designer. He devised a test for what he characterized as weeding out mediocrity: "I asked the other graphic designers that I met whether they would do certain things because I wanted them done a particular way. I intentionally gave them examples that, in my opinion, exhibited very poor taste. . . they said okay; they'd do it." He wasn't impressed with anyone who seemed to be too willing to compromise. Then, after choosing Mike Weymouth, he resisted, as he put it, the temptation to micromanage. "If you interfere and demand mediocrity, I think a smart designer would drop you and your company as a client," he says. The result: annual reports that, unlike many others for growing companies, don't look like low-budget, do-it-yourself solutions. Why don't they all do it? I was pleased to have the opportunity to speak with Dr. Lederman and find out.

Dr. Lederman, several years ago, Business Week *ran a cover story, "Small Is Beautiful: America's Hot Growth Companies." I wrote to the companies for their annual reports and found out that even if the numbers were beautiful, with a few exceptions, the annual reports were anything but. You've done things differently than many CEOs of young companies, for whom extremely low-budget annual reports seem to be good enough. Why?*

LEDERMAN: Many young companies, startups, do not pay enough attention to the market. An annual report is a mechanism to tell the stockholders the status and prospects of their investments. But it is also a mechanism for the company to present itself to the world. If you think of yourself as being "beautiful," to use *Business Week*'s word—even if it's your first year as a public company—it is important to show exactly what is beautiful about you, and it is very important to find someone who can do that well. I have been told (I don't know whether it is true) that the majority of people spend somewhere between seventeen and twenty seconds on an annual report before throwing it away, and that they only look at the chairman's letter and at the photographs, so the design becomes as important as the words.

Well, I've read they spend five minutes in a couple of studies by investor relations firms.

LEDERMAN: I'm glad to hear that. I certainly spend more than five minutes on the companies I follow. Typically I ask, "Why did they decide to show that picture, that product, that person?" or, "Why did they say this or that?" What you think of yourself, your self-image, also applies to a company. And quite frankly, I don't think that the issue of cost is the deciding element in the decision to go with a leading graphic designer. While cost consciousness is obviously a concern, when you break down the cost of making an annual report, there may be a tendency to be penny-wise and pound-foolish. You may try to save on something, and in the long run it costs you more. A good annual report is always a good investment. And if a company is mature enough to realize that the marketing of the company is as important as the marketing of the products, they will pay attention to the annual report. Companies that think small are likely to stay small.

For many small, new companies, budget is the number-one consideration. If they went directly to a printer with pictures from the files and said, "Put these together with our financials, print it, and put a nice cover on it," maybe they would spend $20,000, just to use a round number. On the other hand, a graphic designer might propose, "You need original photography and a much higher level of printing quality." Perhaps the cost would then be between $75,000 and $100,000. And to the client that would be a signifi-cant amount of money that could be spent on something else. The thinking might be, "The securities analysts and shareholders will just look at the income statement anyway, and won't care about all this stuff." Is your feeling that they do care?

LEDERMAN: Yes, but the spread you have given me could be narrower. One can get something very elegant for a lot less than $100,000. And one can go directly to printers and spend more than $20,000. Before we were a public com-pany, we issued literature where we didn't hire a graphic designer—and it shows. But all this is noise compared to the overall cost of going public, and the cost of maintaining a public company in terms of legal, accounting, and other related expenses. You have to put everything in the right perspective. Think of the cost of doing business as a public company, and try to assess what percentage of that should be spent on projecting your message and informing the world and your stockholders of what you have done, are doing, and are planning to do. Again, very small companies tend not to be market-driven. As they mature, companies become more market-driven, so I would think that in most cases, the successful ones will change their minds. Am I right?

Yes, but by then there might be quite a lot of bad work that will need to be redone.

LEDERMAN: Well, not for us. I am very happy we decided to go the way we did with our first report as a public company. And I have to tell you that our marketing staff is also happy because the annual report becomes more than just a financial report to stockholders. It serves numerous functions. It also becomes a marketing instrument for our products. It is also very important for recruiting. When interviewing prospective employees, especially during the phase of building the management team, the first document candidates ask for is the annual report; sometimes they won't even schedule an interview until they've seen it. It is to their benefit to read something that presents the company fairly and accurately, and the report pays for itself in that sense.

How did you meet Mike Weymouth and start to work with him? What was your interview process like? And what were your goals for the report?

LEDERMAN: Since becoming a public company, we have used an outside consulting firm to help us set up an investor relations program. They introduced me to four different graphic designers. Each presented to me a representative assembly of work. I was simply and overwhelmingly more impressed with Mike's work. I have a lot of respect for good photography. Mike doesn't strike me as being the type of person who will do any annual report for any company; he apparently has to feel that there is something of real quality before he takes an assignment. There is a correspondence between the elegant kind of report he likes to do and the type of company that the report is about. It's not just a question of dollars and cents. Our mission is to save lives, and we derive a great sense of pride from our work. Our company's success is not only measured by our ability to generate profit, but by our ability to develop medical technology that will save or improve human lives at a cost lower than comparable or existing therapies. Mike also gets a great deal of satisfaction and pride from his work. I asked him questions, and I asked the other graphic designers that I met —I won't reveal their names, of course—whether they would do certain things for me because I wanted them done a particular way. I intentionally gave them examples that, in my opinion, exhibited very poor taste. Imagine the layout or structure of a very ridiculous type of annual report. I said, "I would like something like this." They said okay; they'd do it.

Do you think that those who agreed weren't very good at what they did?

LEDERMAN: Yes. It meant to me that it wasn't important to them how the annual report was going to end up looking. If the designer doesn't have a strong feeling about his or her work, even if he or she disagrees with me, then I'm not very impressed.

You conducted something that delved much deeper than a portfolio review. You tested people to see if they were just going to be "yes" people and if your report was just going to be another job.

LEDERMAN: Correct. To me that was very important. If the others were as good as I am told—and I'm not saying they didn't do good work—they were not consistent. They were driven by the economics of their business.

They might also have been driven by being intimidated by past clients. The clients may have "made them do stuff" that they didn't feel was right, and they assumed that's the way these relationships had to be.

LEDERMAN: That is precisely what they said to me! When I reviewed their work, I asked them how they could do work like that, and they said, that's how the client wanted it! That may be true. But if you look at Mike's work— whether you like it or not—however diverse and different, he is consistent. Working with him, he voiced strong opinions, and I learned to respect him even more. His attitude is similar to and compatible with our corporate philosophy, our culture. I sense that Mike is a person who seeks long-term relationships. After he thought about and discussed what he recommended as the focus of our first annual report, one can sort of project what the second one should be like, and what the third one, and so forth. I like that. I like the idea of long-term planning. For annual reports and everything else. I would be curious to know how different I am from the others you have spoken with.

Several years ago, I surveyed a group of leading designers about what they found most rewarding and most problematic about client-designer relationships. And to reflect on what you're saying, most designers told me that their biggest overall business problem was that clients seemed to want mediocre solutions. "Seemed to want" is too mild a term. They described clients who demanded mediocre solutions, who were overly directive and would say, "This is the picture I want for the cover; this is what we want on page three." How would you address clients like that? What advice would you offer?

LEDERMAN: I consider myself to be very knowledgeable in my own field of medical device technology. I expect people whose expertise is in other areas of interest to recognize that, and acknowledge that I am better qualified to determine what is extraordinary or what is mediocre about medical-device products. If you have chosen the right graphic designer, he or she should also be considered an expert. I would say that once you have chosen someone you are comfortable with, the design should be driven more by what the designer feels than by what you feel. Mike asked in the beginning, "What is it that you're trying to say? Why are you going to do this?" And then he decided how to implement that. So one must offer the direction, but once the direction is given — if you have retained the right professional — one would think that you're not doing your job if you cannot delegate the creative decisions. If you interfere and demand mediocrity, I think a smart designer would drop you and your company as a client.

Here's an example: to my thinking, photography is one of the most important elements in a report. I am personally an enthusiastic photographer; I have my own darkroom and a collection of cameras. The temptation was high to get involved and try to micromanage. However, I pretty much left Mike alone. When the selection of photography came up, I asked some questions, and made some recommendations. But ultimately, the choices were the shots he selected, except for one photograph that I thought didn't look right and that we should reshoot. He agreed. I don't think that we disagreed about anything in the annual report; it became largely what he recommended. This had never happened to me before. Very seldom have I been able to interact with someone from the outside in that way, and we do interact with a lot of outside professionals who provide us with various services. There are always disagreements. Maybe it's just personality compatibility or maybe that's just how a relationship should be. But I do think the decision maker in a company must choose someone he can rely on to produce a high-quality product that represents the company well.

Sometimes a CEO delegates those decisions to people who don't have his vision.

LEDERMAN: That's a mistake. It's shortsighted. There are certain functions that are part of a CEO's job. You used the right word, "vision," which is one of the things you want to project in an annual report. And that comes from the top. In this company, by the way, there were two people involved in the process —myself and the person with the most marketing and sales experience in the company. He is a very important member of the management team and it is his charter and focus to sell our products. We didn't want to make a product catalog out of the annual report, but we did want to project the credibility of the company to our product customers as well as to the stockholders. Our reports have done that very effectively.

RECENTLY, I FOLLOWED UP WITH MIKE WEYMOUTH.

You do twenty annual reports a year, and many of your clients are high-technology and biomedical startups. What is unique about working in this market?

WEYMOUTH: The majority of tech and biotech companies are headed by dynamic young scientists and management teams who embrace dynamic thinking in their graphic material. Unlike larger companies, where we often work with middle management to develop ideas, with startups we most often work directly with the CEO and can tap directly into his thought process. That's the magic formula for great design.

Do you agree with Dr. Lederman's assessment that many startups don't invest enough in an annual report that will work hard for them?

WEYMOUTH: I think startups generally realize that the annual report may well be their only communications tool. Dr. David Lederman is on the high end of that window. Startups may not want a big, expensive report, but they will more often than not opt for a higher level of creativity and better-thought-out solutions. In David's case, he also has a great sensitivity to good photography, and a sensitivity to visual material in general, which, of course, is one of the primary reasons we were able to do so much good work for him.

I was impressed when Dr. Lederman said that even though he's an amateur photographer and has his own darkroom, he resisted the temptation to micromanage. How rare is that?

WEYMOUTH: Very rare. David is the quintessential great client in this respect. When you know your client has good taste, you raise our own creative bar. It's the best kind of challenge.

What do you think about his test for avoiding mediocrity, i.e., describing what he calls "a very ridiculous kind of annual report" and seeing if a designer would be willing to do it?

WEYMOUTH: He's a sneaky guy. I am nothing but cautious in this respect. The process of feeling your way along in early meetings is tricky. I liken CEOs to supertankers. They have big, unwieldy egos, and they take a long time to turn around. Sometimes, as in the case with David, the tanker is going in the right direction under a full head of steam. With other CEOs it's not so easy to detect their course. They may think the designer only cares about design principles. But in my case I really do care about the CEO's objectives and less about my own, especially in first encounters. Also, if I'm talking to a potentially great client, I tend not to be unnecessarily opinionated. It's all part of the dance. David is just a lot smarter and intuitive when he plays it. And yes, many designers are willing to do ridiculous things, or at least things they aren't very happy about, in order to satisfy clients' wishes.

How do you handle it when you're asked to do something you don't think is in the best interest of the client?

WEYMOUTH: Clients who come to my firm tend to know they're going to get "new and different," and they actually listen to us, believe it or not. They ask us for our advice and, by and large, they take it. The dynamic you refer to happens mostly in the design review stage, in which the interview process weeds out uppity designers or those who do not fit the client's profile. I suspect we've lost out on lots of work at this stage because the clients didn't believe we would do what the CEO wanted and that we'd over-argue our own case. They probably looked at our design solutions and couldn't believe that a client actually agreed to them, when in fact the client was very happy with our work. It only points to the problem of dealing with middle management when the second-guessing-the-CEO game results in a safe, mediocre design firm getting hired.

Last year, when it was on the front pages and the network news that an Abiomed artificial heart was keeping a dying patient alive, do you think the company's attention to marketing put it in the forefront so an event like that was reported so positively?

WEYMOUTH: I think David personally nipped any over-marketing in the bud, knowing full well that there were miles to go with that heart, and that the early trials, however impressive, were going to go through many failures on the way to perfecting the heart for use in humans. So he didn't want to create too large a bubble of expectation.

THE **MILITARY-INDUSTRIAL COMPLEX**

Northrop Corporation *and* Jim Cross, Peter Harrison, Doug Oliver and Mike Weymouth

Northrop's YF-17 is the prototype for the U.S. Navy's F/A-18A twin-turbofan multimission aircraft and Northrop's land-based F-20 Mk. tactical fighter. More than 50 pilots have evaluated the YF-17.

Servicing F-5 fighters

Les Daly retired in 1993 after a thirty-three-year career with **NORTHROP CORPORATION**, Los Angeles. In 1973 he became vice president for public affairs and chief communications officer, with responsibility for producing the annual report. Prior to that he was based in Paris, from where he directed Northrop's communications in Europe and the Middle East, taking a leave in 1979 to become chief spokesman for the U.S. Department of Energy. He lives in Santa Fe, New Mexico, and his articles on a number of subjects have appeared in *Smithsonian*, *Atlantic Monthly*, *American Way*, and the *New York Times*.

JIM CROSS was designer/creative director of eighteen Northrop annual reports from 1961 to 1982. A graduate of UCLA's College of Fine Arts, Cross became Northrop's corporate design director in 1960. After three years there and a short stint as Saul Bass's head designer, he founded Cross Associates in Los Angeles in 1963, which became Siegel & Gale/Cross in 1988. He has been a director of the AIGA, the International Design Conference in Aspen, and Alliance Graphique Internationale and has taught and lectured widely. He is now a fine-art printmaker in Napa Valley, California.

PETER HARRISON, born in England, studied at the London School of Printing and Graphic Arts and emigrated to New York in 1957. Currently a resident of Fire Island, New York, Harrison has taught at Parsons School of Design and The Cooper Union. Known for his work in advertising art direction, graphic design, and three-dimensional design, he headed his own multi-disciplinary practice until joining Pentagram as a partner in 1979. There, he designed the Northrop annual reports for 1991 and 1992.

DOUG OLIVER was chairman of the 1998 Mead Annual Report Conference in New York. A graduate of Art Center College of Design, he worked for both James Cross and Robert Miles Runyan before founding his own consultancy in Santa Monica, California, in 1983. The firm opened a St. Louis office in 1995. The Design Office of Douglas Oliver designed the Northrop Grumman annual reports for 1996 and 1997.

MIKE WEYMOUTH, who shoots much of the photography for the annual reports his firm designs, worked his way up the New England design scene for ten years before founding Weymouth Design, now a twenty-person Boston design firm, in 1973. Mike Weymouth Design, which recently added a multimedia division to provide laptop presentations, Web sites, CD-ROMs and video services to its clients, designed the Northrop annual reports for 1983, 1984, and 1987 through 1990.

Here is a rare opportunity to eavesdrop on a truly privileged conversation. At the 1998 Mead Annual Report Conference at the World Trade Center in New York City, designer Doug Oliver hosted "A Study in Excellence," a panel discussion that paid tribute to Northrop's thirty-six-year history of extraordinary annual reports. Deceptively simple, classic, elegant, and black-and-white, each Northrop report used museum-quality photography and printing to explain how massive aerospace-defense projects like fleets of fighter aircraft are designed, built, and tested. Les Daly, the longtime Northrop senior vice president who directed the annual report process, joined Oliver on the podium, along with design firm principals Jim Cross, Mike Weymouth, and Peter Harrison—who had each, like Oliver, designed a number of Northrop reports. Afterwards I met with the panelists and asked a series of questions that resulted in the following free-flowing discussion. Subsequently, I had the opportunity to have several conversations with Daly and learn how one of the most experienced and respected clients in the business thinks and operates.

Doug, why was it important to you to honor Northrop in this way today?

OLIVER: Northrop was a touchstone of my career. After graduating from Art Center I joined Jim Cross's office, and the 1978 book was already underway. It unfolded before my eyes, showing me the kind of work I wanted to do for the rest of my life. It had beautifully reproduced, dramatic, black-and-white photography framed by sensitively handled white space, elegant type that was correct down to the tiniest detail, paper chosen deliberately only after testing on press. I worked on quite a few reports with Jim, and over the years I learned, among many other things, that you don't chase the Northrop annual report; they call you. My call came in 1995, when I was selected to design the 1996 Northrop Grumman report. I had visions of a long and rewarding run of books, perhaps the most satisfying of my career. But on July 3, 1997, after we'd begun work on the 1997 book, it was announced that Northrup Grumman and Lockheed Martin would merge and do business as Lockheed Martin. It looked like the company and its annual report would disappear, and that my 1996 book, which was black and white and as elegant as I could make it, would be the last of a tradition. I wanted to commemorate that tradition. As it turned out, the Department of Justice blocked the proposed merger and Northrop Grumman will live on. But the genre is very likely gone. The company is no longer a maker of aircraft but a broad-based electronics supplier pursuing a new look and direction.

Les, you were responsible for selecting a stellar group of designers. What were your criteria?

DALY: We didn't want people to pick up our report and say, "That's a great design." We wanted them to say, "That's a great company." Good design — except to designers — is practically invisible. And good design doesn't cost any more than bad design. We wanted to sculpt everything down to perfect, functional design. And we needed solutions that were enduring, solutions with legs. Some designers say they'll "take you to the edge," and they don't even know what the edge is, or they may confuse it with all kinds of clichés like cutouts and wild colors. That's not what we were after. We aimed at the core, not the edge: an absolutely perfect platinum sphere. We didn't always do it right. We made our share of mistakes. But one thing we worked the hardest at — and that I'd advise other companies to do — was to create our own orchestra. By that I mean select the very best designer, photographer, printer. We formed a team, not a hierarchy with the designer in charge of everything. Then the designer could put every ounce of effort into designing and didn't have to worry about managing suppliers. The team would get together and everyone would contribute ideas and learn from each other. When we finished, everybody thought it was "their" book.

How did the process get started every year?

DALY: It started with the written word. What were we trying to say? Then we wanted to use photography to make it real. We wanted real photography, nothing faked or manipulated, no airplanes superimposed on backgrounds with Photoshop. The chairman's letter was real and the product descriptions were real and the numbers were real. The photos had to be real, too. You can't fake an annual report in one place or it's not real in every place.

CROSS: Before all the photography was scheduled we had the photographer take a couple of test shots. Then, looking over the proofs, we gave guidance, saying, "This is what we are after, here's the real direction."

But the direction has remained remarkably consistent, hasn't it?

CROSS: It has, since the early sixties when I was Northrop's design director. I established the black-and-white medium because it was appropriate to the company's products and mission. It's not a colorful, glamorous type of business; it's a serious company involved in serious missions of national security. One year we might focus on the sculptural aspects of a gyroscope or a guidance unit. Another year it might be the people working on prototype fighter aircraft.

Did the best pictures come about through careful setting up, or were there fortuitous accidents when something just happened or the light was perfect?

HARRISON: I think the answer is both planning and magic. Sometimes the photographer will see something no one had planned.

WEYMOUTH: Northrop had a natural instinct to let people go for it, to talk with their eyes, so to speak. There was a lot of control but there was also a lot of respect and giving free reign, letting the designer and photographer do their thing. But always within the framework of the team.

DALY: If the photographer says, "I want to do something else," the corporate staff has to know what to say, whether it's appropriate to go off in that direction or not. Often the answer is, "Go get it. Shoot both. The picture we want and the one you want. Then we'll choose the right one."

OLIVER: Magic can happen, but I try to go on shoots. The photographer and I can bounce ideas off each other, and the shots almost always come out better if the designer is there.

Mike, were you the photographer on the reports you designed?

WEYMOUTH: No. I don't think Northrop was aware of my photographer side when they hired me in 1983. I recommended that Northrop hire Bruce Davidson. We got the great photos and that was all that mattered. Whatever I thought of my own talents as a photographer, Bruce was better. The fact that I was a photographer, though, made me a better designer for Northrop. I knew where the good pictures were. I knew the problems photographers faced. I knew when lighting was needed and how to make it look natural. But I never went on shoots. Obviously not every designer feels the same way, but maybe because I never wanted a designer hanging around when I was shooting for other clients, this was my chance to practice what I preach. And I was never disappointed with the results, although there were many factors besides aesthetics that went into choosing a particular photo.

OLIVER: Northrop has changed. It's more complicated. They make very few aircraft. Now it's radar and black boxes. We're not shooting sculpture any more.

DALY: We were always looking for new talent. The idea today would be to find the young photographers who haven't been discovered yet—today's Jeff Corwins, the young Cheryl Rossums and Marvin Silvers and Melissa Farlows—and to spend the time and work with them.

WEYMOUTH: As just one example of that, one day Les came into a meeting and dropped a bunch of prints on the table and said, "So, what do you think of this guy?" I'd never heard of him, but Les had taken the time to look at his stuff, which showed how much Northrop valued new thinking. He turned out to be one of the all-time-great annual report photographers.

Some photographers in the "great" category have reputations for being difficult. Were you willing to put up with it, Les?

DALY: Some of them, not all. But yes, I was and I did. Sometimes it was almost worth it.

Almost? How many days of photography are required to accomplish results like this?

CROSS: A lot.

HARRISON: Fifteen to twenty-five days. There's a lot of scouting and setting up.

And in fifteen to twenty-five days, how many pictures do you end up using?

HARRISON: Eight to twelve.

I think that will surprise a lot of people.

DALY: The fifteen to twenty-five days they're talking about is just the final stage. An annual report is conceived and crafted by the staff, consciously and unconsciously, every day of the year.

CROSS: And after choosing the pictures we went to extreme measures to achieve certain effects. Northrop is aluminum, titanium, steel, graphite. We'd have the photographer make a whole series of prints, twelve prints from one negative: on Ilford, on Agfa, on Fuji, on Kodak, to find the photographic paper that would result in the right level of contrast, the right nuances. Northrop's products were made with such great care and detail, and we needed to express that. It took a lot of experimentation.

WEYMOUTH: Les used to say, "I want a photograph worthy of hanging in an art gallery." I never failed to be awed, entering Northrop headquarters, by the black-and-white photography on the walls.

OLIVER: I told my photographers, "Go take the pictures you want to be buried with."

HARRISON: Because of that attitude Northrop owned black-and-white in the annual report marketplace.

Isn't the process you're describing too costly for most clients to consider?

CROSS: It can be worked out as part of the photographer's fee. Let's say the photographer was Steve Kahn. I might say, "Steve, can you show how this would look if you printed it several different ways?" The photographer has a vested interest, too. The best print for hanging in a gallery might not result in the best reproduction. And the printer would press-proof different prints, experimenting with different inks. We worked with a chemically dulled ink at George Rice. The first book, '61, was printed in rotogravure, a process using thick metal plates with deep dots that are incised into the plates, which gives you deeper tones.

Les said before that good design doesn't cost any more than bad design. I want to give readers a sense of what a project of this magnitude does cost. What would a company need to budget to achieve this kind of quality?

DALY: We were all over the place, some years up, some years down.

WEYMOUTH: It depends on the quantity.

Let me be more direct. What would you say to a company that had budgeted $100,000 for its annual report?

HARRISON: Even if there was a budget of $250,000 for 150,000 copies, I would say it would be extremely difficult to achieve. Managing the photography takes a lot of planning and scouting, a lot of careful effort. It's enormously complicated. You have to remember that this is about getting the best photographers. They are hard to find, and when you find them they are almost impossible to book. And then, if possible, you have to budget to go on location with them.

DALY: This is where the staff is instrumental. I really want to make this point: designers tend to ignore the staffers' experience and creativity. They tend to think creativity walks in the room in the person of the designer or maybe the photographer. They say they want to deal directly with the CEO. If designers appreciated the talent inside the room, more learning would go on. The CEO probably knows zip about how to make an annual report. And if he's working the annual report, somebody's not doing their job, including the CEO.

With all due respect, I can't tell you how many times designers have told me they worked with the PR or communications staff, only to have the CEO tear the whole book apart at the last minute because he said it didn't reflect his vision.

DALY: That's why the CEO has people like me: so he doesn't have to think about the annual report and can concentrate on being CEO.

You have to realize that you are unique! If every communications manager in every corporation were like you, the world would be a different place. This also relates to what you said about putting together your own orchestra. There's nothing that can sink a designer's heart faster than coming into a situation and learning that the client has already picked the photographer and the printer. I think most of us believe that those decisions should be the designer's responsibility, because the client may choose the wrong people for the wrong reasons.

CROSS: You're right. Ninety-nine percent of clients can't do it.

HARRISON: Northrop is the exception, not the rule. It almost never works. The worst is when they try to hand you a box of photographs. In general that's a lose-lose situation because there's no concept or strategy. Without focus a project usually ends up as something of a dog's dinner.

WEYMOUTH: It helped a lot that Les was astute and knowledgeable. But it wasn't like he was writing a blank check.

OLIVER: And he's left a legacy. People in charge of Northrop books today were trained by Les and have guidelines to follow.

DALY: I worked from the supposition that the designer wants the highest quality, too. It's a question of raising the level, not imposing. That's why we went through this exhaustive process.

OLIVER: Northrop's chairman once said to Jim and me, "If they [the readers] have a good feeling about the book, they'll have a good feeling about the company." That's really it, isn't it? Quality transmits confidence and competence.

Other than the photographers Cheryl Rossum and Melissa Farlow, have any women been involved in this endeavor?

DALY: It was curious. Women played key roles on our staff and brought an interesting perspective to it, but we never saw a woman designer come in the door. I think it's a loss that still prevails today.

CROSS: There were very few women in graphic design firms in the sixties and seventies. Women designers in my office had responsibility for other projects for Northrop in the eighties, but for no conscious reason, not the annual report.

HARRISON: Seventy percent of my students at Cooper Union were women, and that was ten years ago. Inevitably, women will become the principals. You have to remember that you're talking to the geezers here.

OLIVER: My partner is a woman and all the designers in my office are women.

DALY: One of the absolutely best, most original pieces of design we ever got was from a young woman named Cory Fanelli, who worked in Mike Weymouth's shop; she's on her own now in Boston. She designed a brilliant logo for the B-2 stealth bomber, but like the B-2 she was practically invisible in the design world. I saw Mike maybe hundreds of times, but the only reason I knew Cory existed was that she's a good friend of my daughter's. No fault of Mike's, that was the way it was in those days and probably still is; the men doing the selling and the women, if any, doing the work.

HARRISON: The important thing in any annual report is that the design team has to operate high up on the client management food chain, preferably with access to the CEO. It's dealing with people several tiers down that can create a problem. Quite often they're scared and don't have the authority to make real decisions. All the worst reports come about when you can't take appropriate risks. It has to be a passionate endeavor, and sometimes it's the designer's responsibility to push the client to take those risks. Otherwise, you end up with a mediocre book.

Les, did you ever feel pushed, or did any of you push him beyond where it seemed Les wanted to go?

CROSS: There was that famous book with handwritten captions. We weren't totally in agreement, were we, Les? You weren't sure.

DALY: Right. I wasn't comfortable with it. It was a different idea. Maybe I didn't understand it because I have terrible handwriting and this was beautiful handwriting, and it was supposed to be written by someone like me.

OLIVER: It was like an artist signing a portrait.

DALY: I just had to get used to it.

CROSS: And I had to sell it. A lot of designers aren't very articulate. When you present an idea you have to be able to explain why it works. "I like it" isn't good enough.

DALY: Sometimes I had to push. Sometimes the designers did. And when they were doing the pushing I needed to understand the reason for it. How was it going to advance what the company was trying to do, where was it trying to go? How and why will it get the company there?

In defense of designers, the designer needs an almost-scientific explanation to sell an idea. "I like it" is never good enough. You have to be able to say, "Ninety-seven percent of consumers responded positively. . . ." But all the client has to say is "I don't like it," and the idea is killed.

OLIVER: Unfortunately, it's sometimes part of our role to protect the client from himself. Sometimes what they ask for is not really what they need.

CROSS: You shouldn't listen to what a person is saying; listen to what they mean.

WEYMOUTH: It's all in the body language. At one point I spent two or three nights on press and the job still wasn't right. Les let me know how he felt with his body language.

What is it that causes a company like Northrop to change designers? Why are there four of you here?

HARRISON: Isn't it amazing that we're all friends?

I asked that half-facetiously because most companies seem to go through designers a lot faster than Northrop, perhaps every other year. And the designer wonders, I busted my fanny for you, I did a great job, and now why are you changing? Sometimes it's hard to get an answer.

OLIVER: It's important to ask for a straight answer and get one. But I'd rather know why I was hired. You can build a relationship from knowing that answer.

WEYMOUTH: Northrop wasn't a situation of your traditional designer getting fired. At the time [when I lost the account], the cross-country transmission of type proofs between Massachusetts and Los Angeles wasn't working as well as it should.

Les, if that was an issue at the time, why use East Coast designers?

DALY: Our big audience, the analysts and investment bankers, government customers, was back East. We used an East Coast ad agency. We were after a certain mental attitude. Also, sometimes the choice of a designer is a matter of who's available, who's too busy to listen. I won't get in line with twenty-eight other books.

CROSS: After doing eighteen Northrop books Les still wanted me. At the end I wasn't devoting all of me to the account. Losing it was a wake-up call. I'm sure I lost interest to the point where it showed.

DALY: We wanted Jim Cross or Mike Weymouth or whomever, not, to use an art term, the school of Jim Cross or Mike Weymouth or whomever.

CROSS [TO MIKE WEYMOUTH]: But when I saw yours, I said to myself, "I wish I'd done that." It had great elegance, a great degree of sophistication.

MIKE [TO PETER HARRISON]: I felt great when I saw yours.

HARRISON: It's a privilege to be part of this extraordinary tradition.

WEYMOUTH: Aside from a couple of one-year situations that didn't work out because of poor chemistry, we each did our tour of duty, each basking in the tradition like we would in the summer sun. But even good things have their limits. So we left, or rather arranged our departure, through one subtle means or another. I never really felt I was fired when I did my last report. Peter's was stunning and I'd reached the point in the relationship where I couldn't have done as good a job. It's the reason we're like a bunch of old Marine buddies sitting around shooting the breeze now. Sure, we could tell war stories, but instead we talk about the tradition.

OLIVER: If you spread all the books out, it's seamless over thirty-five years. You can't tell who the designer was. And most of them are still timeless. Take that '78 book. If you entered it in the Mead Show today, it would still win.

PART **III**

RETAIL AND ENTERTAINMENT CLIENTS

Today, every retail environment and entertainment
property is a brand and a consumer experience.
And each client requires a graphic identity,
interior design, packaging, direct mail, and print
and interactive advertising that touch
consumers' emotions.

12 THE MEGASTORE

Barnes & Noble *and* Farago + Partners

Leonard Riggio is founder and chairman of **BARNES & NOBLE, INC.**, the parent company of Barnes & Noble Bookstores, B. Dalton Booksellers, and Doubleday Book Shops. Traded on the New York Stock Exchange (symbol: BKS), with $4 billion in annual sales and one thousand retail bookstores in forty-nine states, Barnes & Noble, Inc., is the world's largest bookseller. Active in civic and philanthropic endeavors, Riggio was awarded an honorary Doctorate of Commercial Science from Baruch College of the City University of New York. He also collects contemporary sculpture, operates an equestrian facility, and is working on a novel.

Peter Farago is president of **FARAGO + PARTNERS**, a boutique New York City advertising and marketing agency. Before founding the agency, Farago was an art director at Jordan McGrath Case & Taylor, J. Walter Thompson, and Geer DuBois, where, working on the IBM account, he developed a passion for bringing the benefits of information technology to the creative process. Farago + Partners creates advertising and marketing communications for a national roster of clients, including Pantone Inc., Dow Jones, Brown & Williamson, and Prudential Securities.

When I met with Len Riggio, he had been taking a beating in the press for quite some time, accused of putting small booksellers out of business and of forcing publishers to change their jacket designs. Yet all of a sudden, perhaps with Barnes & Noble's online bookstore coming up strong against Amazon.com and the success of its private-label publishing venture, he was being called "the smartest guy in town" on the business pages and in magazines like the *New Yorker*. As you will see, he knows how to manage an interview. At one point, when asked about the demise of small booksellers, I was afraid he was going to throw me out of his office. "I thought this was going to be about design," he asserted. It was. His agency at the time, Farago + Partners, was producing nearly ten thousand newspaper ads a year, and was responsible for branding the consumer's entire experience, which included the design of coffee bars and shopping bags. In Peter Farago's words: "We — Barnes & Noble — are not what you think we are. We are not a huge impersonal chain. We are a champion of literature and a large version of the family bookstore." It was with a great deal of interest that I visited Farago + Partners at 107 Fifth Avenue, right across the street from Barnes & Noble's flagship store and corporate headquarters.

How did your agency's relationship with Barnes & Noble get started?

FARAGO: Len Riggio and I go back twenty years. Barnes & Noble had one store, and Geer Dubois was its agency. I was a twenty-nine-year-old art director there. At the time it was a sixty-person agency at One Dag Hammarskold Plaza. We'd worked on the account about five years, and Steve Olderman, who headed up the business, came to me and said, "Lenny wants a shopping bag." I'd just seen an illustration show and had fallen in love with R.O. Bleckman's work, that squiggly style, and I did a comp I wanted Bleckman to illustrate. It was a skyline of Manhattan, but instead of skyscrapers there were books — "bookscrapers." I did it to impress the account executive, Jeri Bag (my girlfriend, soon to be my wife). Apparently Len flipped out, he really liked it. I said, "Okay, let's get Bleckman." Jeri said, "Len wants to use the drawing just the way it is." I said, "You don't understand, this is a comp." They printed my layout anyway, coerced me into doing it. Embarrassingly, I'd also signed it like Milton Glaser, with my name, Farago, in a little lozenge shape. But eventually there were millions of those shopping bags around town and it made me crazy to see them. So after a certain number of years — I wasn't at Geer Dubois any more — I decided to sue Len for copyright infringement.

Didn't you get paid for the work while you were at Geer DuBois?

FARAGO: It was done on the side, as they say. That's how it goes in some agencies: the account executive, in this case Jeri, placates the art director with some gift certificates for doing extra work for the client. I'd gotten paid $75 in gift certificates for it and it was my understanding that the use was for one year. After several years I felt entitled to more money. The whole thing was unclear, fuzzy, on both sides. I got cranky that this thing was a huge hit and all I'd gotten was $75. Actually, I had no right to sue. I was a naive kid trying to make my way in a world I didn't understand. Len just kind of shrugged it off, laughed at it, and asked me if I wanted to do more work for him.

Already he sounds like an unusual guy.

FARAGO: He's the son of a prize-fighter from Brooklyn. He doesn't think like anybody else, especially people in literature and publishing. I made a deal with him. I had friends at Apple and Adobe who'd said, "Computers are the next thing." I'd spent the past five years learning about computers. I'd developed a system, a total electronic environment for manufacturing ads. Len saw me walking up the street with some equipment and asked what I was doing. I told him I was opening an agency that could create ads on computers. I said, "You're paying $12,000 an ad to Geer Dubois. I'll make you a deal." I showed him how to manufacture his existing ads for a quarter the price. We currently ship nine thousand ads a year.

How did you accomplish that?

FARAGO: The way it used to work, a copywriter would write a headline and four days later the art director would come back with a layout. The AD's job was to decorate the words, make everything fit. In 1988, we had the first color Macs, the first network Macs, and Adobe's launch of ATM allowed us to see on-screen what real type looked like. We were the first agency at which copywriters and art directors could work together in real time. Our agency developed the system by which everyone worked at a computer and shared the same set of tools. The writers used computers. The art directors used computers. And the enthusiasm bonded them together. When the copywriter could see his or her words set in type minutes later, it would crank up the process another notch and the project could evolve. You could see your layout with an image and change a word to make it work better. Or you could change your image to make your words work better. Then it flowed to production.

More important, when the copywriter and I left here with the ads under our arms, we were wildly enthusiastic about the work because it was so fresh. That couldn't help but be transmitted to the client. Clients can sense that. They know when you believe in something or you're just trying to shuffle off some half-baked idea.

What was your thinking behind the initial presentation to Len Riggio?

FARAGO: I knew that Len, perceived as a newcomer, wanted to be loved by the literary community. So Steve Olderman and I—Steve was by then recruited by Len and working for Barnes & Noble—helped him create a brand that said, in essence: "We support the important works of great literature." I in turn recruited Mark Summers, who was known for his author portraits in the *New York Times Book Review,* and we bought drawings of five dead authors for $500 apiece: Shakespeare, Virginia Woolf, Oscar Wilde, Isak Dinesen, and Theodore Dreiser, everybody's favorites. We showed the world how to take the high ground in bookstore advertising: Let the authors sell the books. It was an instant hit. After the dead authors appeared, we were able to convince Kurt Vonnegut to let us use his likeness. Then everybody wanted in. Authors and publishers.

How do you choose which author gets to play center stage in an ad? Is it related to the book that's being promoted most vigorously?

FARAGO: In the beginning it was related to who we could get. But once it started to go, the concept went like a house on fire. Every publisher wanted their people in our ads. Soon, it seemed to be almost as important to have your picture in a Barnes & Noble ad than to get a good review or to get on the best-seller list. You would be handsomely drawn and presented as one of the icons of literature. Stephen King is in the company of Shakespeare. Mary Higgins Clark is like Virginia Woolf. For the first time, publishers fell in love with and came to support a co-op campaign; they no longer had to be coerced.

Let me see if I understand the co-op concept. Let's say a page in a newspaper costs $20,000. There are ten books featured on it. So each publisher pays $2,000 for the space?

FARAGO: Right, and typically there's a little margin in there. That's where we can do some branding. We chose to give people a brand reason and an emotional reason to shop at Barnes & Noble. That's another way our ads are different from typical co-op ads, like "Nobody Beats The Wiz" [an East Coast electronics chain] ads. The Wiz is so hungry they chockablock every ad. Wiz ads are highly engineered to get in as many products as they can fit. The director of co-op has only one master: the bottom line. That puts you in a commodity business. There's no reason to shop at the Wiz except for selection, selection, selection, price, price, price. Len Riggio has a passion, a belief, a desire to create something of value. That's where the authors come in. For Nike, it's the athletes. For us, it's the authors. That's the people we represent. We give you the works of great authors, so you can be smarter. I see a visit to a Barnes & Noble as a visit to a place where I can get my act together: With these self-help books my life will be better. With these books about health my body will be better. With these classics my mind will be better. If I read this author, my social life will be better. I will have something to talk about. Hell, I might even meet someone in the store.

Your involvement with Barnes & Noble goes far beyond advertising, doesn't it?

FARAGO: We are a combination of advertising people and designers. Greg Crosley, my partner, comes from pure design and he's also a fine painter. You can't sell design any more because it doesn't work fast enough. The average duration of a brand manager is eighteen months, and he has to show increased sales. Farago + Partners is responsible for what we call *deep branding*. It's a combination of design and sales messages. Down to the fax paper and coffee cups. Deep branding means applying the brand identity to every object you as a consumer see. We've done five different trucks. Twenty coffee cups. In-store design. T-shirts. Ads are only 20 percent of the communications. Do people come into a new store because of an ad? Hell, no. They come in because of a sign they saw in a parking lot. Every year we continue with Barnes & Noble (it's been nine years), their brand equity grows. Our job is twofold: to move books and build brand. Move books, build brand. Sell brand. At every opportunity. Right down to the bookmarks. It shows in sales. You can extend the brand into every portion of your business. Or, to put it another way, if you are in business today, and miss any opportunity to brand, you're missing an enormous opportunity.

How about the research side of the agency business? How does that fit into the mix?

FARAGO: To help us create not just a place to buy books, but a destination that's personally involving. For our focus groups, I go into stores and ask people, "What does this store feel like? Does it feel like home?" What we're trying to do is make an experience that people will really love. You want to find out why people come back to one store and not another. You can buy the same books in Borders, but people say Borders looks like their college library. Barnes & Noble looks and feels like home. They say, "It's quiet like my home. It's comfortable like my home. I meet friends here. We come for coffee." The answers to those questions help Barnes & Noble decide, what do I put more of where? More books? More furniture? More coffee?

Were you also involved in the store design?

FARAGO: It started with Steve Olderman walking over here with some William Morris wallpaper, and we'd sit down at the computer and work out William Morris interiors with dark green accents. Of course, Steve worked with architectural firms, too. But he worked out the look and feel with me.

Do you have a background in interior design?

FARAGO: I'd just have to close my eyes and remember what my parents' home looked like! My parents bought their home in Lake Forest, Illinois, a suburb of Chicago, from the Scribners, the late publishing family, for a song. My father was a doctor and one of his patients, Mildred Fitzhew, one of the last of the Scribner family, was nearing a hundred years old. She said to my dad, "You take the estate and I'll live in the guest house. Just make sure I'm well taken care of." It was a Victorian country mansion with suits of armor, libraries, mahogany paneling everywhere, thick, rich, cushioned furniture. There were paintings of great authors all over the place. As a kid I had no appreciation for any of this, but it's amazing to realize how much it's influenced my life. There were lots of other people who contributed [to Barnes & Noble store design] too, but I never had to do any research. I'd lived with the classics and knew how to apply them.

What was the process of working with Len Riggio like, especially in the beginning?

FARAGO: We sat in a room like this. Lenny, Steve Olderman, and me. No minyan, no shareholders, no committee. Steve and I played writer/art director and Len played impresario. Lenny loved getting involved. He's a great collector of art as well as a lover of books. He put everyone in a room and let the sparks fly. Everything emanated from him. Nothing got in the way. It got birthed whole.

It was absolutely joyous. Nobody asked middle-manager-mentality questions like, "Doesn't this compromise the author's relationship with other book-sellers?" Or, "It looks like an endorsement, it looks like he or she is endorsing Barnes & Noble and not the others."

How much time do you spend on the account?

FARAGO: Every day. Every day. As the business grows, we continually rein-force this message: We [Barnes & Noble] are not what you think we are. We are not a huge impersonal chain, a giant conglomerate. We are a champion of literature and a large version of the family bookstore. Hence the easy chairs, places to sit and read, cafés.

Tell me about the case-bound book about your agency's work for Barnes & Noble [Deep Branding: A Case History] *and the other books you've shown me? Are these one-of-a-kind? How do you make them?*

FARAGO: Agencies typically don't have good, current information. No one wants to read sixty pages of account-exec dogma. It simply won't work. We make these books ourselves. We have a skilled bookbinder who wears little white gloves and puts them together in our studio. We make them from 600-dpi color photocopies. How? It's our secret. But they typically take about four hours to make. It's our intention to simply show the pieces of work that relate directly to a potential client's business, and let them and the consultants who recommend agencies to clients decide for themselves.

AS WE CONTINUED TO TALK, PETER FARAGO STEERED ME ACROSS THE STREET TO MEET WITH LEONARD RIGGIO AT BARNES & NOBLE'S EXECUTIVE OFFICES.

Were there a real Mr. Barnes and Mr. Noble, booksellers since 1873?

RIGGIO: There were such people in the nineteenth century. Unfortunately, the history and lore of the origins of the company have been lost. The modern-day predecessor of this company moved in around 1920.

When did you enter the picture?

RIGGIO: The company formerly known as Barnes & Noble was bought by a conglomerate in the 1960s, when conglomerates were buying up all kinds of unrelated companies, whether they had any synergy or not. Essentially they failed. The once-proud fifteen-store chain had shrunk to one, that store being the one right under where we are sitting right now. I bought the flagship store and the rights to use the name.

What had you been involved in up to that time?

RIGGIO: I was in the business of college bookstores. SBX—Student Book Exchange. We have 400 college bookstores in addition to 450 Barnes & Noble retail stores all over the country.

How much of Barnes & Noble's growth do you attribute to Peter Farago?

RIGGIO: Peter and I go back a lot of years. When we met, he was an art director for Geer DuBois, which was a very hot, hip agency that prided itself on having a few exceptional clients. That's what attracted me to them. Most of the clients had a fairly high profile, such as IBM (a specific division of IBM, for which they were doing great work), Foster Grant, Dry Dock Savings Bank. They created "Who's Behind the Foster Grants?" a very memorable campaign, as well as "Dry Dock Country," a very endearing campaign. Their specialty was image creation through advertising. With Peter as an art director, we created many memorable, award-winning campaigns, including the first TV campaign for any bookseller in history. During those years Peter had designed a shopping bag. I'd been shown a sample of it. It was kind of a prototype, almost a sketch. I said, "Why don't we just print it?" They said, "You don't understand, that's not the finished art." But I knew what I wanted. I was the client. The customers loved it. It was the best bag we ever created.

Peter told me he rekindled his relationship with you by suing you over it.

RIGGIO: He'd left Geer Dubois by that time and was starting his own agency. I got a letter saying he intended to sue us for using the artwork. I'd obviously thought I had good title to it, that I owned the bag. When he threatened to sue, instead of being angry I was amused and asked him to come in and talk to me. I asked him, "Why don't you make a proposal?" I had always thought Peter was one of the most brilliant people I'd ever met.

So in that way he wrested the account away from Geer Dubois?

RIGGIO: Geer Dubois was in the process of going away anyway. They did eventually fold. When I started with them they were a cottage company, about a $15 million agency. The agency went out of business at $250 million. All that growth doesn't necessarily help. By getting Peter, I could again have a relationship with a smaller-size agency. I like having a direct creative relationship with the owners.

What did you think of Peter's presentation?

RIGGIO: Most good advertising is the result of a collaborative effort. In the best work, you see the account executive, copywriter, art director, and client all taking credit. As a client, I had a lot to do with it. As did Steve Olderman. He came from Geer DuBois to work for us. It was just a great collaboration.

I wanted our advertising to be distinguished by the richness of the graphic images and the look and feel of our ads—more so than by the copy. Advertisers spend far too much time talking to people and get far too cutesy. We don't do enough about letting the customer decide for himself. Peter's mission, or job—in addition to designing our logo—was to create a look for Barnes & Noble that was both very hip and produced in impeccable detail and quality. His agency had to create a new ad every day—either for the *New York Times* or someplace else in the country. Production costs had to be in proportion to our budget for each ad. Peter was and still is on the cutting edge of computers and technology. He did it. It was kind of marvelous that he was able to turn out that kind of quality so inexpensively.

I'd like to turn to some items from the news. Here's a front-page story from the New York Times *titled "Book Chains' New Role: Soothsayers for Publishers" that reports that publishers are using Barnes & Noble to tell them which jacket designs will sell better, even which book titles. Readers who design book jackets will be interested in knowing whether their clients are ultimately the store chains, not the author or publishers.*

RIGGIO: It just doesn't happen! We buy more than 50,000 titles a year. Once in a while a publisher's sales rep may ask us what we think of one jacket over another. The whole story was a complete fabrication.

And that you are constantly accused in the media of putting small neighborhood bookstores out of business. Is that because you can buy in volume more cheaply?

RIGGIO: We pay the same price as they do. The real question should be, why do independent booksellers charge so much? People in the world of literature tend to look down on people who make a profit.

Here's a story from Fortune *magazine, "Why Barnes & Noble May Crush Amazon,"*
which says you are beating Amazon.com at their own game. I read somewhere else that
you have a hundred people here working on the Web site. Is it making a profit yet?

RIGGIO: No. Of course not.

For what it's worth, I tried to order a book through Amazon.com yesterday, and,
after the book got in my shopping cart, the transmission got cut off three times.
The transaction went through at Barnesandnoble.com right away. Maybe the prophets
at Fortune *are correct.*

RIGGIO: Sometimes it works one way, sometimes the other. But thank you.
Maybe they are.

You were quoted in the New Yorker *this week as saying you envision online stores as*
a supplement to, not a replacement for, the store environment. In an age when your
competitors are trying to sell books without real estate and inventory, tell me about
your commitment to the store.

RIGGIO: The store transmits our biggest message, the message that's central to
our ad campaigns, which are rooted in the store experience: A home away from
home. A book-lover's second home. A place with lots of books and crannies.
Bright, cheerful, warm, promising, full of energy. We try to create an emotional
environment. To make a public space. When you walk into a typical store and
a salesperson says, "Can I help you?" that's a form of "What are you doing
here?" We want to make our stores an extension of people's lives, an extension
of the street. To give them a feeling of ownership. When it's welcoming, they
spend more time. We provide easy chairs, restrooms, even baby changing
stations. Baby changing stations in the men's rooms. Children's sections don't
make money, but they make future readers. Families spend time together
in our stores. Peter Farago had a lot to say and do with our prototype stores.
He was intimately involved in store design, with the emphasis on lighting and
messaging graphics.

Typically, a client's ad agency and architectural or interior design firm would
have little to do with each other. What's behind your thinking on overlapping
these disciplines?

RIGGIO: If you think of an agency to just do ad campaigns you're missing
the full potential of what an agency can do. Your primary marketing vehicle is

your retail environment. Our mission is to make the store the most pleasurable shopping experience possible to the customer. You want the brightest minds designing it.

I RECENTLY FOLLOWED UP WITH PETER FARAGO.

You are not an agency of record any more. What happened?

FARAGO: Tibor Kalman had gotten his start at Barnes & Noble, and when he came back from editing *Colors* magazine in Italy he approached Lenny, asking him to help set him up another company, something like M&Co. Tibor became Lenny's impresario once again, and they held agency reviews. We were in review, along with several others. Tibor said, "It's time for a change; jettison the authors; they're old hat." We refused to do that. We did what we thought was right. We said that *Rolling Stone* would never walk away from the rock stars on the cover. We would never walk away from the authors.

So the business went to . . . ?

FARAGO: To TBWA/Chiat Day, and now it's with Steve Olderman's group at Digitas. We had a great ride while it lasted. Absolutely no hard feelings.

The Nature Company *and* Kit Hinrichs

In 1973 Tom Wrubel and his wife Priscilla opened the first **NATURE COMPANY** shop in Berkeley, California, which sold products related to the observation and understanding of the natural world. Two years later, *Kathy Tierney* joined as executive vice president of retail—responsible for all store operations, store design, and marketing. The Nature Company became a nationwide chain of fifty-five stores and a mail order operation with a circulation of six million catalogs and more than $90 million in annual sales, employing eight hundred people. Today, The Nature Company is owned by Discovery Communications, Inc.

KIT HINRICHS is a partner in Pentagram, the multidisciplinary design partnership with offices in London, New York, San Francisco, Austin, and Hong Kong. A native of Los Angeles and Art Center graduate, he was a partner in Jonson, Pedersen, Hinrichs & Shakery, which became Pentagram's San Francisco office in 1986. Hinrichs has received numerous awards, including Gold Medals from the New York and Los Angeles Art Directors Clubs and the Margret Larsen Award for excellence from the San Francisco Art Directors Club. He is the author of three books, including *TypeWise*, published by Northlight books.

"**W**e strive to operate in a visually exciting, professionally staffed environment in which authenticity and knowledge are balanced with sufficient humor to give our customers an experience which makes them feel good about themselves and the world in which they live . . . this is called The Wow Factor, and you are responsible for creating it." —The Nature Company merchandising guide

Sixties counterculture guru Tom Wrubel's quest was to sell quality products in an environment in which employees could take personal responsibility for sales success, which was closely linked to design. Leafy spaces with waterfalls and natural wood beams, the Nature Company stores that Wrubel founded were designed as places to experience (and buy) field guides and binoculars; wind chimes and sculptures, fossils and crystals; jewelry and scarves with fish and bird motifs. Graphic design was as important as environmental design. Catalogs brought that experience to the printed page and the mailboxes of shoppers across the country. The relationship between Tom Wrubel and Pentagram partner Kit Hinrichs went much deeper than a business plan or a square-inch analysis of catalog sales. As these interviews show, Wrubel and Hinrichs spent time together, visited stores, and talked about life—and about design.

I left your store with a full shopping bag, but I'd like to begin by talking about the mail order side of the business. Has mail order become an American way of life?

TIERNEY: Well, yes and no. The catalog shopper and the retail shopper are two very different consumers, and it's almost impossible to convert one to the other. Catalog is currently under 10 percent of our sales, but it still plays a major role. The catalog is a major benefit to our retail stores; it brings people in. That's why we spend so much effort on it. Actually, mail order in general has suffered greatly in the last several years, for two reasons. One is printing and paper costs. The other is postal increases. It now costs 21 cents to mail a catalog. That kind of overhead defeats a lot of profits. Also, once you open a store, catalog shoppers have to pay sales tax in that state, which defeats one benefit of mail order.

I'm also wondering about the practice of selling lists. And about the proliferation of similar catalogs. Haven't those practices defeated a lot of profits? One year I sent my clients twig wreaths for holiday gifts. Within a few months I must have gotten five catalogs from other outfits selling twig wreaths. You'd think the first company might have wanted to keep my business for itself.

TIERNEY: The mail order industry has definitely killed the golden goose; it's killing itself off. Companies make a lot of money trading names, renting names. Those names are gold because you need to get your catalog in front of someone who's a catalog buyer. So many catalog companies copy each other that the buyer has many choices, but little to choose from that's really unique or of real quality.

Can you characterize the mail order customer?

TIERNEY: Working women make up the largest percentage. Part of it has to do with not having time to shop. But it's really a lifestyle choice. There's a mystique about catalogs. Some people really enjoy getting a gift in the mail that they've ordered for themselves. And when you think about it, it's a tremendous leap of faith: seeing a picture in a catalog, giving your credit card number over the phone, trusting the system that you'll get what you've ordered and like what you get.

And would you say the retail customer is the one who has to feel and touch things?

TIERNEY: Yes, and to have the experience of being in the store.

The Nature Company has fifty-five stores. Can you tell me how the concept began?

TIERNEY: Tom Wrubel had been in the original Kennedy Peace Corps in Liberia and in Africa on a Fullbright. He and Priscilla didn't start out as merchants or retailers; they were idealists and naturalists. Tom was trained as an architect: he was fascinated by design; he had an incredible respect for it. He was back teaching at Mills College, and simply wanted to turn people on to nature. He thought it would be great to open a store in Berkeley where people could buy tools that would enhance the experience of being outside. The Nature Company is just one company — others are Esprit, Banana Republic, Smith & Hawken — that grew out of the Bay Area in the sixties. Tom didn't start out to make a lot of money and have a big company. He wanted to sell high-quality products, to express his love of good design, and do things in unconventional ways. He thought that paraphernalia for the naturalist — things like field glasses — didn't have to be sold in musty old stores, but could gain a larger audience in a new kind of environment. Priscilla focused on products for kids — toys and books that would teach children about nature.

In addition to Berkeley in the sixties, I also sense the presence of the human-potential movement of the seventies. Specifically in language like "taking responsibility" for success. Did anything like the "est" training also influence the concept?

TIERNEY: Yes, we did all that stuff. And Tom really believed in all those movement ideals, and applied them to business. For example, we never use the term "customer service." Instead, we encourage our staff to share their love of nature. It really is a humanistic approach to retail. We choose the right people and let them be themselves, be sincere and honest. None of that phony "How can I help you?" stuff. Tom was fond of saying to our staff, "You have this wonderful opportunity to greet and talk to strangers."

It might be too easy to dismiss all this as a cute merchandising gimmick. But aren't there also some serious ideas behind The Nature Company?

TIERNEY: We don't just dress up things with pictures of animals, we're committed to certain principles. For example, no killing living things, no trophy collecting. We follow Thoreau's words, "Go out and leave only your footprints." We won't sell butterfly collections, or even seashells found on the beach, if that would mean disturbing the hermit crabs that live in those shells. The sixties were a time of heavy political and environmental organization, and Tom could have easily jumped on that bandwagon. But he wanted The Nature Company to be a place where everyone would feel welcome. As soon as you take a political stand, you polarize and alienate people. So we'll never show pictures of whales being slaughtered; we show the beauty rather than the wrongs. People learn by opening their minds, not by being intimidated. Another thing is our alliance with The Nature Conservancy, an independent conservation organization. We've sold over 18,000 Conservancy memberships, and we've donated a percentage of the profits from certain products—to date over $100,000.

When the company was sold to CML, had Tom already expanded it into a chain?

TIERNEY: We had about eight stores then, but Tom would never have used the word "chain." He was driven by the desire to continually evolve and do things better. Every time we opened a store we had the opportunity to refine the concept. The original stores were primarily about books and tools. With every store we added another department—you've seen what we have now. And as we grew and evolved, we needed someone like Kit Hinrichs.

Tell me about the evolution of the catalog.

TIERNEY: It started out as a homegrown kind of thing. There were sketches of products, and Tom, who was a pretty good photographer, took some of the pictures himself. You could say that those early catalogs were folksy and earthy. We outgrew that and wanted a much finer design. When Tom and Priscilla wanted to expand nationwide, CML gave the okay to work with Kit. We finally had the financial stability.

Was money an issue?

TIERNEY: It's definitely a commitment to find the best designer. And as a business you have to see that it's repaid in terms of profits. Our success is measured in sales. The unconventional side to The Nature Company, though, goes beyond sales and means being a leader.

Can you describe how being a leader translates into catalog design?

TIERNEY: Most cataloguers will take all their products and say to the designer, "This is where I want this and that. Here's what goes on the cover, what you should make the biggest on each page. And when I get my sales figures I'll do a square-inch analysis to figure out what's selling best, what to feature next time." We threw all that out the window. You can look at some of the first catalogs Kit designed and see that he took something like a $14 fish potholder and made it four times bigger on the page than a sculpture costing many times more. We're never boring because we never do the expected or the mundane.

It's the same theory we use in our stores. A mixture of fun and serious, inexpensive and expensive. It creates a feeling people love. As you've discovered, we don't sell things you need. We sell an experience and appreciation of the natural world—in an environment of dappled light, streams, waterfalls—that makes people feel good. So they want to buy a piece of the feeling.

I can buy a potholder at Kmart for a dollar. Are you saying that an experience will make me pay $13 more?

TIERNEY: We're definitely not a discounter, but we give people the best, the most value. It's worth what you pay for it. Instead of potholders, let's talk about toys and gifts for children, an area in which there's so much junk. We really do select and edit, find the highest quality, the toys with the most educational value. There's a loyalty and trust in what we're doing.

Some strong voices in the design community are saying that designers have sold out to the capitalist system. That instead of using our talents to create better products, we have become mere decorators in the service of big business. That we are guilty of making products that are in essence the same appear to be better, different, made in "olde England," or whatever. Some designers are saying that we ought to be "bad" and say "no" to our clients.

TIERNEY: I agree. You should. But that's not the way things are at The Nature Company. We're not asking anybody to make anything look better than it is, to make it into something that it's not. Just put it in the right environment.

Do you and Kit ever disagree?

TIERNEY: All the time. In a very healthy way. As a company we're constantly pushing ourselves, and Kit and Pentagram along with us. To lead us to the next plateau in design. To be on the leading edge of catalogs. We spend time together and talk about these things, get that tension going. As I said, many clients will say to their designer, "You will feature this, the product with the most profit potential." Kit will see a $19.95 rubber reptile and say to us, "What a wonderful design element! Look at the way the tail curves!" And he'll use it across two pages.

He makes the photo selections himself? He's that personally involved?

TIERNEY: He spends the time on it. Kit and The Nature Company go back eight years. And we can still call him up and say, "We're concerned about this," or, "We don't like the way that is working." He'll listen. And he can be the same way with us.

So often clients complain that the only time they see the design firm principals is when they're selling or presenting work.

TIERNEY: Sure, Kit has assistants and a photo stylist we work with. But we won't have a meeting without him.

Tell me about your entry into product design.

TIERNEY: Proprietary products are something people can't get anywhere else, and they've become quite important to us; they now account for about 10 percent of our sales. They're often developed with the help of a design firm or another vendor. This happens a lot; someone from outside will come to us with an idea. We may think it's not quite right, and we work together on it.

I'm especially impressed by the level of detail given to visual merchandising. Is this unique to The Nature Company?

TIERNEY: All retailers who are doing a good job have defined how they want their stores to look. Because of our variety of merchandise we had to get very organized. And we must be doing it right because we're getting knocked off all the time. People even come in and measure our fixtures.

Pentagram also consults in architecture, interior design, and product design. Have you worked with them in those areas?

TIERNEY: No.

I don't have to tell you that cross-selling is a big buzzword now, and it's interesting that this hasn't happened.

TIERNEY: I guess it's because our relationship is with Kit rather than Pentagram as a firm. Kit has designed many products for us, though, mostly T-shirts and posters, that are excellent sellers. He's gone far beyond catalog design and into packaging, which has become very, very important to us.

How do you determine when something's right?

TIERNEY: When Tom Wrubel died in 1989 it left a huge hole in the company. Priscilla has been the guiding light, and continues to promote our mission. But we relied on Kit to keep up the creativity. At one time, he served on a committee to review graphic identity, packaging, posters, T-shirts, wrapping paper. From that have come all kinds of ideas and themes. As our needs have changed, Kit's role has contracted and expanded. For example, because we couldn't pass along to our customers the costs of doing all the design work out- side, we put together a strong internal creative department. Instead of being threatened by this, Kit helped us set it up and find and interview the people. What's right is the pace Kit set: warm, friendly, whimsical, lively. When you turn the page or go around a corner you're never quite sure what you'll see. I don't know if you've seen our spring catalog.

You've changed the size.

TIERNEY: Right, we're always experimenting, always trying something new and different. And Kit's right there with us.

LATER, I SPOKE WITH KIT HINRICHS.

Well, Kit, do all your clients value you as much as the Nature Company does?

HINRICHS: (Laughs). It isn't always roses. There are always times when each side needs to test the other. It's important for me to test the edges, to take the client somewhere they haven't been before, to get them to do something they hadn't thought about. As designers, we have to constantly challenge ourselves; that's why we're in business. Tom Wrubel liked to test the edges. He was a counterculture guy with a good entrepreneurial attitude. Businesses have to continue to grow or they die. He knew that. The Nature Company would have been successful and grown without us, but probably not as well or as quickly.

I am especially interested in Kathy's statement about you: "We won't have a meeting without him." Is this much client dedication and contact typical for you?

HINRICHS: I sure like to think so. It's not unique to The Nature Company. Tom and I spent a lot of time together. I was on retainer as a consultant, and we used to drive around to the stores together and spend hours talking. You can always do better work if you know the top person well. And, sure, you can be dedicated to more than one client. It varies. Some clients want to be "your clients." Others want you to do a special project or consult for a specific period of time.

At a conference last year, I opened my presentation by talking about how the best and best-known designers get and keep clients. Someone got up and said, "If you're going to talk about those superstars, I want my money back. I want to know how I can do it." There was a general feeling in the audience that "ordinary" designers have nothing in common with people like Kit Hinrichs. What can readers learn from what you do?

HINRICHS: Well, we can start with how to earn trust. Designers make thousands of judgments on behalf of clients. From the choice of typeface and photographer to how a store is sold to someone who's never been there. For example, someone may get a Nature Company catalog for five years in someplace like Kansas City, and then a store opens up, and you have a pre-sold customer. Over the years we've been able to prove that we are the right people to make the right decisions to accomplish something like that. Whether it's a two-color job or a World's Fair exhibition. If I lose a client—something that happens to everyone—it's because in some way that trust was broken. The Nature Company must have gone through ten designers, one a year, some very good ones, before they talked to us. For some reason—perhaps it's because we were able to visualize Tom Wrubel's philosophy—that trust was able to take root and grow.

Can we talk about some more practical matters? According to Kathy Tierney, few designers are given the freedom to choose the scale and location of items in a catalog. Is this something you were involved with from the beginning?

HINRICHS: When Tom selected items for his stores, he liked the way they looked or felt. It was intuitive. And he just said to me, "Do what you do." At the time we had no experience doing catalogs, so we drew upon our editorial experience with annual reports, magazines, and books, trying to bring in wit and a sense of humor.

What about the photography? I'd imagine that your approach cost many times more than what they were spending.

HINRICHS: They often picked up the manufacturers' supplied photos. We initially showed comps that demonstrated the value of establishing a photographic look and creating a visual tone of voice for all the photos.

Was all new photography a difficult sell?

HINRICHS: We explained that what they were responding to so favorably in the comps was the quality of the photography. And in terms of sales, the costs all come back. Many times over. They're already spending heavily for paper, printing, postage—whether a recipient looks at the catalog or throws it in the garbage. The difference between keeping and throwing a catalog away is often good design and good photography. And the impact on the overall budget is usually less than 5 percent. Without it, you may be wasting all your money. Luckily, a catalog has direct feedback. With most projects, it's the chairman or president who has to like it, and that's as much as you know. A catalog goes out and the phone starts to ring. You know right away if it's successful.

Tell me about the Nature Company products you've designed.

HINRICHS: All the products are collaborative and initiated by the client. They may come to us and say, "We'd like some T-shirts, and frogs are really big this year." Or they'll buy the rights to an idea that needs some work. For example, someone owned the rights to a list of all the multiples of animals, like "gaggle of geese" and "ostentation of peacocks." We thought it was a great idea, and we designed a typographic poster and T-shirt. What we're talking about is not industrial design, it's graphic design, graphic paraphernalia.

What's next for Kit Hinrichs, Pentagram, and The Nature Company?

HINRICHS: Some interesting—and confidential—projects. Overall, we support the growth of their businesses. We're not threatened by the in-house department; we'll continue to consult and work on special projects. Sometimes I don't agree with everything they do; something may not look right, it may not look like it's from The Nature Company, so I make recommendations, help them stay within the family of design we developed. We agree with them that making money and doing good work are not contradictory activities.

14 THE TYCOON

The Grand Union Company *and* Milton Glaser, Inc.

In 1978 London-based financier Sir James Goldsmith purchased the **GRAND UNION COMPANY**, a U.S. supermarket chain headquartered in Wayne, New Jersey. Fourteen years later—during which Milton Glaser, Inc., was engaged in a $500 million redesign— Grand Union had become the nation's fifteenth largest supermarket chain: a $3 billion company with 20,000 employees, operating more than 300 stores in eight eastern states. The company was sold twice since then and liquidated in 2002.

William A. Louttit, who had joined the company in 1964 as a part-time clerk, was executive vice president and chief operating officer during the entire redesign.

Milton Glaser founded **MILTON GLASER, INC.**, in 1974 after he left Pushpin Studios to pursue work in interiors, exhibitions, corporate identity, publications, and restaurant design. Often combining innovative lettering with his own illustrations in a manner inspired by Italian painting and design, Glaser is creator of an influential and distinctively American graphic style. Since 1978, the firm's redesign of Grand Union supermarkets—which has brought together elements of Glaser's personal interests in food, marketing, social issues, and town planning—helped revolutionize the way many American supermarkets are designed and the way America shops. *David Freedman*, senior designer at Milton Glaser, Inc., managed the Grand Union project for fourteen years.

For the late Sir James Goldsmith, buying and selling companies on the world market—oil companies and industrial companies—was all in a day's work. When he bought an American supermarket chain, the object was to redefine the category. "Why don't you just invent a new supermarket for me?" he asked Milton Glaser at a Washington dinner party. Glaser answered, "I know nothing about supermarkets." Goldsmith said, "Good. When can you begin?" Thus began an odyssey that took Goldsmith and Glaser to the food halls of London and Berlin and the open-air markets of Italy—and became one of the more remarkable stories in design history. "Our concept was to present food in a different, engaging way," says Glaser, "to break the up-and-down-the-aisles traffic pattern with piazza-like spaces, to keep the customer interested through the voyage." In the mid-eighties, Grand Union markets sprouted new signage and nifty packages for everything from jam to dog food to pantyhose. But it wasn't just a new "look." The stores now had sections for fresh fish, herbs, imported cheeses, flower markets, bakeries. I was curious about how this massive project was orchestrated, and how, despite its mythic proportions, it retained a certain old-fashioned charm. Glaser explained: "The corporate structure that kept things from happening had to be aborted. People disappeared who were unwilling to support the plan; everyone who remained (like executive vice president and COO Bill Louttit) got behind it with enthusiasm." Surrounded by comps of packages and architectural models of stores, I met with Glaser and lead project designer David Freedman in 1992 in Glaser's sunlit Murray Hill brownstone offices.

I've moved about fifteen miles north of the city, and one of the thrills of our new neighborhood is the full-blown Grand Union with its imported cheese selection, fresh seafood, quality produce, even excellent breads. Tell me, how did all this come about?

GLASER: It all started in 1978 shortly before *New York* magazine was sold to Rupert Murdoch. Clay [Felker] and I were not happy about Murdoch and attempted to find another buyer. At a dinner party, Kay Graham's daughter Lally Weymouth introduced us to Sir James Goldsmith, who unfortunately wasn't interested in buying *New York*. But six months later he called me out of the blue to redesign *L'Express*, the leading news magazine in France, the equivalent of *Time*. We redesigned it and the relaunch was a big success. Then he asked me, "Do you know anything about supermarkets? I have this chain . . . why don't you just invent a new supermarket for me?" I answered, "I know absolutely nothing about supermarkets." He said, "Good. When can you begin?"

Absolutely nothing isn't exactly true, is it, at least about food? There was "The Underground Gourmet" (a column in New York *magazine and guidebooks describing inexpensive New York restaurants co-authored by Glaser and artist/food critic Jerome Snyder),* The Cook's Catalog, *your kitchen featured in various interior design publications . . .*

GLASER: . . . and ventures with Burt Wolf and James Beard and Joe Baum. Well, over the next three months we did a series of sketches, insights, of what we thought a supermarket should be like. We started with the Wyckoff, New Jersey, store—an existing space. Within a year, we went from concept to fully realized store. In three months sketches were done, another three months for detailed drawings, three months for construction. It was an enormous success. Today, this design seems relatively primitive. Our concepts, which have remained, were to open up and use the space generously and to present food in a different, engaging way; to break the monotonous up-and-down-the-aisles traffic pattern with piazza-like spaces. In other words, to keep the customer interested throughout the voyage, making shopping a kind of adventure, not unlike an editorial journey through a magazine.

What was working with Sir James like?

GLASER: We wouldn't have lasted a week without him. At the back of his mind was revolutionary change in all the assumptions of the supermarket business. I haven't met anyone like Jimmy before or since. He's the consummate marketer, a gambler, he risks everything at the roll of the dice. He wanted to see how far he could push it, and was involved in every detail. This was especially interesting because at the time he owned Diamond International and several oil companies; Grand Union was less than 10 percent of his holdings. I would have never done the project without him and my personal enjoyment of the relationship. It was marvelously satisfying. I loved seeing him charm and muscle his way through the world. He raged against "industrial filth," his term for processed food in America, against pseudo-bread, fake dairy products.

FREEDMAN: He was incensed that they wouldn't put fresh bread and fish in the supermarket but that a bakery and a fish market could be located right next door in a strip mall.

GLASER: When the experts said, "You can't do it," he would fly into a rage. Suddenly there was fresh fish, and not necessarily because the store managers or the corporate planning department wanted it. Our relationship with Jimmy was unprecedented in my professional career. Generally, we were encouraged to suggest everything we wanted. The corporate structure that kept things from happening had to be aborted. People disappeared who were uninterested, unwilling, or incapable of getting behind the new plan; everyone who remained got behind it with enthusiasm. Although Jimmy was open-minded, he didn't always agree with every detail we suggested. But he wholeheartedly embraced our philosophy—that the store must be on the customer's side, not on management's side. What made *New York* magazine successful was that it was editorially on the readers' side, not on the advertisers' side. That, in my judgment, is the only way to make a magazine credible.

What kind of presentations did you show?

GLASER: We put together a marvelous industrial design staff under Murry Gelberg and Larry Porcelli. For several years fifteen to twenty people—about 60 percent of our staff—were working full time on the project. Every day was a Grand Union day. After fourteen years, we wound down. But first you do an ideal model, plug in all the things you'd like. Then you deal with real constraints, like the number of running feet of shelf space for cheese.

FREEDMAN: Our presentations showed, "This is the way you might do supermarkets." We used comps and models. Altogether, we created six prototypes, elements of which have been applied to several dozen stores. They demonstrated ideas like fresh herb bars, fresh-squeezed juice bars, a ripening shelf that indicates which fruits and vegetables are ready to eat, custom lighting. The lighting was tricky because it had to illuminate the meat, fish, and produce without speeding up spoilage. We designed new fittings and modified stock items to fit our spaces. The staff included Tim Higgins, Martin Schweizer, and Allen Lubow, top people in interior and industrial design.

GLASER: We knew that the consumer was ahead of the supermarket, that people were interested in nutrition, freshness, and whole grains. This gave Grand Union an opportunity to respond to a market that was not being appropriately serviced. Getting in sync with the consumer required rethinking of a form. Food retailing is a basically conservative business, and margins are so small that a small mistake can mean enormous losses. The entire business operates by stealing tiny ideas from each other. All executives constantly tour the competition. One store puts up a candy stand; within days all the others know that $1,800 worth of candy was sold.

You're Americans, shoppers, food lovers, designers. It makes sense. Who else could intuitively predict what the public would go for?

GLASER: If it hadn't worked, Goldsmith is the person who would have suffered. We might have gotten a slight dent in our reputation; he could have lost it all. And we weren't always perfectly on target.

FREEDMAN: Wyckoff and most of the other prototypes were successful. Stratford, Connecticut, bombed. Sir James often said that if we didn't fail some of the time, we weren't trying hard enough.

GLASER: They hired a research firm to find out what customers were looking for. Grand Union started out at the bottom of the category called "Best Liked." I was intrigued by the "Best Liked" characteristics, and found out that in that category consumers shopped at your store more often and bought more when they were there. Grand Union, however, started off at the top of "Most Convenient." They'd been making their living off good locations because they'd simply gotten there first. So my thinking was if we could move them to the top of "Best Liked," they'd have everything.

What did you have to do to get them there?

GLASER: All our design judgments grew out of answering that question. We changed the lighting. We gave shoppers nutrition information. We changed the spaces so people weren't forced to go up and down endless aisles in a proscribed direction. Quite simply, we tried to make shoppers feel good. It is shocking that these things are still not at the top of management's or retailers' consideration.

Let's take as an example the Grand Union in my former neighborhood, La Guardia Place, which serves Greenwich Village and SoHo. Unfortunately, even after its renovation—which helped a lot—shopping there can still be an unpleasant experience. It has to do with the piles of boxes in the aisles, the dented cans, the endless checkout lines, the surly employees.

GLASER: You're talking about commitment to training and the attitudes of personnel. It's a morale problem, a labor problem. Early on, almost before anything else had been done, I came up with a button for the checkers to wear: "Ask Me. I'm Here to Help." This is an example of benign social engineering that encourages people to be responsive.

And was Sir James pleased that his designer got involved in social issues?

GLASER: Right. At a regular presentation meeting I showed a mock-up and said, "Let's do this button."

Other things were more difficult. It took two years to get the signs off the windows. You know how the windows of most supermarkets are papered over by "sale" posters, "Two for $1.39." The first thing you learn about retailing is to provide visual access. I said, "Your customers have already come to the bloody place to shop. It makes no sense to cover up the windows."

You really talked to management like that?

GLASER: Yeah. The nice thing was that we felt we were dealing with peers. On the other hand, we could be a real pain in the butt.

But they did it.

GLASER: They did it. Grand Union became arguably the best supermarket chain in America. This came about through tremendous investment. Millions of dollars went into retrofitting old stores, new fittings and fixtures, plus opening brand new stores. No other supermarket chain has made this kind of capital or development expenditure.

Today there's news in the papers of another ownership change at Grand Union? But no matter what happens they're not going back to the long aisles, right?

FREEDMAN: Right. They've kept the whole system intact following our models. And remember that key people in top management, like Bill Louttit, who were excited by Jimmy's ideas and Milton's ideas, will continue to lead the company.

Let's talk about the packaging.

GLASER: Like all things in this office, we're not merely interested in the decorative side. The traditional idea of private labeling was to provide low-cost alternatives to national brands; for example, slightly smaller kidney beans at twenty percent less cost. Our new position became: We should have the best, most competitive product. The slogan, "As good or better than national brands at a better price" is now in the company manuals.

So they changed the quality of the products, not just the labels.

GLASER: Yes. If you bought Grand Union cream cheese and thought it was rotten, you'd think all Grand Union products were rotten. You can't deceive the public. The quality was improved, and we designed within categories to compare with the brand leaders.

As I understand it, the concept of "trade dress" is that a certain distinctive combination of lettering style, color scheme, and imagery associated in the public mind with a particular brand is protectable under trademark law. Just when do you get too close?

FREEDMAN: At times we were instructed to include a reference to the brand leader. For example, a cola label or can has to be red, blue, silver, white or cola brown. Our packaging is not knockoff; it just tries to make it very clear which product category it's in.

GLASER: We think that all Grand Union packages, while true to their genre, are recognizable within the company design system. They look good; they don't look cheap. That's why we're still doing it.

FREEDMAN: We brought together staples like flour and sugar with an identity within an identity, kind of a homey Pennsylvania-Dutch look. Now all the baking materials that people keep out on their counters, spices, salt, chocolate chips, are within this group. And perceptions have changed. People know you can get really good stuff under private label.

How much of our perceptions are based on advertising? I wonder if in the choice of something like catsup—and it's Del Monte versus Heinz—we're more swayed by the commercials than the package? But then when the shopper sees the great-looking Grand Union catsup with its big red tomato costing significantly less than either of them, that's the one to choose, correct?

GLASER: There's no doubt that television gives an advantage to the brands. Packaging is only a way of identifying what you've already received many messages about. Our labels sit next to the brand leaders and say, "We, too, promise you quality."

LATER, I SPOKE WITH BILL LOUTTIT.

You've been with the company for twenty-eight years. When Sir James Goldsmith took over, was it a scenario out of Other People's Money, *the off-Broadway show that lampooned hostile takeovers?*

LOUTTIT: Not at all. He was a third party who bought the controlling interest in the company before he had a high public profile, and we really didn't know much about him. Many of us in middle management didn't have a strong opinion one way or the other, but waited to see what changes would take place.

In your view, what was Goldsmith trying to accomplish?

LOUTTIT: Goldsmith looked at food retailing in Europe and the United States and recognized that there was a big void in the fresh food area, that the American supermarket was pretty much a manufacturer's outlet for packaged product. Most U.S. supermarkets were simple buildings with no warmth whatsoever, fluorescent lighting, maybe walls painted with red and blue stripes. He wanted to change all that. With Milton, he led us in opening what we call our "food markets," the first phase of the revolution in style and decor. The next phase was the products themselves. Then we took another look at the stores and said, "This is all wonderful but we still aren't offering clearly superior perishable products to the customer." Milton got very involved in that, also. We took big steps forward in terms of quality and had phenomenal improvements in both sales and profit.

As I understand it, the capital investment was unprecedented in the food retailing industry.

LOUTTIT: It was unprecedented in the industry in terms of the amount of money spent in proportion to the total sales of the company. Safeway may spend that much, but we spent $125 million in one year, which was more than 4 percent of sales. That was twice our cash flow, an infusion of capital into the company.

And it all came from Goldsmith?

LOUTTIT: Absolutely. It was both his identification of the opportunity and his support of the capital program.

So if the resistance wasn't a money problem, was it a worry that the public wasn't going to appreciate all these changes, that only a few gourmets in New York's affluent suburbs are interested in fresh fish and pretty packaging and so forth?

LOUTTIT: We had approximately eight hundred stores at the time, stores in the areas where we currently operate, plus in the Carolinas, Florida, Texas, and Washington, D.C., some in not-so-affluent neighborhoods.

So you questioned whether one design concept was going to serve everybody?

LOUTTIT: Right. Question number one was, "Is this going to be equally effective everywhere?" Question two was, "How do we get from our old format to this new format?" And question three was, "How do we advertise if some stores are fully converted and some stores aren't?" And then there was the, "All of these things have been tried before and haven't worked" mentality. For example, fresh seafood departments had been popular thirty years ago, but supermarkets got rid of them as technology developed ways to freeze seafood and deliver it effectively. So there were the "times have changed" arguments and the economic issues. Yet if you examine Goldsmith's concepts, many of them aren't profitable in and of themselves, but they add tremendous appeal to a store and attract customers who buy other items. That can be a tough proposition to measure.

I guess the most overused quote around the design business is Thomas Watson, Jr., of IBM's, "Good design is good business."

LOUTTIT: Yes, but there is another important aspect of Grand Union's repositioning we have to consider. Not only did we change our design and merchandising, we took our pricing down significantly. Some of our food markets met with mixed success because our pricing was not what it should have been. So in 1983 we took a strong position and matched the leader in each market. For example, in New York, you'll find the prices of Kellogg's corn flakes and Hellmann's mayonnaise are the same as they are at ShopRite or Pathmark. This is a Goldsmithism: "You can't sell a uni-dimensional product," which means you can't sell a product for more than what the competitor is selling it for — there's no reason for the consumer to buy it. At first we took a bloodbath on the bottom line; we lost $120 million in 1983.

But that had nothing to do with Glaser's design, right?

LOUTTIT: No. Gradually, though, with this new price position and as we converted more and more stores, it's been uphill. Every year since 1983 has shown compound improvements.

How was consumer reaction to the redesign? Did you get letters?

LOUTTIT: The reaction was outstanding. We got lots of letters. We have a very thorough method of evaluating our customer comments and we break them down into all different categories, compliments, and complaints. But the financials are the true measure of success. We saw that the business in a single store could double when it went from a standard supermarket to the food market. In the upper-income areas it has been better than that, even during the recession of the past few years.

Were you present at Glaser's presentations?

LOUTTIT: Milton came to most of our store planning committee meetings, and he's just a wonderful person to work with. He combines artistic ability with fundamental common sense and a realistic approach to practical business matters. He doesn't have his head in the clouds and isn't daydreaming about what could be; he talks about what we can do and how it will work. In the early days I had no idea what his skills or reputation were and I was just amazed how well an individual with so much artistic ability was able to fit in and work with an old-line organization like ours.

Well, he used the phrase "pain in the butt" to describe himself, in terms of making suggestions some executives were not all that keen on.

LOUTTIT: Some people might characterize him as much worse than that. But I thought he was progressive and clear-thinking and not only one of the best graphic communicators I've ever met, also one of the clearest verbal communicators. In meetings there was plenty of give-and-take and he didn't back off if he believed he was on the right track. Some people thought he came up with crazy, zany ideas, but that's what we expected. He worked with us as a member of our team, not as an outsider, and helped us improve things we were doing as well as put new propositions on the table. In the beginning there was some resistance to a few things like the pet food package (using half a cat's face each on two package styles that lined up on the shelf), but we got everybody out of the way and let Milton do his stuff, and it's been great for us.

Some people in our profession think graphic designers are valuable enough to be paid as much as major league ball players. Others are sure we'll always be undervalued and our work thought of as frivolous decoration. When you talk about sales doubling I wonder if the former isn't true more often than we're given credit for.

LOUTTIT: Well, Grand Union has enjoyed two major benefits. We not only attract more customers, the customers who come into our stores buy a lot more product.

And, to me, your private label products often look more appealing than the nationally advertised brands.

LOUTTIT: That wasn't our intention, but that's what can happen. Our objective in private label is to match the national brand quality, and if we can't find a supplier who can do that on a particular item, we just won't carry that item. For example, we renamed our cola Penguin Cola because we didn't want our name on something that wasn't clearly equal to the national brand. This is something that Milton proposed and has been very involved in, not just from a design point of view, but from an actual strategic direction. And the package designs are all his firm's, with very little input from anybody here.

When you speak about reputation, Milton has been known for many years not only as a leading designer; but also as someone involved with the stars of the food world, with restaurants, someone who knows what good food is all about.

LOUTTIT: Every year we would take a trip with Floyd Hall, the chairman of Grand Union at the time, Goldsmith, Milton, and maybe one or two other guys, to look at the best supermarkets in the United States or the best retailers in Europe. One year we flew from New York to London and met Goldsmith, who had chartered a jet to see a department store in West Berlin with a 60,000-square-foot food court. Two limos met us at the airport; Jimmy and Milton were in the car in front of us, and our driver said, "I know who that guy in the front car is," and we said, "Yeah, that's James Goldsmith, he's a billionaire, owns Grand Union plus around ten other companies worldwide and you've probably seen his picture in the papers." And the driver, a kid who probably went to the West Berlin School of Art and Design, said, "No, no, I mean Milton Glaser. He's the best graphic designer in the world."

No matter how good a designer might be, clients sometimes behave in ways characterized by designers as nit-picking: "We don't really like this typeface. Isn't this color a little too bright? Aren't there too many polka dots per square inch?" What would you say to management in other industries? How would you describe the most successful way to work with a designer?

LOUTTIT: I'd say, to the greatest degree possible make the design part of the internal processes. Retail companies have many processes by which they operate, meetings, internal communications. The designer needs to understand the mechanics of the organization in order to become effective within it. He also needs to get to know the people. The more people in Grand Union Milton knew, the better he was able to function. When he was kind of an outsider in the first couple of years, there was resistance. We got him heavily involved in the organization, in the processes, and got him working with the people. He could see if they had a valid reason for objecting to something and they could see the real beauty of his ideas.

IN SEPTEMBER, 2002, I FOLLOWED UP WITH MILTON GLASER.

I watched with dismay as Grand Union stores returned to the standard configuration of long aisles, and innovations like the herb bars and cheese shops disappeared. Grand Union declared bankruptcy in 2001 and its stores were sold to other supermarket chains. What happened?

GLASER: They went through a series of leveraged buyouts after Goldsmith, the guiding force, decided to cash out all of his businesses and become an ecologist. He owned forests. He was worth a billion bucks.

What would you say to people who, noting the return to the old paradigms and ultimately the bankruptcy, would call the Grand Union redesign a failure?

GLASER: We managed to move the company from the bottom of consumer preferences to second. Everything was working. Goldsmith intelligently sold it all at the top of its form. Then there was a series of purchases, new owners. None of the new owners were interested in investing, so the company got weaker and weaker. The company lost its vitality and its customers. Eventually there was a financial collapse.

Which had nothing to do with the design program . . .

GLASER: Everything we did caught on across the entire supermarket industry! Everything we introduced that worked was immediately replicated. A new generation of supermarket owners moved in our direction. They brought in fresh fish, fresh herbs. They're doing it now at the Food Emporiums, the A&Ps. This isn't the story of the demise of Grand Union. It brought about a change in the whole supermarket industry.

Do you have any advice for young designers who would like to develop working relationships with their clients along the lines of yours with Goldsmith?

GLASER: Generalities are nonsense. These are very individual occurrences. Goldsmith and I liked each other. There was personal chemistry. With every client, you have to accommodate yourself. What is it that you want? What is it that the client wants? Your concepts should address the client's concerns, but ultimately you should do what's pleasing to you and that is of high quality.

THE **DOWAGER BRAND,** REVIVED

Brooks Brothers *and* Desgrippes Gobé

As president and CEO of **BROOKS BROTHERS**, *Joseph R. Gromek* orchestrated the retail chain's metamorphosis from a traditional men's wear store to a "lifestyle brand." Mr. Gromek was previously senior vice president at Ann Taylor Stores, which expanded into fragrances and other accessory items during his tenure. With a BA in history from St. Peter's College, he began his career at Lord & Taylor and later held management positions at Bonwit Teller, Saks Fifth Avenue, and The Limited. With 235 stores in the United States, Japan, and the Pacific Rim, Brooks Brothers was a wholly owned subsidiary of Marks & Spencer PLC, the U.K. department store, until the chain was purchased in December 2001 by Retail Brand Alliance, which is launching another remake that will focus on premium-priced merchandise.

Marc Gobé is president, CEO, and executive creative director of the **DESGRIPPES GOBÉ** Group. With $20 million in billings and 150 employees in offices in New York, Paris, Lyon, Brussels, Tokyo, Seoul, and Hong Kong, Desgrippes Gobé specializes in "emotional branding" of fashion, beauty, retail and consumer entities, packaging, and architectural interiors. Clients of the firm, in addition to Brooks Brothers, include Ann Taylor, Christian Dior, Gillette, The Limited, and

Sears. A native of Paris, Gobé studied at the Ecole Superiéure de Design. He has served on the board of the International Package Design Council.

Principal and executive creative director at Desgrippes Gobé, *Peter Levine* has been responsible for strategic planning and direction for The Limited and Ann Taylor, as well as Brooks Brothers. Formerly senior designer at Wang Laboratories and an art director at the American College in Paris, he is a board member of the Art Directors Club of New York and has taught visual communications at Parsons School of Design. He holds a BFA from California Institute of the Arts and an MFA from Yale University.

Step inside the Brooks Brothers flagship store on Madison Avenue and Forty-fourth Street in Manhattan and you're greeted by an array of hot-pink-checked dress shirts paired with tiny-patterned red and royal blue ties. On a mannequin, a shirt's sleeves are rolled up and a pullover is nattily tied around the waist. Lime green and deep blue shirts are displayed with iridescent purple ties. And you haven't even gotten to the sweaters and sport jackets. Clearly, this is not your grandfather's Brooks Brothers. Yes, the oxford button-downs are there, and so are the red-and-blue repp ties and the navy blue blazers with gold buttons. But it's a younger, hipper Brooks (not that Nine Inch Nails will be shopping there any time soon). The store interiors are brightened, and the traditional graphics on the shopping bags are done in turquoise-on-navy. You are experiencing the revival of a dowager brand and, in the end, it all looks so easy. As this story demonstrates, it's anything but elementary. Such a task requires the expertise of a design firm that specializes in consumer experiences, that undertakes rigorous research, and can communicate its findings and recommendations using a methodology that gets all layers of management on board. I spoke about this with Marc Gobé and Peter Levine.

How did you and Brooks Brothers get together?

LEVINE: Joe Gromek had been general merchandising manager at Ann Taylor back in '93 when we helped them reposition their brand and refocus on their core customers, career women. We sent Joe a "congratulations on your new position" letter when he became CEO of Brooks Brothers.

I'm glad to hear that those things work. What was the situation at the time?

LEVINE: The Brooks Brothers customer was over fifty and nothing was being done to pass the brand along. The image didn't communicate that Brooks Brothers was about fashion. The customers they had were very vocal, even crotchety. They were complaining, but not shopping. They might come in twice a year and stock up on white shirts and underwear, maybe buy a blue suit or a gray suit. The rest of the wardrobe was up to the wife or girlfriend—presents. Brooks Brothers needed to attract a younger customer, a more casual dresser, someone who says, "I can wear a colored shirt, a more interesting tie, spruce up that blue or gray suit." They needed to leverage socks, bathing suits, other kinds of purchases.

Do you consider yourselves fashion specialists?

GOBÉ: We like to specialize with clients that have a very high level of emotion.

Can you describe what you mean by emotion?

GOBÉ: Clients who reach customers with messages that make them respond emotionally. We are better at beauty and fashion than we are at industrial products. For example, a fragrance is nothing without a package that makes people respond. On an emotional level, a fragrance is a ten; cereal is a five. We also have Coca-Cola and IBM as accounts and they came to us because they want to be more sensorial.

"Sensorial"? A new word for me.

GOBÉ: "Sensorial" refers to all the senses: appealing to the eye, the sense of touch, smell. All the senses trigger emotions. That is part of shopping, too. The act of shopping needs to be a total experience for the consumer. When you design an identity for a store from packaging to interiors you try to create an experience. You connect all the senses. Retailers have a unique opportunity to build branded experiences.

How did this particular assignment unfold?

GOBÉ: Joe explained to us his understanding of the business. We met with people who were responsible for store architecture, interiors, visual merchandising. It's critically important to line up everyone who might have a piece of the truth. Nobody has the whole truth. It's the same way in most companies. In order to create a really strong, focused visual identity you have to get everyone together. We call this process "BrandFocus." It's a proprietary technique we developed, an incredible tool to get people together. We get top management in one room and have them respond to visual stimuli, which are identified and classified in different categories.

Can you give an example of a category?

GOBÉ: A flower. We show pictures of six different flowers. We ask, "Which is a Brooks Brothers flower?" We want your first, visceral, response. Then pictures of cars. "Which is a Brooks Brothers car?" Then people, situations, accessories. There are thirty or forty categories. Then we have conversation, dialogue. Someone writes down every single word. The session is videotaped. Some words and phrases come up over and over again.

LEVINE: They are the core cues. At the end of an intensive one-day workshop you have a mosaic, which becomes the vision of the brand pillars. And the advantage is that the people are all in sync—they are part of its creation.

GOBÉ: Then we start working on the basic expression. It takes two to three months to develop. We generally come in with one strong recommendation and show the steps, how it evolved.

What about the logo? Still the sheep hanging from a ribbon?

LEVINE: The Brooks Brothers golden fleece has a heritage as the mark of an American luxury brand. A destination, like Henry Bendel and Tiffany. It is a status symbol of America for Asians and Europeans. There is an expectation to see that logo. We cleaned it up, made it more energetic, introduced the repp-tie pattern, an angled stripe in navy and bright turquoise blue, as a symbol icon for the shopping bags and other collateral. Just like Hermès orange, it is a distinctive characteristic. We developed a typographic vocabulary, the stacked booklike type that also communicates the heritage. We then undertook a huge labeling program for garments, internal labels for suits, and external for casual weekend wear.

Here is the Brooks Brothers insert in the current issue of Vanity Fair. *How would you distinguish this expression, this look, from J. Crew and Banana Republic? Prosperous-looking twenty-something people, khakis, white polo shirts . . .*

GOBÉ: Banana Republic is very European in nature. More put together. Predictable. Slick. European designers dictate how an outfit should be put together. There is something inherent in the Brooks Brothers brand that makes it an American icon. It has more heritage. Here the shirt is out. There are bare feet. It's energetic, highly personal, relaxed. This has a lot of appeal not only to Americans, but worldwide. Brooks Brothers has a great opportunity to grab that niche, to own it.

What's happened to the man with the blue blazer and repp tie?

GOBÉ: Today he is more of an individual. On the weekend he wears loafers, no socks. The American attitude is personal, eclectic, not dictated. It's something felt. It spans generations. The father can be wearing his blue blazer with gray flannels. But the son wears his with chinos and a different combination of tie and shirt. The tie will be slightly open.

Tell me more about how Brooks Brothers appeals to Europeans.

GOBÉ: Well, my own first stop in America was at Brooks Brothers.

Did you want to look like an American?

GOBÉ: Yes, and get extremely good quality, fashion-right clothes.

How long did the entire design process take, up to the point that Brooks Brothers was ready to begin implementation?

LEVINE: A year, with a team of seven: Marc and myself as creative directors, a design director, a marketing director, two graphic designers, and a retail architect. We had a lot of group meetings; Joe is very team-oriented. They were trying to figure out how far they could go.

Do you push clients to go farther than they think they want to?

LEVINE: We never surprise clients with radical departures. That's not how we work. We collaborate. The client is focused on changing merchandise with the seasons, changing windows. Sometimes they lose the big picture. That's when we can help rebuild that visual portrait and regain the core cues of the brand.

You are very brave for describing all this, because now Desgrippes Gobé may have a rash of imitators. "Is this flower the — name any client — flower?" How did you learn how to do this?

GOBÉ: My family has always been in the retail business. My grandfather had an operation in France that included clothing, millinery, a restaurant. We always talked about retailing. On our staff we have graphic designers, product designers, architects. On the client management side we have planners, headed by Peter. We are constantly looking to create useful tools for building brands.

The people who head companies are the true visionaries, though. They don't necessarily have the time to think of their business in visual terms, in the creative sense. They think in numbers. But when you put them in a room and ask them to respond creatively, it's totally amazing how brilliantly they can respond and focus on their brand.

A FEW DAYS LATER, I MET WITH JOSEPH GROMEK IN HIS OFFICE ABOVE THE FLAGSHIP STORE ON MADISON AVENUE AND FORTY-FOURTH STREET.

What problems was Brooks Brothers facing when you took over the leadership role?

GROMEK: It had stopped evolving. Once any business stops changing it finds it's in grave trouble. Brooks Brothers was struggling badly, suffering from ten years of negative store growth. We needed to move forward without alienating the existing customer. Actually, we needed more than to move forward. We needed to be shocked. This was not a remedy for a cold. The patient would have been terminal without what we did and without the support of Marks & Spencer, our parent company.

What were your first steps?

GROMEK: A new store design. We changed from dark, clubby mahogany to cherry. We made the stores open and inviting. We took the merchandise out of cabinets and put it on tables. We took dress shirts out of cellophane bags so the consumer could touch and feel them. I'd much rather have a few shirts get dirty than have all of them under glass. We developed programs for the sales staff to help them be more friendly and engaging.

No more "Can I help you?" in a tone that sounds like "What are you doing here?"

GROMEK: No more, and we lost some good people in the process. Along the way, we made as many mistakes as successes.

Can you describe a mistake?

GROMEK: We had a big miss in the women's line in terms of quality and sizing. As just one example, we tried to sell cotton sweaters in autumn and that just didn't work for our customers.

How would you describe the difference between your new positioning and that of Banana Republic or J. Crew or Calvin Klein?

GROMEK: We're all vying for the same customer. But our campaign is one of family values. A father and son story. We show happy, smiling faces, and that's not true for the other brands. We are less about style and more about relevance. We're not cutting-edge high fashion, but we are very upscale Middle America.

How does the lavender tie with the mint-green shirt fit into this?

GROMEK: Brooks Brothers was always about color. A fifteen-year-old red-and-blue striped tie was colorful for its time. That's one thing that made the business successful for 180 years. We are authoritative about color, that's part of the heritage and history of the brand.

You are the inventors of the button-down shirt, are you not?

GROMEK: One of the original Brooks Brothers originated it. John Brooks was at a polo match in the U.K. where everybody's collars were flapping around. He said, "I can solve that problem." We are also the innovators of the seersucker suit and the repp tie.

Cheap Chic, by Catherine Milinaire and Carol Troy (Harmony Books, 1975), recommends that women who want to be fabulously dressed for little money shop in the Brooks Brothers boys' department. The authors devote a spread to what they call "The Ivy League Look" and illustrate Brooks Brothers shirts, sweaters, Bermuda shorts, and white bucks. Did that book affect your sales?

GROMEK: Yes, and then the Condé Nast editors discovered us. They're next door and would come in to buy boys' suits and polo shirts.

How did the entire reengineering and redesign process work?

GROMEK: On the product side, we hired fashion designer Jarlath Mellett, who had twelve years experience with classic contemporary clothing at Fenn Wright and Mason, to be senior vice president, design director. He did all the right stuff. We hired Derek Ungless, who had been at *Rolling Stone*, as creative director, executive vice president for in-house advertising and promotion. On the real estate side, we worked with several firms. We keep tweaking it. The product is the same in 85, 90 percent of our stores, but we tweak the store design by climate. In one city we may add more wood to the walls, in another, more limestone to the floors. Of course, we focus more on suits in business locations and on casual wear in suburban malls. We also changed our windows. There's a new color story in our windows. Bright shirts and ties and the sportswear to go with them. Now we appeal emotionally, rather than to filling needs.

And behind all of this was Desgrippes Gobé?

GROMEK: They consulted on window presentations, merchandise presentation, in-store graphics, logo, and packaging.

That you kept the logo may surprise some people.

GROMEK: The golden fleece denotes the finest quality in wool. It was originally the mark of the British wool-makers. A guild sign that I think originated in ancient Greece. It may or may not stay over the long term but it served us well through transitioning.

What was the process like that ended with the updated golden fleece and the new shopping bag?

GROMEK: It took months. Desgrippes Gobé came in with a range of options, from solutions with the highest degree of drama to those that were very conservative. It was a work-in-progress situation.

One of the legends in the design business is about how Paul Rand presented the NEXT logo to Steven Jobs. Rand came in with one solution and a little book demonstrating how he arrived at it. How would you have reacted to that kind of presentation?

GROMEK: That isn't how we like to work around here. We like to look at different solutions and ask each other, "What do you think about this?" Does it reflect our heritage in a way that is newer and fresher? That's very important. We felt comfortable with the process all along and ultimately got to a point when we said, "That's it." They pushed us, but they made compromises along the way.

And everything grew out of the brand focus session?

GROMEK: Let me show you . . . (Mr. Gromek leads me into an adjoining conference room where framed boards with collages of "swipe" photos from magazine editorial and ads line the walls) . . . the Brooks Brothers customer (pointing to the first of seven boards) is distinctively correct, casually elegant, genuinely eclectic, smart, and sexy. He's in his late twenties or early thirties, very active. He's social and athletic. He spends time with friends, day into evening. He's action-oriented. In his work environment he's got a more relaxed attitude. He's not a stuffy banker. He's a father. He's a son. He may have young children. He drives a BMW.

And he likes Michelle Pfeiffer, BV Cabernet Sauvignon, and Rolex watches.

GROMEK: You're getting it, and his home is an open, airy environment.

Hmm, from the looks of that house, he's rich.

GROMEK: You have to remember, this is aspirational.

Another new word for me, one I'll remember.

GROMEK: He's affluent, but not stuffy. He likes to have fun. He's healthy. He works out. He reads. This is all about wardrobing. We want to dress this guy from head to toe. We can supply his business and weekend attire, his tux, his tennis clothes. The details are important. The buttons. The correct shoe. The right briefcase. It's all American traditional. All this is in place in this country now, and we're going through the whole revamping process in Japan. Europe and Latin America will be next. Desgrippes Gobé did a brilliant job.

THE **GREAT DESIGNER** HIMSELF

Joseph Abboud *and* Tyler Smith

JOSEPH JOSEPH
ABBOUD ABBOUD

Former Louis, Boston clothing buyer **JOSEPH ABBOUD** was associate director of menswear design at Polo/Ralph Lauren before forming a company under his own label in 1986. The company, J.A. Apparel, a joint venture with Gruppo GFT, has grown into a $50 million fashion empire that includes men's, women's, and accessories lines, available at department and specialty stores as well as Joseph Abboud stores. In 1991 he introduced his menswear at the Milan market and opened his first European store in Rome. Abboud won the Council of Fashion Designers of America Designer of the Year for Menswear Award twice, in 1990 and 1991.

TYLER SMITH specializes in branding, communications, and design, primarily for the fashion industry. He started his shop, Tyler Smith Creative Direction, in 1976 with one client after leaving Creamer/Lois, the Providence, Rhode Island, branch of a New York advertising agency owned by George Lois. One month later he began his relationship with Louis, Boston, the account that has established him as a specialist in menswear. He has remained in Providence as an independent creative director and attracting an increasingly international clientele. In 1984 Smith was named Rhode Island School of Design's Alumnus of the Year. He recently created the award-winning "wave" license plate for the state of Rhode Island.

To some graphic designers, a fashion designer who challenges himself to win top industry awards might be a dream client. Others, who like to take control and take credit for the work, might not be as contented working with someone who views the results—the identity and marketing materials created by fashion industry specialist Tyler Smith—as the issue of a meeting of two creative minds. Abboud gives his colleagues—fellow fashion entrepreneurs—excellent advice: "Great art direction, great logos, great coloration, it all captures people's attention. If you are small, do a little bit, but do it well. If you grow, do a little bit more, and make it consistent. And you do have to spend some money." He puts his company's money where his mouth is. In Abboud's New York showroom, where I met to speak with him, high above the corner of Fifth Avenue and Fifty-second Street, the look and feel of the identity, the logo sandblasted on panels affixed to fruitwood cabinetry, resonates perfectly with the earthy, tweedy colorations and textures of the suits and ties, shirts and jackets. Abboud's shopping bags, ads, brochures, and hangtags are appropriate, elegant, and consistent—and the work of a single individual, Tyler Smith, who proves that you don't have to be a big design company to do work that has a big impact.

Would it be fair to say that in the nineties, Joseph Abboud joined the top tier of elite menswear designers, which includes Calvin Klein, Ralph Lauren, and Georgio Armani? And that graphic design has had something to do with that success?

ABBOUD: Yes, but I didn't go to somebody and say, "Give me an image." I already had an image, and I asked Tyler to embellish it. I asked him to help me look like myself.

Generally speaking, a client who hires a graphic designer is not an expert in design. You are a client who is a designer himself, an increasingly renowned designer. How did the relationship with Tyler Smith get started, and how does it work? Do you ever have any conflicts about how things should look?

ABBOUD: I met Tyler at Louis, Boston, fifteen or sixteen years ago, and I always knew I wanted to work with him. I have a great, energetic relationship with Tyler. We enjoy each other's company. It's really two creatives working together. I love the creative process, working together and within boundaries. By boundaries I mean consistency. Consistency for me is two complete clothing collections a year, the merchandise, the advertising, the shops. It's all one vision. I've gotten where I am today by following a singular path. Some companies have one look in their advertising one season and another, completely different look or campaign the next. I don't agree with that. Tyler is on my wavelength. We always see eye to eye. He doesn't need to convince me of anything and I don't need to convince him. When he shows me something I like, I know I like it. Working with him is fun. This business can be tough sometimes, but I still want it to be fun.

Can we back up a little bit? Where did you go to school? How did you get started?

ABBOUD: I went to U. Mass and have a degree in English and French comparative literature. I spent my junior year in Paris at the Sorbonne. I don't have a design degree; you could say I got my design education at Louis, Boston. Louis gave me the platform of quality. As a buyer there, I would coordinate clients' wardrobes. I would use things that were in the store, things I was able to buy for them, and things I designed myself. When I had a thought, a design idea for an article of clothing, I was able to get it made, put it in the window, and put it on my clients' backs. I spent twelve years doing that.

What inspired you to go into business for yourself?

ABBOUD: It's the old Peter Principle. I wanted to see how far I could go before I couldn't go any farther. For example, I always wanted to win the Designer of the Year for Menswear Award, and I won it twice. I always felt strongly about my own point of view: that there have to be a lot of men out there who want to dress the way I do.

Can you describe that way of dressing?

ABBOUD: My image is an American image, but sexier than the old American image. We started a look that is softer, looser. No more uptight, button-down guys. It's the new American international look. Kind of restrained passion, restrained sexuality or sensuality. If you put Ralph Lauren—the wholesome American preppy look—on the right, and Georgio Armani on the left, I would fall right in the middle where those two circles overlap. Our look is one that people are chasing now. A lot of other people have gotten on the bandwagon. Here's another thing I feel strongly about. I hate plagiarists. There are so many uncreative people out there. But our look is original; it's about sophistication, about people being themselves.

How does that translate into your marketing communications?

ABBOUD: It's simple. Show people and the clothes. I don't like copy. I like images. I want to get an idea from a picture. The pictures we use do it all. Sometimes we have to use copy, like on the last page of the image brochures. Other than that, it's show, not tell.

And the interiors, the showrooms, the shops?

ABBOUD: From the color of the metal on the door hinges, to the way the fabric swatches are shown to buyers, to the shopping bags and carpets and uphol-stered furniture, the whole company is design driven.

What factors do you think clients should consider when choosing a graphic designer?

ABBOUD: I get calls all the time from slick salesmen representing supposedly the hottest marketing companies in town. They say, "Why don't you try someone else, try us?" I say, "No, I don't want to." I don't want to change. The hottest new look is not for me. This company may be relatively new, but it's rooted in tradition, and I need someone who understands that tradition.

Do you think it's essential to work with someone who specializes in your industry?

ABBOUD: No. Someone with absolutely no experience in menswear can do a good job for a menswear company. Although almost everyone in my business knows Tyler, people who are good can catch on very quickly and come up with original ideas.

A colleague told me that she recently got a call from a "friend of a friend" in the chil-dren's sportswear business, who asked, "I need a logo and hangtag design for a new line of boys' pants. How much?" She answered, "About $10,000," which to me sounds rea-sonable. He apparently said, "That's crazy, I was planning to spend about $500," and practically hung up on her. Isn't there kind of a Seventh Avenue mentality that means cheap, cheap, cheap?

ABBOUD: A lot of people don't believe in advertising. In my opinion, they are not going to succeed in today's market. So much, psychologically, depends on it. Great art direction, great logos, great coloration, it all captures people's atten-tion. If you are small, do a little bit, but do it well. If you grow, do a little bit more, and make it consistent. No matter how much you do, make it all consistent. And you do have to spend some money. My partner, the Italian company Gruppo GFT, which is also behind Armani and Valentino, understands marketing and strategy. The Italians seem to have design in their blood.

True or false: A company makes a product, a bicycle, a teapot, whatever, that functions just like its competitors' products. But the company's investment in design—the product's appearance as well as the design of logo, the collateral, the packaging, the sales promotion—will distinguish that product in the marketplace and cause it to be perceived as the best?

ABBOUD: If two products are equal, graphics can make one win over the other. But you can't fool the public and try to cover up a bad product with a good logo. A few companies have tried that and it doesn't work. I think most companies with good logos usually make good products; they are committed to quality all around.

Tell me how the Joseph Abboud logo evolved?

ABBOUD: Tyler and I were playing around with some things in a coffee shop in Providence.

And the colors?

ABBOUD: We played around with those, too. I like warm colors. When we got around to where we wanted to be, we stopped.

What kind of presentation did Tyler make?

ABBOUD: None. The first thing we said was, let's get a photographer and take some pictures. Then we knew we had something beautiful. We tried not to create a logo that would mess things up.

How do you work together?

ABBOUD: When we're working on something, he sends me a fax with a note, "Do you like this or that?" We cut through all the bureaucracy. I call him all the time and ask him things, "What do you want to do about this invitation? Is there any new paper I ought to see?" We talk all the time.

And now you have it all together, the products, the logo, the showroom, the shops, the advertising, the collateral? What is it that actually moves the clothing off the racks and into the shopping bags of the customers? What makes a man think to himself not "I'm going to buy a new suit today," but "I'm going to buy a Joseph Abboud suit"?

ABBOUD: It's a complicated process. It starts with the trade press reviewing our runway shows at market week. In January we had two shows, in New York and Milan, the fall 1991 collections. At the same time retailers, department stores, Saks, Bergdorfs are being contacted by our sales staff. In August and September we run ads in consumer magazines like *GQ* and *Esquire*. At the same time, the retailers are featuring our merchandise in newspaper ads. There are shows and personal appearances. I've been on *Donahue, Attitudes, Today*, all of them. Bryant Gumbel wore my clothes at the Olympics and gave us an on-air credit. He looked terrific. If everything goes right, the clothing is featured in magazine editorial spreads, showing the magazine's interpretation of the collection.

But remember that the designer name, the label, means nothing without the product. Some people try to put a product behind a name. That doesn't work. The product has to come first. If it's good, then people remember the name.

The sense I got by looking at your graphics and stepping into the showroom was that your product would be special. Had I found the clothes not to live up to the promise I would have been disappointed, felt cheated. When I looked at the women's line especially, I was reminded of great Chanel suits of the forties — not the lines, which are quite different — but the quality of the fabrics and workmanship.

ABBOUD: Correct. It's hard to find people today who make things like this. Everything we do is handmade in Italy by incredible tailors. It costs money. A lot of money. Of course, we think it's worth it, that these things will become collectors' items.

LATER THAT DAY, I SPOKE WITH TYLER SMITH.

Tyler, if typical agency people and graphic designers were characterizing their average client, it's likely that they would describe someone who rejects their best ideas and asks for what the competition is doing. Will readers of this book be able to relate to your dream client, Joseph Abboud?

SMITH: Joe is admittedly the other extreme. Sometimes he knows more than I do. That in itself can be a challenge.

In what way?

SMITH: He expects new and stimulating ideas without me doing a stunt, without doing things that are ridiculous and decorative. They have to make sense. For example, the way the type on the image brochure covers works, the picture is swimming through the letters. Some clients might say, "This doesn't look right. I've never seen anything like this before." Or, "You can't read it, it's illegible." Instead, Joe says, "That's great, it's a whole new way to look at logos, now the logo is part of the photography." Or I might show him the idea of printing a page on vellum, and he asks, "Can we do the whole book on vellum?" And I have to pull him back, to explain why not, why it wouldn't work.

Have any of your ideas been rejected?

SMITH: I get more static from Joe's people than from him. For example, the texture in the pictures. There's kind of a woven texture in every photograph. Joe does very unslick things, nothing shiny, everything earth-toned and textural. So we photographed some fabric, some hopsacking, and I put a weave right into the pictures with a Scitex. Sort of like a living logo that goes though all the images. A lot of people in his company did not like that, but Joe appreciated it right away.

What was the process of designing the logo like?

SMITH: A real collaboration. Joe really understands the idea of a label and how it can create an image. The logo is a traditional American look, repp stripes, burgundy and green, and it was actually created to work, first and foremost, on a woven label. We didn't go about it in the usual way. It was mostly done on the phone, faxing back and forth. I started with a "JA" and got totally away from it. But don't think of the label alone as "the logo." In this case, the entire company look is the logo, the corporate signature. It's the Copperplate Gothic typography and the type arrangement, the way the letters line up. I put an awful lot of thought into that, and got lucky, the same number of letters is in Joe's first and last names. It's the paper and the colors and the textures and the models we pick, the way they look, and especially the photography. Fabrizio Ferri, our photographer, is a big part of all this. We wanted our brochures to be like movies, with no copy interrupting them; we wanted them to be the real visual experiences of the clothing. Choosing the right photographer is very important, and Joe picked Fabrizio. Joe wanted an American art director but an Italian "eye." Fabrizio's eye expresses a certain sensibility, a European sense of style.

Let's take a moment to talk about the material aspects of the relationship.

SMITH: I have no contract with Joe. It's all done on a handshake.

Was there a proposal or a written estimate?

SMITH: No.

Do costs matter to him?

SMITH: Everybody wants to know the approximate amount of money. I work on a retainer-fee basis. You have to have a certain faith in what you're doing, what it's worth. I work out different arrangements with people. For example, my fee sounded too high to one client, a law firm; I wasn't going to compromise, but I said, "You can pay it out over twelve months." They said, "Okay."

As you know, so-called industry expertise can be a problem for graphic designers. If you've worked for other companies in the same industry, potential clients cite "possible conflict of interest," saying they can't risk letting their competitors know their secrets. If you have no experience in that industry, then they might not hire you either, saying they have to see something in your portfolio that's exactly like what they're looking for. How have you dealt with this?

SMITH: When I started my little agency in Providence, I got a call from a writer in Boston, asking, "Do you want to work on a store called Louis?" Since then, other clothing stores and manufacturers have just called; I've never had to go out and hustle. After a while—if you do great stuff—everyone in that universe knows about you. There's not that many of them. So I've carved out a little niche and become a specialist. But I have to be very, very careful and really dig and figure out what each one is about. And express that distinctive personality. Today, some designers give the same look to every client. I can't stand that stuff. I give a different look to every client.

Chicago, The Musical, and Spot Design

Barry Weissler is president of Namco (National Artists' Marketing Company), producers of **CHICAGO, THE MUSICAL**, which has been running on Broadway since 1996. Namco, founded by Weissler and his wife, Fran, has been producing professional theater since 1982. The company has twenty-five employees in New York and eight in London. Broadway productions include *Othello* with James Earl Jones and Christopher Plummer, *Cat on a Hot Tin Roof* with Kathleen Turner, *Zorba* with Anthony Quinn, *Gypsy* with Tyne Daly, *Fiddler on the Roof* with Topol, and *Grease* with stars including Rosie O'Donnell and Brooke Shields. *Chicago* is currently running in New York and London and recently opened with a Russian company.

Drew Hodges is creative director of **SPOT DESIGN**, a New York studio that specializes in the entertainment and media industries. A 1984 School of Visual Arts graduate, Hodges worked with Terry Koppel and Paula Scher at Koppel and Scher for four years before founding Spot Design 1987. The studio produces posters, book covers, CD packages, and media kits for such clients as Dreamworks, Bravo, and Nickelodeon, in addition to Namco and other theatrical producers. In 1997 Hodges founded SpotCo, a full-service theatrical advertising agency that provides creative strategy, media planning, and placements for the print ads and radio and television commercials Spot Design creates and produces. With the successes of *Rent* and *Chicago*, the whole look and feel of theatrical advertising has changed, most notably through such Spot-designed campaigns as *Wit*, *The Tale of the Allergist's Wife*, *Seussical*, *The Vagina Monologues*, and *True West*.

Until *Rent*—with its hardware-store-stencil logo and solarized, tinted, taped, scratched, photographic portraits of angst-ridden young performers—most stage productions were advertised with a kind of metaphorical, illustrative symbol (the *Phantom of the Opera* mask, the *Les Miserables* little girl bearing the French flag). Drew Hodges created a new paradigm: sell a Broadway show based on the talent of the performers, on how the audience is going to feel, not on the plot line. It worked. On the first day a *Rent* ad ran in the *New York Times*, half a million dollars worth of tickets were sold. *Chicago, The Musical* was Hodges's next big challenge. This Bob Fosse revival set in the 1920s, with music and lyrics by Kander and Ebb, opened in November, 1996. Thanks in part to Spot's campaign, it has run for more than 2,500 performances on Broadway; it's an international hit in five other cities. Soon Hodges had a client list filled with Broadway producers. But doesn't "producer" really mean a whole roomful of egos to satisfy: the director, the playwright, the stars, the backers, as well as the producer himself? Not for Barry Weissler, who sees himself as a creative collaborator. "Drew gets me to delve more fully into my creative psyche," he says. The son of a minister, Hodges has a sixth sense how to work with all kinds of show-business clients, so that all psyches (as well as the box office) are satisfied.

The first time I visited you, to talk about Rent, *you were working at your kitchen table. Now you're in the middle of Times Square and, I understand, soon moving to an even larger space.*

HODGES: We're moving to 38th and Seventh, 14,000 square feet in a former bank, a very grand building.

You told me in 1996 that when you came in to present the concept for Rent, *the attitude of the people in the meeting was, "And you are?" Obviously a lot has happened.*

HODGES: Well, we now do the advertising for 50 percent of the shows on Broadway, a dozen at a time, all over the world. We work for cable TV stations like Bravo, we do movie posters for independent and big studios. We did the advertising for *The Dangerous Life of Altar Boys* with Jodie Foster. We work for arts organizations like the Bill T. Jones Dance Company; for rock and roll; for institutions like the New York Theater Workshop, where *Rent* came from. Right now we're working on the Big Apple Circus campaign. We have thirty-five people, two art directors including Gail Anderson from *Rolling Stone* and Vinnie Sainato from Comedy Central; four designers, three production-layout artists, two writers, three broadcast producers who do commercials, plus account executives, billing people, and a CFO.

And you still have that aw-shucks, this-can't-be-happening-to-me attitude.

HODGES: Yeah, we built this advertising thing, SpotCo, because it was obvious with *Rent* and then with *Chicago* that the agencies placing the ads were the ones making the money. I think we billed $40,000 and they made about $1 million.

Understood. What is it like to have Broadway producers as clients?

HODGES: They're all different. One is not like the other. A lot of different kinds of people do this. Some of them worked their way up in the theater, they'd always loved Broadway. Some of them are former marketing people from TV or film. Some of them made a lot of money in other industries. For example, the woman who founded the first biotech temp agency is now a producer. There are a few heiresses who always wanted to be involved with the theater. All you need is money. You can buy your way in. Let's say you have $5 million. You can say, "Give me a theater. Give me a press agent. Give me a casting agent. Give me a writer." Some of them have a philanthropic bent; they're doing something useful with their money. You could give your money to the Cancer Society or you could produce a show, in which case you might get to stand up with David Mamet and get a Tony on national television. You can enjoy the community, the glamour, the challenge. Few of them have any sense of working with an agency or a designer. Maybe their closest experience was working with an architect.

And the producers of Chicago?

HODGES: Barry Weissler worked his way up in the business, from touring companies to *Grease* to being one of the top theatrical producers in the world.

There are a lot of people involved in a show and in making decisions, but the producer is the one who pays your bills, right?

HODGES: Right. Everyone works for the producer. A show is like a startup corporation. There are the legal papers, the business plan, the team of people who don't know each other very well. The producer hires the playwright, the set designer, the costume designer. Every show is a brand-new palette with brand-new imagery. Even if it's a revival, like *Chicago*—especially if it's a revival—they don't want to use old imagery. We, the designers, the agency, are just one more piece in the mix. All producers are total entrepreneurs of some kind, even the ones who come from a media background. Some of them enjoy the marketing aspects, the making of the advertising. The trick is to completely get to know each of them and what they need.

How did you learn how to do that?

HODGES: My father is a minister. I was brought up in a church, the Methodist church in Hyde Park, New York, near the FDR mansion. As a minister's son you learn how to talk to people, how to intuit what they want. It's all about personal relations. Some people want you to tell them what to do. Some people want to tell you what they want. Some people want a collaboration, a group thing.

To get to know them, do you spend a lot of time entertaining, taking them to lunch and dinner?

HODGES: Nobody has the time for me to take them to lunch or dinner. Maybe I'd be more successful if I did more of that. We're here working all the time. Broadway is a way of living your life, morning, noon, and night. I see clients at opening nights. Every show has an opening night. That's where I see new clients, old clients, successful clients, not-so-successful clients. If the show you're associated with wins Tonys, everybody is aware of your work. And every year one of our clients is up for "best play" at the Tonys. The fact that we did the poster might make the producer of another play call us to design theirs. The success of a show rubs off on everything associated with it. And when we do get a new client, they all want to imagine that we don't have another client, that we're 100 percent committed to them and their production.

What's your biggest challenge?

HODGES: Broadway is always fighting to stay relevant—important and relevant. Especially in the face of film, which has the sense that there's no other type of entertainment. Every show is a defining moment for the producer, personally and professionally. Is it a hit or a flop? Their whole life is about this show until it succeeds or fails.

Your expertise goes way beyond the visual aspects of design, doesn't it?

HODGES: We help plan the campaign. Who is the audience? When will the ads break? Will there be a TV campaign? What are the buying patterns? *Harlem Song* on 125th Street is very different from Albee's *The Goat*. We do a written statement for each show, ending with a mission statement that's two or three sentences. This is what we want it to feel like. Each one is different. We did the *Annie Get Your Gun* revival and it needed a sense of nostalgia, nostalgia for an old-fashioned musical western. To do this, you need experience in tactics. We develop a strategy. What the show needs to sound like, feel like, walk and talk like. You keep half your head in design: is it stunning, beautiful, surprising? You keep half your head in results. How many tickets did it sell? Our strategy is calibrated to produce very specific results. We have to sell eight thousand tickets a week per show. When that's not happening, we look at the reasons. After September 11, Barry Weissler and I worked with the whole community to revive Broadway with the stars singing in Times Square commercials. Sales were down again on the Fourth of July weekend, but it was predicted that New York was going to blow up, so it was expected. At other times we might change tactics: we'll try a price discount, we'll do a direct-mail piece, run an insert or another ad; we might do an e-mail campaign to a list of people who are former ticket buyers. Sometimes you look for something new to promote, the cast changing, a new star. For three months, Michael C. Hall, David in *Six Feet Under*, starred as the male lead in *Chicago*. His new wife in real life, Amy Spanger, played Roxie. Here's the ad [the headline is "To Die For"].

I love it. It's hard to imagine the pressure of having to sell eight thousand tickets a week, though. How often do you get the numbers?

HODGES: Every day. The general manager of the show faxes them every afternoon. We evaluate design and advertising based on its real-world effect. This is all about investors getting their money back. It takes a long time. *Lion King*, which is one of the most successful shows of all time, didn't make a dime for five years.

How did you get started with Chicago?

HODGES: We had just done *Rent*, and Barry and Fran Weissler of Namco called, saying that they wanted to meet. *Chicago* had just had a short, successful run with Bebe Newirth and Ann Reinking at Encores at City Center, which does short-run revivals of classic shows. The Weisslers wanted to move it to Broadway just as it was. A concert. They needed positioning, a logo, media, TV, radio.

What drove your design?

HODGES: I had a real concern, no, make that *fear*, that it was going to be hard to charge Broadway ticket prices — $75 — for a more-stripped-down version. According to union rules, in the Encores setting, the show couldn't have sets. It could have platforms, but no sets. Sometimes the performers had to have scripts in their hands. It was an almost-bare stage. No helicopters, no swinging chandeliers. The story was based on a real-live crime of the 1920s; the original show opened in 1975, with full sets, and it was not a hit. It was considered too dark at the time, and *A Chorus Line* was the only show that people were paying attention to that season. But we often try to support a show's weak points. This was my thinking: This is about two women who kill their husbands; about press, fame, corruption, injustice. It exists in the general sense of time, which makes it more modern. We had just had O.J., so the public was ready for it. What did we want the show to feel like? Well, we had to find a way to *own the minimalism*. How could we give the minimalism form and style? Let's make it look as if we always wanted it that way. Let's use black-and-white. Let's use fashion photography in which minimalism is an asset. We picked Max Vadukal, who was known for his editorial spreads in *Vogue*. We comped up the campaign using his existing photographs. This is one of the hardest things to do, to get a client to understand what it will look like with the star in it. For the logo we used wood type from the Rob Roy Kelly book. But it was more about the pictures than about the logo.

Did you present more than one idea?

HODGES: I always want to see a bunch of ideas. So do my clients. They want to have a role in it. They want to be choosy. I always say, "I think this is the one," but I show at least half a dozen concepts, with several variations each. There are always different ways to solve something. Four or five different ad campaigns could be equally successful. The decision is based on answering the question, what do we want the show to feel like? Sometimes the porridge is too hot, sometimes too cold. Here's a funny concept. Here's a sexy one. Here's a classic one. Ah, this one is just right. *Chicago* needed to be sexy. Dangerous, modern, minimalist, and sexy. When Barry saw the comps, he said, "I love it!"

And since then?

HODGES: It's been six years. Twelve productions in six different cities: New York, L.A., Washington, D.C., London, Vienna, Moscow, Mexico City. The movie came out at Christmas, with an amazing TV commercial. Did we do it? No. Miramax wanted a departure.

How has the buzz for all the Golden Globes and Oscar nominations for the movie affected the marketing of the show?

HODGES: Traditionally, movies are the death of Broadway shows. Producers like to wait until theatrical runs are over before a movie can be made, but in this case the movie rights had been sold in about 1979. So we embraced this movie and made it work for us. The first thing we did was a press kit with everything you'd ever want to know about *Chicago*: the 1924 real-life murder, the original 1926 Broadway show, the 1942 "Roxie Hart" movie with Ginger Rogers—every fact and figure about the event and the Broadway show. We mailed it to all the movie reviewers. The idea was to try to get them to write about us, too. They did. Some reviewers said that the movie audience would be experiencing the same thrills they could get in the theater. Our idea is that you can see the movie—or you can see the real thing—live. We just recut our commercial to make it more filmic. And we're doing a new print campaign, "Chicago Live," that breaks the wall between real life and what's on stage. We're taking the girls—the cellblock tango girls, the merry marauders of Cook County Jail, in their black fishnets and all—out in the street, into Grand Central Terminal, into beauty shops and department stores, and shooting the public's reactions. The photographer is photojournalist Larry Fink, today's Weegee. Sales are way up. During the blizzard on Presidents' Day, we were sold out. That's amazing. Now a bigger audience knows the show because of the movie.

LATER, I SPOKE WITH BARRY WEISSLER.

When you saw the graphics for Rent, *did you know that Spot was the creative team you wanted for* Chicago?

WEISSLER: Drew came in to see me before he had his agency, when he was an art director on his own. I didn't even know he'd done *Rent*. I'm usually suspicious of people coming in to market services. But when I met him I knew right away he was my man. He thinks the way I do. We march to the same drummer. We have the same feelings about advertising and marketing and about how to communicate with the public.

To you, what's the most fun about being a producer?

WEISSLER: We've produced some of the great shows. I can't even count how many. We began on Broadway with *Othello* with James Earl Jones and Christopher Plummer in 1982, which won a Tony. There was *My One and Only* with Tommy Tune, *Zorba* with Anthony Quinn, *Cabaret* with Joel Grey. The most fun is when you have a success, and you transport thousands of people each night to a magical place. That's what's really exciting about what I do. When you have a failure it's like being in an inferno. Saddam Hussein should have a failure on Broadway.

You work with several kinds of designers, right? Lighting designers, set designers, costume designers. Is there anything all designers have in common?

WEISSLER: Their creativity. Each one is different. Each one applies him or herself differently. All the good ones are passionate about what they do.

How many ideas do you remember seeing for Chicago? *What was it about the one you chose that made you say, "I love it"?*

WEISSLER: I know that Drew presents several ideas to some of his clients, but that's not how he works with me. We begin alone. We talk to each other. He always begins by asking me what I think and what I feel. We work together like partners. Not only on *Chicago*, but on *Sweet Charity, Seussical, Annie Get Your Gun*. After we come up with the idea, we show it to our people. He wants his staff to love it. I want my marketing staff to march to it.

Drew said that one of the most difficult things for an agency to sell is a concept using existing photography, because the real pictures of the show, with the stars, haven't been taken. What's your experience with that?

WEISSLER: It was Drew's brilliant choice of photographer that made this campaign what it is and has been. I had never heard of Max Vadukal before and didn't know his work. I said I wanted high fashion, sex, and danger. This campaign began with six narrow vertical shots of the women, spliced together, black-and-white, with red type. That succeeded perfectly. I didn't need to be sold.

Do you really hold the agency responsible for selling eight thousand tickets a week? Aren't there other factors at play that have nothing to do with advertising and promotion?

WEISSLER: Of course. There is word of mouth. That's as important as advertising and promotion. I have my own marketing division. We join hands with Drew's agency. If sales are down, we talk about what's been happening and what we can do. For example, shall we try this or that? Should be put a wrapper around the whole *New York Times* on Thanksgiving and own that space for the weekend?

Last week, I saw people standing in line for the Wednesday matinee of The Tale of the Allergist's Wife *fanning themselves with* Chicago *fans. Tell me about those fans.*

WEISSLER: We created those years ago, and we update them every summer. When it's hot people love fanning themselves. So the fans are all over town.

How important is a Web site for a show today?

WEISSLER: It's tremendously important—vital. Just ask my marketing director, Scott Moore. More and more people are shopping on the Web, so it's a portal to ticket sales. Sales from the site are increasing by the double-digits, and now account for one-quarter to one-third of the total. People may visit the site because they're curious. And the site can turn them from merely curious to committed buyers. They can buy tickets before leaving their hometowns, without leaving their chairs, without dealing with a ticket agent. Also, fans go to the site for updates on the show. We get about ten e-mails a day from fans asking questions like, "How long is Michael C. Hall going to be in the show?"

Drew told me that after September 11 you and he came up with the idea of the TV commercials with all the Broadway stars singing in Times Square. Do you think the American public would have rallied behind New York and Broadway anyway?

WEISSLER: That idea was born when I was sitting in my summer home trying to think of what we could do. I gave Drew the idea and he executed it. He made it better. In the execution you have a commodity that's as valuable as the idea itself. Everyone involved with that commercial donated their time, and the air time was either donated or the New York Convention & Visitors Bureau found the money. In the beginning it worked brilliantly, but now ticket sales are falling off again. It's the economy. People, both Europeans and Americans, are not spending in New York the way they used to. There are many fewer international tourists than there were last year at this time. Hotel occupancy is down by 15 percent and tourist spending is down by about 10 percent.

What's next on the agenda for you?

WEISSLER: We're about to open *Chicago* in Russia, and we have a beautiful Italian production in Milan. *Sweet Charity* is opening in New York this season.

When you begin producing a new property, thinking about the marketing, do you consider different creative talents, different agencies, pick the one that's right for the show?

WEISSLER: No. Spot's my organization. Drew's my man. He's the best in the industry, heads and shoulders above everyone else. There's no reason to go anywhere else. He gets me to delve more fully into my creative psyche; I come up with better ideas because of him.

PART **IV**

INSTITUTIONAL CLIENTS

Institutional clients include schools, colleges,
and universities; churches, government
agencies, charities, foundations, hospitals, and
museums. Fulfilling their complex branding and
marketing needs, including raising funds
and recruiting constituents, requires increasingly
sophisticated skills.

18

THE INSTITUTION
OF **HIGHER EDUCATION**

Harvard *and* Corey McPherson Nash
MIT *and* Korn Design
Northeastern *and* Robert Davison

Andrew Tiedemann is **HARVARD** University's communications director for alumni affairs and development. He heads the team responsible for all Harvard College publications and for developing, designing, and maintaining the University's alumni affairs Web site. Previously with Northeastern University and, before that, California Federal Savings and Loan, he is a graduate of Boston University.

A partner at Boston design firm **COREY MCPHERSON NASH**, *Michael McPherson* has been creative director for several key projects for Harvard. Before cofounding his firm, he was design director at Northeastern University and a book designer for MIT Press. In 2002 he received the "Fellows Award" from AIGA/Boston for a "significant contribution to raising the standards of excellence in the Boston design community." He is on the advisory councils of the Design Management Institute and AIGA/Boston and on the part-time faculty at RISD.

Cambridge-based writer and communications consultant *Martha Eddison*, former head speechwriter for New York governor Mario Cuomo and Massachusetts attorney general Scott Harshbarger, consults and writes for nonprofit institutions, often as they launch major capital campaigns. In addition to working for Harvard Medical School, Williams College, and the Children's Museum, she has been lead consultant in **M I T** 's ongoing multibillion-dollar fundraising effort.

Denise Korn heads Boston-based **K O R N   D E S I G N** , which provides branding and corporate identity, strategic positioning, and design services to corporate and nonprofit clients. The firm has been working closely with Martha Eddison on MIT's capital campaign. Korn previously worked in New York as a senior designer at Corporate Graphics and as a designer at Carbone Smolan Associates and the *New York Times*. Over the past eight years she has served on the board and headed business outreach programs for AIGA Boston.

Caroline Jorgensen directs the communications strategy for undergraduate admissions and alumni programs at **N O R T H E A S T E R N** University, a position that encompasses the strategy and design of all letters, brochures, magazines, postcards, and invitations sent to prospective students, alumni, and donors. She began her career in undergraduate admissions at her own alma mater, Mount Holyoke College, and was also an admissions officer at Regis College.

Designer **R O B E R T   D A V I S O N** is Northeastern's director of publications. With a BFA from Massachusetts College of Art and an MFA from Boston University, he heads the team responsible for defining and maintaining the university's visual brand. He was previously principal of his own graphic design firm, and before that, the design director at the marketing agency Philip Johnson Associates. He is a senior visiting instructor at Massachusetts College of Art.

Of all the things graphic design does—sell products, change opinions, give people positive experiences—recruiting students and raising funds are two of the most significant. Colleges and universities are in increasing competition for the best students and the ever-rarer donor dollars. As all college alumni and every parent of a seventeen-year-old with decent SAT scores knows, it's highly competitive. Every year the need is greater and the stakes are higher. Producing materials for this market is a science and an art. Whether you are an in-house designer or an outside consultant (and I've been in both positions), you can often feel pressured to satisfy too many constituents, in too short a time frame, with inadequate budgets for photography and printing. However, at some institutions clients and designers have been able to use the power of design to produce work they are both proud of and that achieves mutual goals. In April 2002 I had the privilege of moderating a "Clients and Designers" panel at the CASE Design Institute in Cambridge, a three-day conference sponsored by the Council for Advancement and Support of Education, a Washington, D.C.–based organization. Here is what the panelists had to say:

Harvard and Corey McPherson Nash have enjoyed a nine-year relationship. Andy, you and Michael have worked on many projects together. Harvard also has an in-house design staff. You've told me that at least five different design firms are among your choices, when you go outside. All this sounds very complicated. When and how do you choose a design firm and when do you use your in-house people?

TIEDEMANN: The choice usually isn't very difficult. We're a small shop, five writers and two designers. We're responsible for communicating with about 300,000 Harvard alumni and producing all the publications for Harvard College. Generally we have twice as much work as we can do in a year. We meet with our in-house designers every three to six months to look at the projects coming up. They decide which ones they want to work on. The remaining ones go into the competitive bidding process.

The in-house designers get first choice?

TIEDEMANN: Correct.

I think that might be a surprise to many college and university designers who think that the really good projects go to outside firms, who get the opportunities to do the great work and win all the awards.

TIEDEMANN: It doesn't work that way for us. Our group will get together to brainstorm about whether a particular project is something we want to take on. What are the chances for success? Or that it will get into a political quagmire? If it looks like it might become politically difficult, we might call a freelancer or a firm like Michael's.

When you call an outside firm, do you invite people to come in and present their capabilities, tell you why they're the right choice for the project?

TIEDEMANN: We have a small retainer with a few firms we work with quite a bit. Every year or so we try to work through that retainer. Then there are situations in which we will entertain bids. But we try not to waste designers' time. If we're leaning towards a particular firm, we're not going to invite twelve firms if each only has a one-in-twelve chance of getting the job.

Is that chance based on price? Or do you evaluate other criteria?

TIEDEMANN: Price is part of it. But if we've had a good experience with a firm, if we know they can deliver, even if the cost is higher, we'll go with a firm we know is going to come through for us.

Can you describe your team structure?

TIEDEMANN: We have a kickoff meeting in which we define the audience and marketing problem the project is intended to solve. There will be myself as creative director, the project manager, the writer, the designer from the firm we've selected, and our internal client, plus the person who will have the final say on the project. This could be the president of the university, the dean of a school, the vice president for fundraising or for alumni. I also include one of my in-house designers, even if we're using an outside firm. We talk about what the deliverables will be, the delivery date, whether a particular event or university happening is driving that date. We talk about past projects that are related to that piece. After that, meetings will involve the creative team only, and we'll brainstorm about design approaches, like whether we're using an illustrator or a photographer, and if so, who.

I'd like to talk a little bit about this brochure, which you did with Michael's firm: "Twenty-Five Years: A Celebration of Women at Harvard." Here is a striking image of a fully dressed woman sitting on a diving board, her sweater color-coordinated with the pool lane markers. The caption reads: "Suzanne Gove '97 faced a choice. A successful swimmer in high school, she had to decide whether to continue her sport or try something new." How did this image come about; who chose the photographer, the setting?

TIEDEMANN: We chose the twenty-fifth anniversary of women moving into the freshman dorms as the occasion to do a major piece that profiled twenty-five Harvard women. Our marketing problem was that women felt Harvard ignored them and that they didn't have a place here. Some of the women pictured are students, some are graduates, some faculty. Each gave a short statement about her relationship to Harvard. We took some risks, which was not characteristic. So there are statements like, "I was the only black woman here and it wasn't fun." Michael and Rich Rose, a colleague at his firm and the designer of this piece, brought in portfolios from local photographers. We decided on Tony Rinaldo. Tony has an unbelievable eye. The way he frames situations is unique. He shot in Cambridge, in Los Angeles, Washington, D.C.

One thing that strikes me is the luxurious use of white space. One might say half this spread doesn't have anything on it, which is not at all unusual in corporate projects, but very unusual in college and university publications. Looking back at the brochures I critiqued [at the CASE Design Institute] this morning, I realize that many college designers are forced into fitting ten or fifteen or more pictures—pictures of people at events or smiling at the camera and shaking hands—on a page. How do you rationalize your use of space?

MCPHERSON: This is a one-in-a-thousand project. When we proposed devoting a spread to each person, Andy and the client agreed. Rich and I sort of looked at each other and said, "Wow." We are often in the position of having to put ten photos on a page, too, and you just do your best. This piece needed to have impact. We made it oversized; we made it not look like just another piece of Harvard propaganda.

As I understand it, there is no Harvard identity manual that suggests typography, page grids, how images should be used. As a communications consultant, do you wish there were more of a Harvard look?

MCPHERSON: Yes. At one point we had five different clients at Harvard— the School of Public Health, the School of Education, the Divinity School, the School of Art and Architecture, Admissions—and none of the projects were related to each other.

Doesn't that give you a lot of freedom? Freedom to do the most effective thing on each project?

MCPHERSON: Well, most Harvard clients start a meeting by saying, "We want this piece not to look like Harvard," which means no serif type and not a lot of crimson. But there are lots of unwritten rules, different for each internal client.

Is there a standard Harvard crimson?

TIEDEMANN: There is a kind of mindset or cliché of what a Harvard piece looks like. And you're always working against that. The cliché piece would be black and crimson—and no one can agree what that crimson is; no Pantone color is quite right—on cream stock. It would have shields on it, small serif type. It might be quite beautiful. You have to remember that we are in a unique position. We have 17,000 applications for a few thousand positions. We are trying to maintain a certain level of selectivity and diversity.

To reflect on what you're saying, last year I wrote an article entitled "Rating the Art and Design School Catalogs" for Print *magazine. We received lavish viewbooks and catalogs from RISD, CalArts, Parsons, Art Center, and so forth, all filled with dazzling color photography and all kinds of design tricks. Yale submitted a simple six-by-nine booklet on cream stock. It had a little Yale shield on the cover, serif type set in a single justified column, no pictures. Informal panels of prospective students and parents judged the books; everybody looked at them laid out on tables. Ultimately, most people said they thought that Yale was the best school. So a lot of what drives the choice is reputation, correct?*

TIEDEMANN: Yes. But we need to make sure that each marketing problem is solved on its own and that we don't rely on the reputation or the cliché.

Michael, you also have corporate clients and have been an in-house college and university designer yourself. For you, what are the special rewards of doing institutional work?

MCPHERSON: Designing for clients in education aligns with my beliefs about what is really important. Like all designers, I love to learn new things, and that's what schools are about. Colleges and universities create experiences for young people. We work hard to identify and understand the different cultures of schools. Superficially, some schools may seem very similar to one another; for example, two fine small liberal arts colleges will be completely different once you get inside: the texture, the attitudes, the kind of student. As consultants, we try to discern the differences and speak with an authentic voice so the pieces reflect a deep understanding of each institution and its culture. By deep, I mean that every decision, style, typeface, paper stock, photograph, has to feel like it's speaking from that school. And that requires a certain invest-ment. Institutions don't have deep pockets and some don't understand the necessity for designers to do an in-depth exploration, a discovery process, up-front. They want you to come in and start working on the brochure, but that's not going to yield the best results.

Andy, when you say that in-house designers get first choice, do you believe that they do have a certain advantage, that deep understanding Michael is talking about, without having to go through a briefing process?

TIEDEMANN: Definitely. They know the client, they have an innate sense of the client's hopes and desires. That's the reason we have one of our designers on every creative team, whether or not they're doing the designing. They guide the consultants that are working with us. It's a balancing act. One of the advantages of using consultants is they're less afraid to take risks. We often involve outside firms on the projects we've collectively decided we want to take some risks on; we want some new thinking; we want someone to think out of the box and take the risk, politically.

Martha, as an independent consultant, what can you do for MIT that no one in-house can do?

EDDISON: My job is to get you, the reader, to fall in love with the institution as I have. And that can be a difficult task for people who are there every day. I can come in and spend six weeks interviewing forty faculty members and can communicate what's going on in a way someone in-house never could.

What was the situation at the time you started your engagement?

EDDISON: MIT was gearing up for a capital campaign that was twice as big as anything they'd ever done before. They were doing this within an institutional culture that did not value graphic design; everything pretty much looked like an engineer typed it. Case statements—brochures that use words, numbers, and images to build the case for making a major donation—in the past had been viewed as necessary evils. You've got to have one if someone asks, but frankly most were in boxes acting as doorstops around campus. The MIT administration knew they had to produce one, but weren't sure how to go about it. There are no in-house designers at MIT, so MIT always goes outside. MIT has an in-house team of print brokers who try to help internal clients under-stand the value of design, the value of working with professional writers. The in-house team started by hunting around for a firm that could give them the kind of writing and design they wanted. They couldn't find one firm, so they decided to make a team of a design firm and me. Bringing in Denise helped MIT to learn the strategic value of design.

I'm intrigued by your assessment that the culture at MIT doesn't value design. Has there been a big change? In his textbook, The History of Graphic Design, *Philip B. Meggs singled out the high level of quality and imagination in the MIT graphic design pro-gram, which he called a paradigm of the International Typographic Style in America. He was referring in part to the posters designed by Jacqueline Casey in the seventies and in part to the MIT design program that enabled all members of the university community to get free, professional design assistance. The MIT Media Lab has been known as an incubator of design technologies. Faculty members like John Maeda are speaking at conferences on such topics as the future of design.*

EDDISON: The design program you're talking about was not anything that came up through the capital campaign design process. The MIT group that helps internal clients find good outside designers certainly took an interest in what we were doing, but they didn't play an extensive role.

Denise, you have called your relationship with Martha collaborative and unique. How do you work together?

KORN: Both of us believe that what we're trying to communicate on behalf of our clients is equally carried by the words and the visualization of them. A lot of clients don't understand that for words and images to mesh in a meaningful way, the process of designing and writing needs to start together. We need to generate the questions to ask the client together. And when the client answers them and we develop a concept that reflects those answers, at the end poetry can happen. Usually a concept will roll out naturally. This is a hard thing to explain to someone who's never been through the process with the right kind of team. Just hearing an explanation like this could seem overly academic or artsy, but it's strategically based. The correct solution allows a client to be brave. Because it's not just based on something that's blue and green, it's something that has meaning for them.

How can you convince a large institution, where, as it's been pointed out, there might be thorny political issues, to be brave?

KORN: It's important, whether you work in-house or are an external consultant, to understand the chain of command and the approval process from the beginning. You have to know who needs to be engaged and included in the voyage you're going on together. Sometimes you find out that you've never met the key decision maker until it's too late.

MCPHERSON: It's important to have everybody who can say *no* together in one room.

TIEDEMAN: Sometimes that's a lot of people.

EDDISON: Our immediate clients at MIT got nervous at the approval stage, looking up a tree of command, or rather, at a kind of lateral stripe of people who perceived themselves as equals. They didn't know what to do if any of those guys said *no*. So I said, "I'll take it to them." I took the piece, marched off to their offices, virtually read it to each of them, and more or less got their sign-off right there. It was kind of hard for them to disagree with me: They weren't going to throw me out; they'd gotten to like me by then, so there was a great advantage for my internal client to let me take that risk.

Can we back up to the design-brief stage? Your overall mission was to raise 1.5 billion dollars for MIT. When accomplishing something of that magnitude, is that the problem stated by the client: "Martha and Denise, help us raise 1.5 billion dollars"? Or are the deliverables more concrete: "We need two brochures, a case statement, a Web site"?

KORN: A campaign is an amorphous, organic thing. The project evolved out of a process of discovery. Over a five-year period it has taken several different turns. Originally there was an RFP that stated, "We need collateral, we need a case statement that focuses on the following initiatives." We were brought in to produce those items. Martha undertook months of research studies, strategic analyses, and interviews with donors, and we came back and said, "You don't need this, you need that, and you're asking for way too much stuff." For example, donors don't want a big party; they want facts, they want to be engaged about what is compelling about this institution now. Some of the pieces that now exist evolved from the original list, and others were not even on their radar screen.

Do you bring written documentation, so that the strategy you are recommending cannot be considered an opinion, but is based on research?

KORN: Yes and no. A lot of what's going to work is intuitive as well as based on research. The solution might be based more on an understanding of the soul of the institution, in this case an understanding of MIT's alumni and what would be needed to get their financial support. We shared a lot of documentation with the client, but in the end it was the combination of Martha's content with the design solution that delivered that.

MIT's colors are maroon and black; every piece in this campaign is chartreuse and blue. People can get very emotional about color. Did you have to fight any battles on this?

KORN: They wanted the brand identity for the campaign to be robust and bold. This is an institutional identity for a five-year campaign. It was gutsy of them to go with that.

EDDISON: There's an advantage in not having an organized design culture. So why not do green and blue?

KORN: Can I just add that the color green is never an easy sell?

TIEDEMANN: Clients hate that green.

Overall, there is a strong theme and look to these MIT pieces: the color scheme, the typography. Did you set out the parameters of the identity first and then design the individual pieces?

KORN: We inherited the mark for the campaign and refined it and made it functional, big and small, on the Web, in color and black-and-white. We wove it into all the materials, moving forward in an organized way in terms of an identity structure. We posted a palette with colors and typography on the MIT Intranet for everyone who would be producing campaign materials over the five-year period to subscribe to. We created templates that people can pull down to create brochures. There's no design police, but there is a tool that many people in the institution can use to keep up the consistency.

Caroline and Rob, you are both employees of Northeastern University. You're doing some strong work together, and I suspect that until hearing from Andy and Michael, most in-house designers thought that outside design firms have all the fun. Not true, right?

DAVISON: Not at all. Like Andy's situation at Harvard, we have requests for double the jobs we can do in a year. We select the projects we want to handle internally, and work with outside freelancers to produce the rest. There are lots of interesting projects to go around.

The work you've done together also has a very strong look, a lot of red. Is this today's campaign look, or is Northeastern's red like Coke's red, a forever look?

DAVISON: Red is Northeastern's color. Similar to what Michael said about Harvard, for years numerous Northeastern reds were being used, and it was interpreted loosely at best. Sometimes it was crimson, sometimes more orange or even maroon. We standardized the color, creating a special ink mix that is distinctive and specific to Northeastern, so I'd like to think there is a parallel to Coca-Cola's red.

When can a look go from fresh to tired? How do you keep it fresh?

JORGENSEN: Students go to college fairs and pick up materials from twenty, thirty different schools. A student has expectations about what an institution should look like, and it's up to us to keep them interested and excited. If a ten-year-old brochure looks similar to the one we have right now, students will pick up on that.

DAVISON: The materials we develop have to be an accurate representation of the university at a moment in time. A university is a fluid entity, and the challenge is to capture and package its spirit. Our goal is to showcase not only who we are but what we're becoming. Projects that were effective even a couple of years ago often don't hold up as well as we would like.

Rob, you had your own firm. Can you characterize the difference between being a design firm principal and managing an in-house department?

DAVISON: I've worked in several environments, from small design firms to larger agencies, as well as having my own firm. Whenever you connect with a good client, you hope for continuity and the opportunity to evolve things over time, but it's never guaranteed. Northeastern is my first in-house experience, and I've had the chance to really look at the nuances here and refine decisions I've made. While my work now revolves around a single institution, it's not too different to having my own firm. Working with design and branding standards reminds me of the Paul Rand essay, "Design and the Play Instinct." A limited pool of ingredients challenges you to bring out the richness in your design solutions.

Caroline, the goal of your capital campaign was to raise $200 million. And every year you need to recruit nearly three thousand students. How do you evaluate design work? Whether it meets certain design criteria or achieves those goals?

JORGENSEN: The goal of an admissions office is to have a successful and talented class enroll, exactly the number we want. We had the highest number of applications in history this last year, and we're seeing more higher-ability students than ever before. Our retention numbers are up as well. Our publications play a key role in this, and we see a direct effect on the caliber of students. Recruiting used to be a passive and standardized process. No more. We have a sophisticated communications strategy. We're implementing a system that can track the distribution specifics of our publications: who receives them, how many times each student gets a publication, what kind of student they are, and whether they apply and enroll. There will be an opportunity to test various communications and get a sense of our success rate in certain markets and with different types of students. This feedback will be an invaluable indicator of how well we are doing.

DAVISON: Caroline and others in admissions often share comments from students and parents about what they respond to in our publications as well as what they would like to see. For high-level projects we often use research firms that run focus groups. In terms of fundraising, development officers pass along comments on our capital campaign materials from prospective donors. There is very direct feedback, and we learn if a publication was persuasive or if it fell flat.

We love to create brochures; they're like our children. But what if you learned from some higher power that you didn't need print materials, photography, any of that stuff, to accomplish your goals? UCLA has current students call and make the annual fund pitch on the phone and it seems to work pretty well.

DAVISON: Print plays a vitally important role in informing and persuading people to make important, often emotional decisions. Is it necessary to print a high volume of data sheets? Probably not. Accessing them online is generally a better way to deliver that kind of information. But we continue to hear that folks want a brochure they can hold in their hands: a viewbook that can be passed around the kitchen table, a capital campaign piece to display on the coffee table. A phone call may be able to successfully close a donation from an alum, but recruiting is a more complex process. For our primary audience, high school students, the game is how to get their attention and then keep it. Photography plays an increasingly important role, as it quickly sets the tone and leads them into the piece.

How important is the Web site to recruiting?

JORGENSEN: It is important, but there are a lot of ways for prospective students to connect. Part of reputation-building is looking at every point of contact as an opportunity to shape and evolve perception. It could be the site, a meeting at a college fair, an open house, campus tours, or word of mouth. Research shows that with all the media options available, students still want something physically in hand to carry with them when they visit a campus, to reference throughout the day during an open house. I don't believe even the best Web site would be as effective without printed material.

What is the best way to manage projects internally? The big complaint I've heard at this conference is, "Our internal clients don't listen." How do you get them to listen?

DAVISON: As Denise, Michael, and Martha said, by getting all the decision makers in the room at the beginning of a project. We host brainstorming sessions with the deans and selected faculty so they feel invested, have a sense of ownership, and so the approval process will go much more smoothly. Northeastern, like any large university, is decentralized. Various offices and departments create their own communications, some of which have no connection to the University brand. There are isolated fiefdoms around campus that are not interested in our design or messaging standards. We in the publications office can act as a consultant, educating them about the value of embracing the standards. This process can include a communications audit of their materials and a strategic plan for improvement. There's often resistance, a lot of fear. But when they see that they can maintain their individual identity while working with us, it's a win-win situation.

A few years ago, when my son was a high school junior, the recruiting materials were coming to our house fast and furiously. My son sometimes wouldn't even open an envelope, saying, "That's a dorky place," (he'd read all the "Insider's Guides to Colleges") and he'd throw the brochure in the trash. Or he'd open the envelope and look at the pictures and say something like, "They have old computers" and then throw it in the trash. From your perspective, what is it that causes a prospective student to choose one college over another?

JORGENSEN: Our job is to demonstrate to prospective students and their families how we can be the right match. One of the best ways to accomplish this is to have them visit our campus. The majority of students who do so end up applying. Our marketing promotions create a window onto what they will see, feel, and experience once here. In choosing a college, students want a personalized experience. Right now, we are developing a whole new interactive experience, personalized URLs. Applicants will be able to check their status, and be given information specifically about what they're interested in.

DAVISON: Word of mouth is everything in academia, so any way we can create positive buzz is worth it. Students are savvy and pick up on visual cues quickly. They want to get that big picture overview of campus and its proximity to things. They see things like technology hardware and what students are wearing as signals to what a place is about. They want to see how they would fit in. Each year I push for an ample photography budget to ensure we have an updated pool to pull from—no old computers. How an institution's defining characteristics are represented visually is pivotal. We are located in the middle of a city. We have 14,000 students. We link classroom liberal arts learning with workplace experience. These aren't things that you want to gloss over. We make the most of them. When you truly capture the spirit of the institution in a way that speaks to the student, you bring him or her a big step closer to making that choice.

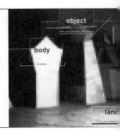

19

SCI-Arc *and* April Greiman

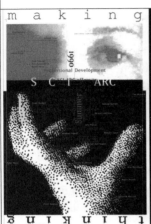

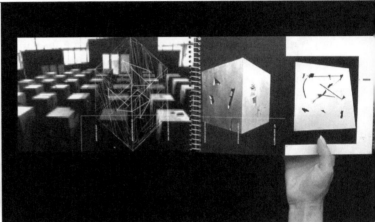

Los Angeles native *Michael Rotondi* is a 1973 graduate of **SCI-ARC** — Southern California Institute of Architecture — which he helped to found in 1972. He was the school's director in 1987 to 1997, and remains on the faculty. SCI-Arc, which relocated to downtown Los Angeles from Marina del Rey, has 450 students and a faculty of fifty, and aims to "advance the field of architecture by producing architects who are truly artists and thus inherently subversive." Mr. Rotondi also heads the firm ROTO Architects, which he founded in 1991 after working independently and in various collaborations. He was co-recipient of the American Academy and Institute of Arts and Letters Award in Architecture for 1992.

APRIL GREIMAN was born in suburban New York and studied at The Kansas City Art Institute and Allgemeine Kunstgwerbeschule in Basel, Switzerland. Since opening her practice in Los Angeles in 1976, she has been a leader in graphic, environmental, motion, and interactive formats. As an early and enthusiastic user and adapter of computer technology, she established her reputation in new media. Greiman's company, Made in Space, is in her words "a central spirit for meta-branding trans-media, an idea and approach that crosses all media: print, motion, virtual, and three-dimensional/environmental."

Michael Rotundi is the kind of client every designer wants but few can have. He understands the ambiguities of design and doesn't tremble in fear (or change his strategy) when his colleagues say, "The new letterhead looks messy, like somebody spilled their lunch." He sticks to his guns, lets people engage themselves and learn to appreciate the work. He is articulate and visionary when it comes to broader issues, too. For example, on the subject of typical corporate identity manuals, he says, "That kind of fixed identity comes out of a static culture that believes things have to be immutable; a culture in which very few people make decisions that affect very many." Ten years before it happened, he predicted that identity was going to change into "unmediated open communications systems." April Greiman says that the most valuable lessons to be learned from her relationship with SCI-Arc is "to see that it's possible to collaborate creatively on an idea and an aesthetic that pervades not only the various formats and applications of design, but enters into the bloodstream of the client's environment." To delve into this synergy between two visionaries, I spoke with April in her studio just east of downtown Los Angeles.

You have commented that you "built an entire career on accidents." What did you mean by that?

GREIMAN: Although I'm a rational, reasonable, sometimes articulate person, my main foot forward is intuitive. I accidentally bumped into the work of the Basel School at the Kansas City Art Institute, where I had three European instructors. Then I studied in Basel until Armin Hofmann recommended that I teach at Philadelphia College of Art. I've never hired marketing consultants or gone after clients, mostly because work that is market driven is quite different than work that is a true integration between culture and commerce. I still prefer to put the design at the fore, and then figure out to work within a budget or specific financial constraints. So far, it has proven successful.

Actually, I thought you were referring to computer accidents—an image that might suddenly appear or transform itself.

GREIMAN: That's true, too. I've always subscribed creatively to the chance principle. Before computers, it was video. One time I traded half-inch video cameras with a colleague, Harry Marks, who said, "Don't forget to adjust the white balance." I asked, "What's white balance?" He said, "Now I know how you get that great color!" You see what I mean? Often I'll watch the computer build an image and have to go back and capture it so we can create it again for another project or purpose.

Are your clients concerned about fees?

GREIMAN: Is there a client who isn't? Usually they will give us a budget rather than having us work on a proposal that we have to revise three times. I ask if a potential client is getting other bids, and can tell by whom they're dealing with how educated they are about buying design. We know who's in our league.

How did SCI-Arc become your client, and what was the situation at the time?

GREIMAN: When Michael Rotondi was newly appointed director, he was a partner at the architecture firm Morphosis, which had hired me to do the Japan PGA Golf Club identity. SCI-Arc was a twenty-year-old architecture school with an identity that looked like someone had put it together at an instant printer— a photocopy of a photocopy of a rubber stamp. Michael felt that the school couldn't get to the next level of professionalism without a professional image. He trusted me and identified with the kind of communications work we did; he felt I was a world-class designer who could help him achieve his objectives. I toured the school, talked to staff and faculty, looked at student work, absorbed the philosophy, which is that architecture is part of a bigger culture: buildings can be read as icons of other, bigger ideas. Architecture is about transformation and should emanate from ideas rather than stylistic or decorative notions.

Tell me about the letterhead, which seems to be a cornerstone of the identity.

GREIMAN: I've always considered a letterhead—any piece of paper—a "space." And I wanted to transform it. We scanned an airbrush gradation into the graphic paintbox, and I kept enlarging it. I wanted to see the deeper structure of that gradation—like discovering the DNA. We used the anti-aliasing feature, and the pixels for each dot, instead of being hard-edged squares, softened and broke into at least 16 million different colors. No two dots were alike. It really was architecture. I chose an early Macintosh typeface, even though architecture was one of the last disciplines to go Mac; the early Macs didn't have enough power for modeling or 3-D. I wanted to speak to technology and the new spirit of the age, since architecture and design have always been aligned with technology and new materials.

Did you present more than one direction or solution?

GREIMAN: In my career I've rarely showed more than one thing. But sometimes I present more than one version when I need the client's input to ascertain which is the most appropriate, since details can be quite subtle.

You sprint between three or four different computers overseeing several projects at once. Can you describe your relationship with your staff? Can you roughly define how much of a solution is "you" and how much is "them?"

GREIMAN: It's all me, and it is truly all them as well. We have such a small staff that I can spend a majority of my time doing design and not design administration. My main responsibilities are concept and design, meeting and presenting to the client. Others in my studio are responsible for picking up my lead and developing, enhancing, or managing the projects once the main direction is set. While SCI-Arc is "my" identity and carries a particular spirit of that concept, everyone who works with me on it is either directly or indirectly part of the whole. Working with new technologies, it is a team and collaborative effort. That is perhaps the new paradigm: sharing, networking, and creative pluralism.

Can you describe your relationship with Michael Rotondi?

GREIMAN: Entangled and entwined with SCI-Arc. I go to lectures and events, and I also teach there, which gives me greater insight into the diverse ideas that are prevalent. I've worked with quite a few architects and architecture firms on color, finishes and materials, signage, and environmental graphics, and therefore have become immersed in that world. We socialize, have lunches, meetings, talk about the various cultures and contexts of design. We discuss things such as "Will the world need more architecture as it moves rapidly into the virtual world?" "Can there be great buildings any longer which do not reintegrate spirit and sensuality?" I feel that in the eighties, in particular, time and money were wasted on building for skewed reasons. Signature work (architecture with a capital *A*) had no higher ideals or purpose. I truly believe architecture—and design—can inspire and transform people at the cellular level.

For example . . .

GREIMAN: Spaces that have powerful symbolism that combine the material, physical worlds with the spiritual, like Chartres, many Louis Kahn buildings, the Salk Institute as a prime example, Frank Gehry's Vitra Museum, Michael Rotondi's home, especially his studio.

Graphic designers often wonder whether they should be having dinner, going to shows or ball games with clients? Especially women designers with male clients. That kind of client entertainment seems artificial, very likely boring, but occasionally a business necessity. You seem to be talking about socializing at a very different, more cerebral, level.

GREIMAN: I tend to be pretty antisocial. Shy mostly. I never enjoyed doing those kinds of things. I was never motivated by strictly business or money, although I love both. I socialize with people, clients, whom I feel connected to ideologically and spiritually. At a certain level, if you will, I don't have much competition, so I attract a unique, perhaps unusual, kind of client, and they tend to be the kind of people I'll have to my home for dinner, and vice-versa. Again, there seems to be an affinity towards the ideological. It would probably be a good idea for me to go to a ball game sometime.

Does anyone ever complain that the SCI-Arc pieces are hard to read? Do you ever get comments like, "Students won't be able to tell what time the class is offered."

GREIMAN: No, not really. They're designed to be copy-light and image-strong. We're never interested in disregarding legibility. I'm not of the destroying-the-word ilk. I'm interested in fine and refined typography. But we push it to the limit, sometimes by doing things like printing olive-green ink on fluorescent pink paper. You do have to work harder to read it. It's always the same conflict: readability versus memorability. I go for memorability, but not at the risk of losing readability. But if we were on press and something was illegible, I would pull the job. And you have to remember that the majority of this work is designed for potential students. They like to be stunned and want to see more image. For younger people, word is image. It's all about image. SCI-Arc has lower budgets and is less endowed than other architecture schools. But perhaps its philosophy is stronger, its message more relevant. One could spend a lot on high-end photography, six-color printing, and still not have a clear message to communicate. Everything that comes out of SCI-Arc speaks with one voice. However, we are speaking about unity through diversity. It reinforces itself and builds on itself.

Do you ever come across clients who ask for dark type on light-colored paper, or demand any particular sorts of things? What do you say to them?

GREIMAN: They never insist on anything. If there's something they're insistent on, it's usually something I notice myself, and we decide on it together. You usually don't notice these details until you comp up the piece at the last minute, and the client asks, "Do you think the type is big enough?" I'll say, "No." Those concerns should not be theirs. Having identified with my aesthetic, ideologically, they give me freedom. My clients have done their homework in terms of which designer they've chosen. I don't interfere with the way they manufacture their products or run their organizations. They don't question my aesthetic or interfere too much with my design. And I invite the client into the process, "We feel it could be red or green." Then we may show them two different files on the computer and ask for their participation. "Let's look at them and decide." But I don't invite them on day one. I wait until I've gone through all the preliminary exploration and I have a reasonable concept at work.

Tell me about the Student Workbook.

GREIMAN: This was the first time SCI-Arc published student work, although all other major architecture schools do it every year. The *Student Workbook* is used for recruiting, but it's also a commercial product sold in bookstores. Rizzoli was interested, but SCI-Arc published it themselves, and it became the second-best-selling book on architecture. People read it from cover to cover. It's in two sections: undergraduate and graduate. In undergraduate, the emphasis is on process, the philosophy, the assignments, and basic exercises given. In the graduate section, the work "product" is treated with more reverence. Additionally, we used "zap-shot" images with a still video camera to capture the new texture of technology. Michael requested every spread to be a poster, which is exciting, but which ultimately was very time consuming for me. Never to be repeated!

Once upon a time, you published a nude image of yourself in Design Quarterly. *What effect did that have on your career?*

GREIMAN: I understand it was fairly scandalous at the time and caused a lot of debate, but I ultimately only got positive feedback, and of course it was a sellout issue for the Walker. I guess it is now a landmark piece in the history of graphic design. The questions it brings up are, "What's personal, what's professional?" and "What's fine art, what's graphic design?" It was a big deal to decide to use a digitized portrait of myself. But it isn't "me"; it's ink on paper, a representation of the female form. If I'd wanted to be a pinup, I would have made it a whole lot hotter. I think the sad thing is perhaps the main point has been lost, which is that this project represents a revolution. It was designed in cyberspace, output onto 8½ × 11 bond paper, given to the printer, and then printed "life size." Even more importantly, it signaled the end of "tangible art" and the beginning of working entirely digitally and manipulating light. With it, design was no longer reminiscent of the past, but indicative of the future.

In an article in Communication Arts *magazine, "Women in Design Speak Out," one of the panelists said, "All the really famous women in this profession—you were named—don't have families." The panelists seemed to agree that women can't have children and put in the time it takes to do innovative or distinctive work. If you had been present at that event, what would you have said?*

GREIMAN: Many famous women designers have families. Look at Sheila de Bretteville and Lella Vignelli. I never consciously made a decision not to have a family, it was just that the men I was with weren't into it. I guess you could say my work is my family; it's what I created. And I never set out to be famous. I was always interested in my work, which was the big adventure of my life. But if I'd had children, I wouldn't have let it hold me back. My career would have been different; I might not have been so prolific. But you get famous for quality, not for quantity.

LATER, I SPOKE WITH MICHAEL ROTONDI AT SCI-ARC, IN A FORMER HUGHES AIRCRAFT PLANT IN PLAYA DEL REY.

As I understand it, SCI-Arc began with fifty faculty and students and is now considered by some to be one of the leading architecture schools in the world. Tell me how that happened.

ROTONDI: SCI-Arc is a place where a lot of the most active practitioners in L.A. work. It's like a laboratory where a lot of experimentation is going on. Teaching is an outgrowth of research, and by that I mean any time you have an idea you can pursue it and give it form. It's a place of experiment and invention. The dominant group of students and faculty are doing experimental work.

Because of this reputation, people who are among the best students and faculty around the world come here to search for and test out their ideas. When those activities are happening in a teaching and learning environment, surprising things arise.

Is there enough demand for experimental work for your students to find employment?

ROTONDI: It's easier to get a job when you're inventive and you've found your own voice. Your work is identifiable. The passion comes through. Clients want to work with somebody who's committed. They also require the skill level, manual and intellectual. We are getting young architects to think and make simultaneously, to be good with both their minds and hands. The kind of work that you do attracts clients. Period. Those who don't grasp this simple relationship continue to wonder how to get better projects. If you do cheap, crummy work you attract cheap, crummy clients. If you push the limits, then you attract clients who also expect this.

This morning I was looking through Architectural Digest *—which is not an architecture magazine in a sense that would be recognized here. Nevertheless, especially in light of my conversation with April, I was struck by how wealthy people have used and will use architecture and interior design to create fictional environments for themselves. "I might be just a schmuck who made a lot of money," seems to be the thinking, "but if I surround myself with pilasters and pediments, marble and gold, the right draperies and paintings and books, then I will be like European royalty." Do you think that catering to that impulse will remain part of the role of architects?*

ROTONDI: There are a lot of different ways to practice architecture. I've staked out my way, which is to make buildings that reflect the way our lives really are, not the way we'd like to pretend they are. First, visualize your whole life; second, ask what the "big idea" is; and third, construct it of parts that will perform spontaneously and with similar purpose. Continuity, integrity, and generosity are essential aspects of any system — life, mechanical, or aesthetic — and will perform the best for the longest duration. We have been exploring every corner of contemporary life, and to be able to do that for other people is a great reward. The building or interior that clients get might not be something they recognize as familiar. It might be at the same time something strange and comfortable. They've never seen it before, but they can live in it.

How did you meet April Greiman, and how did you present what you needed?

ROTONDI: I knew her work. It was one of a kind, yet not repetitive. A graduate student who had spoken to April about a lecture series poster introduced us. We met at a restaurant I'd designed and talked for hours. Part of the conversation was about SCI-Arc's need to grow to a higher and more sophisticated level in every way. I felt strongly that the aspirations of the school should be embodied in its entire graphics program—print and motion.

When April describes herself and her work, one has the impression of being on a different plane, in a different universe, from other graphic designers—even the most well-known ones—who are still at the effect of carrying out clients' wishes. April says that her clients never "demand" anything. In a world where graphic designers are sometimes viewed between word processors and interior decorators, what is it that makes her different, that commands that level of respect?

ROTONDI: Her spirit. She's an evolved spirit. She's energy. You go near her and it's like you plug yourself into a wall socket. It feels good. You just want to keep doing it.

Kinda like sex?

ROTONDI: Yes, but it's pure energy, somewhere between sexuality and spirituality. The quest is tapping into that. You just look at her work and know it's the way it should be. Her work is about ideas. It's not about selling or about marketing, although it ultimately does that. SCI-Arc has a very definite structure, but it's as invisible as possible. One event bumps into a second event to create a third event. You can look at one of April's posters, and it seems to be complete chaos, too. But the more you look at it, the more you can see the order and reason. It's a process of discovery, a terrific feeling.

Does anyone complain that SCI-Arc's materials are hard to read? Parents, alumni, trustees? What do you say?

ROTONDI: Yeah, some of them do. I say, "Don't be so impatient. Everything isn't a quick read. Sit down quietly, spend some time with it, and engage yourself." Remember, we're not doing these materials for sixty-year-old CEOs. They're for eighteen- to twenty-five-year-olds who can take in and process information faster than you or I can imagine. I asked April to learn about the school, who we are, what we do, and what it means. Then I asked her to make the Student Workbook accordingly, which outlined the curriculum and the projects in a way that requires all the senses to be engaged to read it. Just like an experience with architecture. It should be an experience of the school, not merely the ideas of it. This workbook has attracted many students. The board of directors is pleased with the enrollment statistics.

Can you describe how you work together with April, and how you evaluate the results?

ROTONDI: I start by discussing, generally, the ideas and feelings I have and then in some detail the nature of the problem. With some designers it is wise to let them help define as well as solve the problem. April is an excellent collaborator. When you work with her you don't have to worry about the quality or precision of the outcome. You may wonder what it is you are going to end up with, but if you remain open and flexible and have the wonder of a child, the results are surprising and enchanting. The more she has done — postcards, brochures, books, and Web sites — the more the quality of this work has influenced our students. It did not take long before the students petitioned me to ask her to permanently teach.

Did you appreciate the letterhead design when you first saw it?

ROTONDI: I had asked, "What if you made a piece of stationery that made you feel like the page is already covered, like an aerial view or map of the city?" Then April said, "What if I were to put a line through it so it looked like someone had put their hand to it?" When I'm outside architecture I always try to suspend judgment as long as possible, but when I saw the design I thought, That's it! I knew you didn't even have to put a letter on it to convey a message. In the beginning, everybody complained about it: "You can't write a letter on it." "It looks messy, like somebody spilled their lunch." But eventually it engaged people. It's interactive. We've reprinted it many times.

When many people think of corporate or organizational identity, they think logo and logo sheets with reproduction art for sizes from a quarter-inch to building signage, a palette of corporate colors, a manual, and so forth. Do you think the paradigms of identity are changing?

ROTONDI: Many institutional structures are predicated on systems theories that have time structures that are static and synchronous. This exists only in our minds; our behavior is inherently more spontaneous and fluid. The type of fixed identity you describe comes out of a static culture that wishes for an immutable world. Until now, we've lived in a society in which a very few people make decisions that affect very many. All that is changing. Print and digital are enhancing each other's performance and spheres of influence. The identity of an organization must be fluid and multifaceted, yet be an integral part of its character. Integrity is based on ideas, not the marketplace, so designers and clients will have to be clear on what the "big idea" is that gives a human organization a sense of real purpose—a purpose that is humanist, not merely economic. Throughout history the best things with enduring life cycles have balanced culture and commerce for the common good. My intention working with April was that these values and ideas would be more deeply explored and understood as we progressed through the creative process.

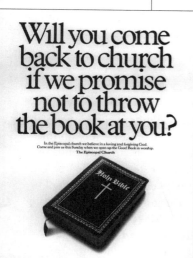

The Rev. George H. Martin, formerly pastor of St. Luke's **EPISCOPAL CHURCH** in Minneapolis, is executive director of the Episcopal Ad Project, an independent, nonprofit ministry that offers print advertising for other churches to use. The initial market for the ads was Episcopal churches, but interest from many other churches led the project to release its ads for use in all denominations. The Ad Project also produces posters, Christmas cards, and calendars. Rev. Martin is a graduate of Hobart College and Bexley Hall Seminary, and has done graduate work at Virginia Theological Seminary, where he is a consultant to the national Episcopal Church in the areas of communications and new church development.

Dean Hanson is a group head at Fallon Worldwide (formerly **FALLON MCELLIGOTT**), the Minneapolis-based advertising and branding agency founded in 1981 by account manager Pat Fallon, copywriter Tom McElligott, and art director Nancy Rice "with more hopes than money." Not long after the agency opened, *Advertising Age* magazine named Fallon "Agency of the Year," and from its inception the agency quickly gained a reputation as a daring and imaginative shop, garnering numerous awards and national accounts, including the Federal Express

Corporation, Timex Group Ltd., and Porsche U.S.A. Famous campaigns have included "Perception/
Reality" for *Rolling Stone, Time* magazine's "Red Box" campaign, and Prudential's "Be Your Own
Rock." Now part of France's Publicis Group, with offices in New York, London, Singapore, Hong Kong,
and São Paulo, the agency has annual billings of more than $1 billion. The ads described on these
pages were designed by Nancy Rice and by Hanson, a graduate of the Minneapolis College of Art
and Design, who was the seventh employee of the then-fledgling agency.

Not too many agencies can claim that among the clients who gave
them the opportunity to do their coolest work is an Episcopal priest. Great
work. Is its purpose to get a job done or to win awards? Perhaps the answer can
come from a higher authority. Certain firms and agencies, on their way up the
ladder to recognition, glory, and national clients, launched their reputations by
doing free work for local merchants and nonprofits, who ostensibly allowed
total creative freedom in return. Fallon got its start with ads for a Minneapolis
barbershop, which featured a stock photo of Albert Einstein, white hair sticking
up in disarray, under the headline "A Bad Haircut Can Make Anyone Look
Dumb." Ads for the Episcopal Church were equally smart and funny. The
agency cleaned up at the New York Art Directors Club awards show, and its
next clients included FedEx and Porsche. This practice became the subject of
a rather scathing advertising column in the *New York Times*, I was most interested
in hearing from the client. Did he feel "used"? Or did the ads work as well
for the church as they did for the agency? Reverend Martin retorted: "We have
one of the most successful campaigns in the history of advertising!" Here's
what else he had to say.

What inspired you to first think about advertising?

MARTIN: I wanted to reach the unchurched people in the immediate neighborhood of the church I served. The original purpose of the campaign was to
change people's Sunday morning habits. We had a community newspaper, and
I figured some good advertising might set us apart and bring badly needed
attention to our church.

*Here's one ad that shows Moses and the Ten Commandments. The headline reads, "For
fast, fast, fast relief, take two tablets." Some people would say you are selling religion like
Alka-Seltzer. Do you think that's a necessity in a culture brought up on TV commercials?*

MARTIN: When I read the prophets, the sermons of Paul, and the parables of Jesus, what I find is a language that was contemporary at the time. I don't think we're doing anything new under the sun. I mean, you don't have to use religious language to communicate about God. You use ordinary language and ordinary examples. Jeremiah once took a pot and smashed it and said, "This is going to happen to us if we don't change our ways." That's great advertising.

Did any clergy of any other churches or people in your congregation object to the ads?

MARTIN: There are always people who look at things from a myopic point of view. They're too concerned with appearances. For me, if we disturb some of the purist types within the institution, it's almost like a litmus test that says we must be doing something right. Getting people upset is not our primary mission, but I've learned not to be disturbed by it.

When you began your relationship with Fallon McElligott, who approached whom?

MARTIN: I went to Tom McElligott, we had lunch together, and I presented the case, as it were. At the time, my urban congregation wasn't in a terrible section of town, but it certainly wasn't in a growing area. We needed to attract new people. I presented an advertising problem, and he was intrigued by the idea. Our first ads were done on the side.

On the side of what?

MARTIN: On the side of our regular work. At the time he was employed at Bozell and Jacobs. He and Pat Fallon had a side business called "Lunchtime Limited," or something like that. They had a few clients they took on the side, and we became one of them. An initial set of six ads was developed, and we've kept within the same basic format. There has been evolution and change and, I think, greater sophistication throughout the history of the project.

When you saw the presentation of those first ads, what was your initial reaction?

MARTIN: I really enjoyed them because they had a sense of humor and a fresh, snappy quality. They addressed the key issue we identified, which was how to get people who are not in the habit of going to church to at least give it a try. As time went by, we also confronted some of the more troubling aspects of our secular culture and its values. We also turned our attention to certain people within the religious world who were giving religion a bad name.

Have you ever rejected any headlines or artwork as too far out?

MARTIN: Yes. There was one that showed a picture of the devil. It was an attempt to say something about free speech, which wasn't an issue we needed to deal with at the time. Another one had a picture of Jim Jones back in the days when we were questioning cults, and I remember the headline saying something like, "Before you accept Christ into your life, make sure it's really Christ." It was just too blatant.

Can you usually tell what's right or not from a gut reaction?

MARTIN: Yes. Here's an example, we had a monumental struggle with the agency folks over an ad headlined, "Where Women Stand in the Episcopal Church." It took them two years to understand what I was saying; why we needed an ad that addressed the fact that women participate fully in the ministry and life of our church. In many churches, especially the Roman Catholic, women are excluded. We needed to make our position clear and positive to people with feminist concerns. The struggle with the agency was over the visual. They wanted a pulpit and I wanted an altar, and we went round and round. They kept saying, "It's got to be a pulpit." I kept saying, "You don't know who we are if you say that." I wouldn't give on it, and we finally shot it as an altar. It was an award-winning ad that has really worked well. They were real stubborn, but I wouldn't go along with them because we're not a pulpit-centered church; we're a sacramental church.

Can you explain the distinction?

MARTIN: In a pulpit-centered church, which tends to be true of many Protestant churches, the most important thing that happens is the sermon. In our church, the most important thing that happens is the Eucharist, or the Communion. In the Catholic tradition, whether Episcopal or Roman, you have to be an ordained priest to celebrate.

Did you want to show a woman offering a wafer or wine at the altar?

MARTIN: The neat thing about that ad, and what makes it work so well, is it doesn't show anybody. It just shows an altar—a very clearly identifiable Christian altar. In the parlance of the trade, it's a quick read.

You say it was an award-winning ad. I'm going to read you a quote from a New York Times *article headlined "Ad Agencies' Obsession with Winning Awards":*

Many executives also detect a frenzied effort among agencies, particularly new ones, to do work strictly for its award potential. The strategy, they say, was perfected by Fallon McElligott in Minneapolis . . . "Part of Fallon's strategy," executives of other agencies said, "was to seek out small clients and pro bono accounts (among them a Minneapolis barbershop and, more recently, the Episcopal Church) for which the agency could do highly creative, even daring, work without risking the client's rejection. The strategy paid off in a spate of Gold Pencils at the One Show. It also helped the agency win *Advertising Age*'s agency-of-the-year award in 1983."

There are a lot of questions that come to mind. First of all, I want to address the phrase, "highly creative and daring work without risk of the client's rejection." The assumption is because they did the work for free, you had to accept it. Were you in that position?

MARTIN: No. It's true that Fallon and McElligott don't want to work through layers of committees. They want to know who has the responsibility for approval, and if it involves a huge process that takes months and various meetings, they avoid that client. In terms of our relationship, I'm the only one who says *yea* or *nay* to things. But I do, occasionally, reject things.

According to that article, there is the feeling in some agency circles that the work they did for you was used to attract national accounts—that you were used, so to speak.

MARTIN: We have one of the most distinctive campaigns in the history of advertising! I like Fallon McElligott's commitment to awards. That's how we know that they think, "We're not just in it for the bucks; we're in it for our quality." There's a freedom, too, for the people who work on our campaign. They can get real tired of writing copy for cereal. An account like this comes along, and it turns on their creative juices. And it has not all been easy. Once you move beyond creating ads to doing a successful campaign, there has to be a momentum to keep it going. We struggle to keep freshness in it because the history of advertising is the history of campaigns losing their edge.

Then you don't see awards as creative people patting each other on the back? To you they really are a mark of excellence, acknowledged excellence?

MARTIN: Absolutely. What's interesting is that when Fallon McElligott goes to pitch a client like Dow Jones or Armour Foods, they take our religious stuff along. You might think they would say, "We better not show that God work."

Here's another quote from the Times *article, "Awards create imitation." They show a couple of award-winning campaigns and how they were knocked off by other agencies, other products. Did other churches or nonprofit organizations copy your advertising concept?*

MARTIN: Not directly. There are a few other examples of sparkling religious advertising. But that's it, a very few. I'm surprised that we have had the field to ourselves for so long. But we have a willingness to express a sense of humor. Some people say, "You shouldn't laugh at religion." There's a risk factor that we assume most institutions are not willing to take on, which is why so much advertising with institutional connections is bland and boring and dull.

Did you meet your initial objectives?

MARTIN: The ultimate tragedy is that we have these wonderful materials, and yet, in terms of individual churches, there still is the issue of how do we begin to make use of them?

Do you mean that they can't afford the ad space?

MARTIN: Yes. We're dealing with small organizations, individual churches, that for the most part have limited discretionary budgets. It's too bad because my experience is that when we do run an ad, the results are astounding. When our diocese could pay for it, we had the ads blown up into billboards at our local airport. I have seen the arresting quality of this work. It literally stops people in their tracks in the middle of a busy airport. Their heads jerk back and they say, "What did I see?" And they stop and they read it.

It says in your brochure that the Episcopal Ad Project was founded in 1979 at St. Luke's Episcopal Church. There's kind of a success story there, too, correct?

MARTIN: We started by running the ads in a community newspaper. Then, we saw the average age of the congregation gradually drop lower and lower; the hair in the congregation turned from gray to varying colors as they exist in God's world. We saw the Sunday school grow. People would say, "I never heard of the Episcopal Church before, but I came to check this church out because I wanted to see if you really matched up with what the ads were saying." Or, "I'd been away from church; I didn't think that anything could get me started again, but gee those ads were good."

Was your thinking that if the ads spoke the twentieth-century American vernacular, people would sense that the priest would, too? That the church would, too? And that the people who would be attracted might not necessarily be Episcopalians to start with?

MARTIN: Exactly. They were all kinds of Christians who had left the fold, so to speak. We do have some people who are still part of the old, stuffy Episcopal Church, and they'd like to keep it that way.

So it wasn't just that you ran some ads. You made some fundamental changes in the church.

MARTIN: That's true across the board. The Episcopal Church had been changing. It isn't just the church of the establishment anymore. The irony of this is that we have no control over accuracy. The Episcopal Ad Project distributes these ads, and we have no way of saying, "You can only use these ads if the reality of your particular church matches what the ads say." But I think there tends to be a fair correspondence between a church that has vision enough to use our ads and what goes on inside. I know that there are some real medieval places, but they're probably not going to use our material.

Let's say you were addressing people with administrative responsibilities for other churches or service organizations that weren't attracting enough people. What advice would you give about advertising and promotion?

MARTIN: I'd say, you've got to be willing to be provocative and approach things with a sense of humor, or you're not going to get people to pay attention. We really err when we take ourselves so doggone seriously all the time. But the willingness to provoke and to ask the tough questions has got to be there. And you always have to keep up the struggle to keep the campaign fresh.

I RECENTLY FOLLOWED UP WITH DEAN HANSON.

Dean, how long have you been with Fallon?

HANSON: I was one of the original hires. It's been more than twenty years.

And you've seen the agency grow from a five-person shop to a $1 billion global agency. What were some of the biggest changes on the creative side?

HANSON: The public has become much more sophisticated, less tolerant of bad ads, and more appreciative of good ones. Technology has made our job much easier technically, and more difficult from a turnaround standpoint . . . shorter deadlines. Copy length has shortened dramatically, in both print and broadcast.

When people, like newspaper advertising columnists, presuppose that doing pro bono work means never risking the client's rejection, what do you say?

HANSON: For a small client it's a challenge to communicate in a way that anyone notices. Your budget just doesn't let you outspend anyone you're up against. So you've got to push things a bit to get noticed. Balanced against that is the reality that just about every client has a group they can't afford to offend in the process, so that means walking a fine line. And inevitably, if you're doing your job right, sooner or later you're going to push up against somebody's comfort zone.

Besides having the opportunity to do those fresh, snappy, award-winning ads, were there any other rewards to working for the Episcopal Church?

HANSON: No matter which client we're working for, we try to accurately reflect their personalities and their value systems. With this client, we were fighting misconceptions. It was an interesting exercise to shake the public's perception that the Episcopal Church was a staid, humorless, judgmental entity. And to communicate that it has tremendous relevance in the modern world for the way people live today.

Does Fallon still do pro bono work?

HANSON: We continue to do pro bono. It's always been an important part of our culture. A couple of current examples are the Children's Defense Fund, a children's advocacy group, and Camp Heartland, a camp for HIV kids and their families. Actually, the work for Camp Heartland goes way beyond communications. Every spring our entire Minneapolis staff spends a day at the facility, building and maintaining the camp. Think art directors with chain saws.

How do you convince institutional clients, who can be very conservative, to take a chance on humor and other creative strategies they may think are risky?

HANSON: If it's done correctly, humor connects in ways that a serious tone often can't. The average person can easily put up a mental barrier to ad copy and visuals that play on tragedy or guilt. Very few people can resist humor.

I've been advising students and young designers who complain that they have nothing but school assignments in their portfolios to find themselves some local nonprofit clients —or retailers or barbershops—and do great work. Do you agree?

HANSON: It's worked since the beginning of the industry. I've never met a good creative that didn't follow this route to some degree.

What is your advice to young people who would like to be art directors at agencies like yours? How should they get started?

HANSON: Pretty simple. Study *Archive, Communication Arts,* and award show annuals. Memorize them. Find a good partner to collaborate with to develop your book. Get the best job you can out of school and then work nights on your own stuff. Don't be afraid to jump jobs frequently. If you're not doing better work each year you need to move.

The Des Moines Metro Waste Authority *and* Pattee Design

21

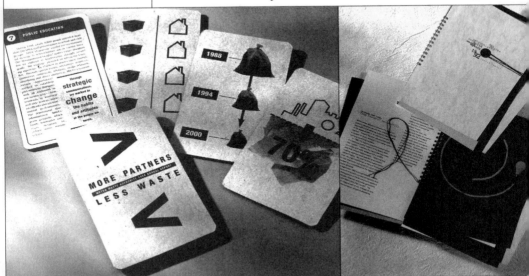

Catherine Huggins is communications administrator for the **DES MOINES METRO WASTE AUTHORITY** (MWA), a $12 million organization that manages a regional collection center for household hazardous waste, a landfill, a compost center, and a transfer station on behalf of its twenty-one member communities. A graduate of Drake University, Huggins is a past president of the Central Iowa Chapter of the Public Relations Society of America and was formerly chief speechwriter and deputy press secretary for Iowa governor Terry Branstand.

Past president of the Art Directors Association of Iowa and president of AIGA/Iowa, *Steve Pattee* founded **PATTEE DESIGN** in 1995 with designer Kelly Styles. Pattee's work has been recognized worldwide in design exhibitions and industry publications. Two of the firm's annual reports for MWA have been on view in an environmental exhibit at the Smithsonian in Washington, D.C. A graduate of the University of Iowa, Pattee is a member of Trout Unlimited and the Federation of American Rivers.

Catherine Huggins was faced with a typical client dilemma: how to continue commissioning groundbreaking design within the growing political and budgetary constraints of a large municipal agency. Three-quarters of the way through these interviews I realized that this story could serve as a paradigm illustration for the battle of Designers (Pattee Design) versus Philistines (Iowa Waste Haulers): Dedicated designers work miracles with impossibly low budgets in short time frames. They spend late nights mixing shreds of newspaper and grass clippings into paper pulp, sweet-talking printers into running the results through their presses, getting local binderies to make special dye-cuts, affixing grommets, hand-knotting twine. The results are met with wild acclaim of the design community and regional and national design awards. Haulers and city administrators don't see things quite the same way, though. To them, the reports are examples of government excess that contribute to ever-rising fees. Battle lines are drawn: the client is told by board members to "curtail those designers," who almost lose the account to a big agency. The story has a happy ending, though. Designers are given the mandate to blend educational content with fiscal responsibility, to produce more "green" design that won't make the audience see red.

At the AIGA/Minneapolis competition, the annual report for the Des Moines Metropolitan Solid Waste Authority just jumped out at the judges. It seemed to be daringly original as well as appropriate for the client. How did you meet the MWA and start working with them?

PATTEE: They were working with another design firm and something went haywire, some timing issue on a newsletter, and we got a call. Generally we don't do newsletters, we're involved in business-to-business collateral. But this time we thought, "Hey, why not? This might be a good entree." The next project was the annual report, which also started with a call: "We need three hundred annual reports."

Did the assignment to produce such a small quantity signal that you had the opportunity to create something unique, virtually handmade?

PATTEE: All of a sudden you're in a different world of production criteria. And because the MWA's image — progressive-minded, ecologically up-to-date — had to be demonstrated as well as projected, the worst thing anybody could do would have been eight colors on virgin, bright-white paper.

Was the client open to unusual ideas from the beginning?

PATTEE: Because they had no experience creating communication tools, they were very open. So the first thing I said was, "If you only need three hundred reports, we're going the stop at grocery stores and pick up boxes." We built a paper dummy and had it Wire-O'd.

Then these covers are real corrugated boxes, not printed to look like boxes?

PATTEE: Right. The inside cover might read, "Charmin'"; it might read, "AA Large Eggs." Because these are reports from the organization that manages the city dump, the mandate has always been to use as little virgin material as possible, cut out the steps, simplify the process. We still operate the same way. Our pictures are shot with a Polaroid camera, photocopies are used as art, we make our mechanicals from laser prints, photocopies, overlays. In terms of press OKs, we say, "Just run it." There are no exact color matches or trapping issues.

Don't conventional mechanicals use a lot more material—boards, overlays, tissues, flaps—than sending a disk to the printer?

PATTEE: Paper consumption has not gone down because of the computer! Think about the number of reams of white 8½ × 11 laser paper everyone goes through a month.

One year the report had a torn cover. Was that intentional?

PATTEE: I can't tell you how many people asked that! We wanted to reintroduce the orange color and have the report look a little, well, trashy. In the office, we tore all three hundred covers one by one to achieve what we were after. But there were quite a few calls, like "We really like this report, but our copy came in damaged."

I imagine all the time you spent tearing those covers was done for love, not money.

PATTEE: Yes, ma'am.

Tell me about the report with the cover line, "This Annual Report Is Trash." Are these pieces of old newspaper I see in the cover stock?

PATTEE: The paper maker, Jerusalem Paper Works in Omaha, manufactured it to order for us, using thousands of old copies of the *Des Moines Register*. The situation was, "What can you come up with this year? Can you bring us some other ideas?" This time, we hand-punched the reports and tied them with jute twine.

Isn't all this handwork very time-consuming?

PATTEE: You can do it when the press run is three hundred to five hundred copies. We spent five to six weeks—tops—on each of these reports from start to finish. And the budget has ranged from $11,000 to $18,000, including design, writing, and production. We've let some serendipity get into the process. Two weeks before the deadline, Kelly and I were beating our heads against the wall to come up with an idea. She threw some paper samples down in frustration, we loved the way they looked when they fell, and said, "That's it!" The pages were die-cut by the guy who printed it, one step up from a quick printer. The red tabs are waste from the red sheet. Again, we tied the string on ourselves.

It sounds like working for this client has meant a lot to you.

PATTEE: MWA has made us more conscious about what we can do for all our clients. You can't be 100 percent environmentally correct on every project, but you can be more sensitive. For example, our biggest client is Principal Financial Corporation, an entirely different mindset. The Principal annual report press run is 300,000 copies. Last year we cut the trim size by one-half inch and saved the equivalent of 44,000 pages. So we're always asking ourselves, "What can we do that saves resources?" It's not like the phone is ringing off the hook with people wanting us to do recycled annual reports. But when I talk to prospects, these books demonstrate that they're not going to get a canned look from us.

Another year, you used a pretty big embossing die on the cover. Is there ever a perception that these techniques are too expensive?

PATTEE: Embossing is just as environmentally correct as you can get! You're not using any ink at all, just changing the shape of the material. And this book is 5½ × 8½, half the size of a normal annual report. That year we had to reestablish ourselves with new marketing people who had come in from ad agencies and were used to a certain kind of process. Also, the reports were sent out to the public for the first time, so the report had to reflect the agency's decree: reduce landfill by 50 percent. Every year the message has become more pointed: you—the consumer—have got to think differently and behave differently. We reasoned, "How do people learn? Flash cards!" That was the germ of the concept. We created a series of icons that identified the facilities citizens needed to become familiar with. Readers were asked to forward the reports to a school when they were finished with them, and over 80 percent did. The reports were reused in classrooms.

You said that new marketing people came in. What happened?

PATTEE: We were let go on the account! They wanted to consolidate everything at this high-test agency who'd come in with a big dog-and-pony show. We got the annual report back, but they said to us, "You have $11,000 to produce 3,500 copies." Seven times as many copies for two-thirds of the cost! I said, "We'll do it." Then I had to get as down and dirty as you can get. The result is this "To Our Trashholders" book.

Which looks like it's printed on your average 50 lb. offset.

PATTEE: It's hard to convince printers that we don't mind all the show-through. But it's part of the effect: we make the corrections by cutting in patches of laser prints, and there are differences in color when the type patches don't match. It doesn't matter; things that would be considered mistakes or imperfections in another kind of job are part of the nature of the beast. We made the illustrations out of public-domain clip art, did Monty-Python things with it, cutting by hand and collaging it. It was like three or four people in our office were playing Scrabble with pictures.

Am I looking at grass clippings in the cover stock this time?

PATTEE: Yep. The same manufacturer, Jerusalem, used over 750 lbs. of real yard waste to make the paper. And the printer was not too happy about running it through his press! Our suppliers know their presses will get gunked up, so we're always cultivating relationships so they'll be willing to work with us and make these things happen.

It looks beautiful enough to sell to the Pottery Barn for photo frames and lampshades. Maybe they can recoup their losses by doing something like that . . . In addition to the annual reports, you've also done some informational brochures.

PATTEE: They're all about managing waste without adding to the waste stream.

What about this logo? Had you been hiding it from us all along?

PATTEE: That was the agency's doing. Speed lines! I was so steamed I got the client on the phone. They said, "We needed an identity that made us look progressive and strong."

Some people might say it looks like a late-seventies cliché.

PATTEE: They spent about $70,000 on that thing!

How did that make you feel after you spent all that time cutting corners by hand, literally and figuratively?

PATTEE: Well, I'll just say that the MWA is now positioned in the industry as leaders. The message is going out all over the world. They are an example to their peers in other municipalities and states. We've demonstrated how good, solid creative has value and achieves results.

What's ahead for the next report?

PATTEE: We're looking into these guys who are doing plastic board, kind of like compressed bubble wrap, made out of used disposable diapers.

LATER, I SPOKE WITH CATHERINE HUGGINS.

I should start with a friendlier question, but Steve Pattee says that you were one of the people who came in from the agency side and burst the bubble on the annual report. What happened?

HUGGINS: It was a different era. In the early nineties the organization had a stable financial future and could afford the luxury of annual reports of that stature, with unique materials and design. A Supreme Court decision changed all that; they struck down "flow control" laws that had in essence given munici-palities and states virtual monopolies so they could count on a certain revenue stream. Waste disposal is now considered interstate commerce, so if haulers can get a better deal in the next county they'll take the trash there. In 1996 alone we lost over $1 million in fees. Plus, there are increased regulations: We have to reduce the amount of waste in landfills by 50 percent by the year 2000. We've spent $26 million since 1990 on curbside recycling programs, teaching people how to compost yard waste, and creating byproducts that can be used by other industries. So we can't have a perception that we're spending a lot of money on the annual report.

I also understand that $18,000 was the top budget for any of these reports. To a corporation that spends a quarter of a million dollars or so on an annual report, isn't $18,000 minuscule?

HUGGINS: You have to look at the cost per unit. If we're printing three hundred copies, that's $60 per book. We had to reassess those costs, and have brought it down to $5 to $7 per copy, which is in line with what corporations spend.

Didn't those early-nineties reports have a benefit to the MWA that can't be measured in dollars, positioning the organization as a leader and so forth?

HUGGINS: Yes. The best example of that is the flash cards. They were written up in the *Des Moines Register.* The report had three audiences: The reports were first sent to our usual audience—business leaders, regulators, board members, elected officials, the general public. An enclosed letter and label asked them to send the reports, after they were done reading them, to middle and secondary schools for use in science classrooms. Then the students were asked to send them to graphic design schools. And from there they were sent back to the MWA. About 80 percent of five thousand came back. It was amazing, and wonderful. A recycling-in-action story.

Several months ago, the New York Times Magazine *ran a cover story claiming that recycling is one of the biggest farces ever pulled on the American people, that it costs much more to recycle than to dump waste in landfills, there's plenty of land available, etc. What do you make of that thesis?*

HUGGINS: Encouraging people to change their lifestyles does cost money. Recycling is expensive—it costs us $2.03 a month per household recycling bin for education and maintenance and transportation, and we only get 13 cents back. But it's an investment in our future. There may be plenty of land, but it's not permittable land—we're not going to get permits to dump on it—and the airspace has to be maintained. Recycling now diverts over 5 percent of the waste stream, and it's finally becoming engrained in our culture.

Are you saying that you won't be able to do anything like those flash cards again?
That the glory days of MWA annual reports are over? What about getting
corporate sponsorship?

HUGGINS: With our $1 million shortfall, our board only lets us do what's
absolutely necessary to run the landfill. And with so many other needs, I don't
think corporations will sponsor something like our annual report.

What's it been like to work with Pattee Design?

HUGGINS: Steve and Kelly like to take creative risks, but they're easy to work
with. You don't think, "Oh, here's another meeting where we'll be knocking
heads with the creatives." And when you go into their facility everything is
very environmentally conscious. The floors are recycled textured wood. The
desks have brushed metal bases. The walls are plyboard. They reuse their
graphic design as wallpaper.

To you, what's the key difference between working with an ad agency and
a design firm?

HUGGINS: With a design firm, there's less layers and more accountability.
You can just sit down and talk. Designers can't push the accountability
onto other layers: "Such-and-such was the copywriter's fault" or "the account
service team didn't tell me about that." Often it's the difference between
a larger and a smaller firm. At a large firm you can always find someone to
talk to. If the account supervisor's not there, you can talk to the president.
A smaller firm can make you more nervous at deadline time because the
principals may be serving other accounts, and sometimes you have to wait
patiently until they get back from a meeting. But Pattee Design has never
missed a deadline.

Steve told me they got temporarily fired when the agency people came in.

HUGGINS: Not true! Several years ago we wanted to pull together our advertising, public relations, and design and put out an RFP to 100 agencies, most of
them local. Pattee Design was one of them, continued to work for us on an ad
hoc basis, and in fact ended up among the six finalists.

What was the process like?

HUGGINS: The RFP had an eight-page questionnaire that covered such questions as, "Describe your strategic planning process for clients." "Does your firm possess environmental design experience?" "Do you have an in-house recycling program?" "What is the one strength of the account team you would assign to the MWA that sets it apart from its competition?" All the agencies were rated in the areas of stability, solid-waste-industry knowledge, average billable rates, account team depth and expertise. We undertook an exhaustive search in which we reviewed the formal proposals , took agency tours, and had what we call a dog-and-pony show by each contender. CMF&Z—Creswell, Munsell, Fultz and Zirbel Inc., a Young and Rubicam affiliate—was designated agency of record.

Did you ask any of the agencies for spec work?

HUGGINS: The agencies were more than welcome to bring in whatever they wanted to.

Did they bring in anything that surprised you?

HUGGINS: Not really. One group brought in some confetti, as if the whole thing were a festive event; another, some brown paper bags. I took great care to make sure there was a level playing field, and that even though I had been at CMF&Z, that wasn't going to influence our decision. The first thing we undertook with the agency was a communications audit; the board thought Des Moines Metropolitan Solid Waste Authority (DMMSWA) was too bulky. So we conducted benchmark research—focus groups—first asking whether it made sense to change the name, then identifying eight to ten possible names and positioning statements. It was ultimately decided to change DMMSWA to MWA. The logo was created by Bill Fultz at CMF&Z. His forte is developing symbols; he's just great at it. The decreasing lines communicate a subtle message of waste reduction. We use PMS 576 green, which is an environmentally appropriate color, and Proterra paper for a consistent look.

Do you know what Steve Pattee thinks of the logo?

HUGGINS: No.

Well, not much. It sounded like he was more than a little upset that after they put in all that time doing $18,000 annual reports and tying on strings by hand—and not charging the MWA for the time—you were able to find $70,000 for that logo.

HUGGINS: It was $47,000 for everything, including focus groups and the name change.

Graphic designers are very sensitive to the fact that PR agencies, ad agencies, everybody else, seems to get bigger fees. Anyway, in the last few years there's hardly been a design annual—type directors, communication graphics—that one could open without seeing an MWA annual report. What do awards mean to you, if anything?

HUGGINS: It's fun to do award-winning design and have your work acknowledged by your peers at industry conferences. It's great when somebody says something is really neat or when the *Des Moines Register* writes up your annual report. Awards make us feel like the partnership works. But right now we're into cost-effective creativity. We have to prioritize our limited dollars while respecting the audience's perceptions. When we do the right things with our budget and educate the most people, then I consider the project a success.

Are you saying that it could be a problem for you if something looks expensive that was actually done for free?

HUGGINS: Yes! The early-nineties reports were perceived as excessive. The ultimate-end audience did not see the value. In fact, those reports made them hostile. It was a real love-hate thing. The reports were memorable to designers and to business and civic leaders, elected officials and the general public. But they were sore spots to our board members, waste handlers, city administrators, public works directors, regulatory officials—important members of our constituency. They said, "You've got to curtail those designers!" There was a public outcry. Years later we still get letters; they're still talking about them.

What do you think accounts for that disparity?

HUGGINS: The people who hate them are the people who pay our disposal fees! In 1985, the fee was less than $5 per ton. It was more than $30 ten years later. That's a sixfold increase in a decade.

So they made the annual report into the scapegoat?

HUGGINS: Those people do their own reports in-house—they're real boring —but the thinking is, "All I need is a printout of the financials and that's X less dollars I'll have to pay."

That must put you in a tough position.

HUGGINS: It's a challenge. Our most successful projects will have an educational component rather than being created to look flashy or win awards. People need to be able to see the purpose. Now we have a standard communications work plan, which includes identifying areas such as, "Who is the target audience?" "What awareness or action do we want to communicate?" "What benefit should the communication promise?" "Why should the target audience member believe us?" The mandate from Washington is, "Create a government that works better and costs less." For us, it's reuse and recycle. We are doing 4 × 9 brochures. Instead of sending a resource directory, we'll ask what the caller is looking for and fax the relevant page. We aim to maintain the quality level without going over the top.

The Wadsworth Atheneum *and* Peter Good

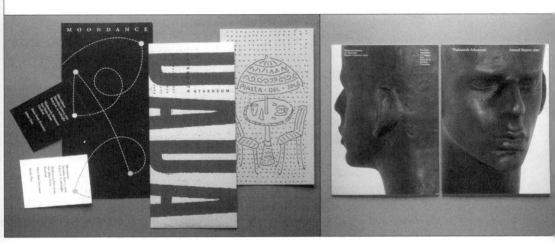

Patrick McCaughey became director of the **WADSWORTH ATHENEUM**, American's oldest public art museum, in 1988. Founded in 1842 by philanthropist Daniel Wadsworth, the Atheneum has grown from a single structure housing 80 pictures to a five-building complex with more than 45,000 works of art, including American and European paintings and sculpture, contemporary art and works on paper. In 1989, the Atheneum hosted the controversial Robert Mapplethorpe exhibition that attracted 72,000 visitors. Dr. McCaughey (pronounced "McCacky") received his doctorate from Monash University, Melbourne. Previously he was visiting professor of Australian studies at Harvard and, prior to that, director of the National Gallery in Melbourne, where he was also a newspaper art critic. He has held prestigious academic appointments, including a Harkness Fellowship and a fellowship at the Museum of Modern Art in New York.

A graduate of the University of Connecticut's School of Fine Arts, **PETER GOOD** is known for his graphic design and illustration work for corporations, museums, and arts organizations. With his wife, Janet Cummings, he is principal of the six-person graphic design studio

Cummings & Good, based in Chester, Connecticut. Good's work has consistently received awards from all major U.S. graphic design publications and institutions and has been exhibited in museums internationally; several of his posters toured Russia as part of Design USA, a United States Information Agency cultural exchange program. Having provided a coherent system to the museum, Good continues to be involved, currently as a board member.

Wouldn't it be marvelous (to use one of Dr. McCaughey's favorite terms) if each of us had the opportunity to learn about art history — instead of from slide shows in sleep-inducing, darkened art history lecture halls — from an original, energetic museum curator or director like Dr. McCaughey? You would follow the flying coattails of the director through the galleries. And when he'd momentarily brake in front of a painting that you'd never paid much attention to, you'd be transfixed as he said something like: "Just look at the Thomas Coles. These are about finding the real truth in the American landscape. Is America a wild, untouched place, or is it cultivated, tamed, the road paved to expansion and commerce?" All of a sudden, you'd see so much more in that painting (or sculpture or print). Perhaps at museums like Hartford's Wadsworth Atheneum, such a stroke of luck is possible. And wouldn't it be marvelous if each of us had the opportunity to be the graphic designer for such a museum? Dr. McCaughey gave Peter Good that opportunity. Other designers — and leaders of nonprofit organizations — can learn much from how Dr. McCaughey and Peter Good met the museum's goals within the constraints of institutional tradition, a board of directors, local politics, and tight budgets.

You've been here about four years now, and it's a generally accepted fact that you've made quite a difference. Which of your accomplishments are you most proud of?

MCCAUGHEY: It's an evolutionary story. We raised $17 million. We've renovated the galleries, of course, and cleaned lots of pictures. We installed new access ramps for the handicapped. I'm quite proud of our collections of African American art; 85 percent of the residents of Hartford are minority, and it's their museum. But I guess I'm most proud of exhuming the basement. Did you know that there's enough art in the basements of American museums to go around the world three times? It's about time we got it up and let the public have a look at it. I've had one major disappointment: I put forth a proposal to make museum admission free to residents of Hartford. I mean, if they can borrow a book at the public library, why can't they come here for free? And the foundation refused. We did get a grant, however, for $150,000 for the "Colt 4," artists working around Hartford. So you count your blessings.

What are some of your plans for the future?

MCCAUGHEY: To make the museum absolutely sing this year. To raise the level of seriousness of the temporary exhibitions, to do more things on the level of the current Ralph Earl show — Ralph Earl was the leading portrait painter of the Revolutionary War era, and this show was the keynote of our 150th anniversary. To mount more traveling exhibitions from our collections, such as the *200 Years of American Painting*, which went to Paris in 1989.

When J. Carter Brown resigned as director of the National Gallery in Washington, the New York Times *reported, "The age of the imperial museum is ending." Is this a tougher decade for museums?*

MCCAUGHEY: Museums will have to do different kinds of things. Because there will be less money for blockbusters, there will be more emphasis on the permanent collections. New resources are being explored, for example, theme exhibitions. We might do an exhibition on American Impression, drawing on the resources of three or four museums right here in New England.

Let's talk about the importance of graphic design and communications in all of this.

MCCAUGHEY: Oh, enormously important. Hiring Peter Good was one of my key accomplishments.

Well, in the current Wadsworth Atheneum annual report, you write: ". . . Peter Good was chosen from a group of highly gifted graphic designers working in Connecticut. . . . Largely through Mr. Good's inspiration and vision the Wadsworth Atheneum now boasts one of the liveliest quarterly magazines produced by any museum in the northeast of America. . . . It has won awards for its innovation and liveliness." You go on to praise Peter's "gifted mind" and "imagination." How rare that clients publicly praise their graphic designers! Tell me about how Peter Good and his firm were chosen. What were you looking for at the time?

MCCAUGHEY: When I first came here, the situation was graphic anarchy. The membership office would get its designer to do certain things, the public information office would get another designer to do the annual report and a third

designer might be working on the newsletter. The museum projected a graphi-
cally disjointed and incoherent message. We wanted a graphic designer who
could give a real sense of unity to everything from catalogs to posters to the
newsletter to gift cards and tote bags—the whole thing. The pioneer and great
model for this was, of course, the Museum of Modern Art in New York. You can
tell a MoMA catalog or poster from fifty feet away, and it was with that idea in
mind that we set out to find a designer. And it so happens that in and around
the Hartford area there were at least three or four very able graphic designers.
They all knew each other and competition was fierce, so we held what we
frankly called a beauty contest. We wrote to each of them and explained what
our graphic needs were. We were very up-front about the fact that we were
approaching the others, and asked, "If you're interested, would you like to come
in and make a presentation?" We felt that Peter Good made the best case.

How were the designers' presentations? Did you find them similar or dissimilar?

MCCAUGHEY: Oh, they were very dissimilar indeed.

*In what way? What kinds of things did people do or say that caused you to respond
positively or negatively?*

MCCAUGHEY: One designer came in and told us virtually how he thought we
should be running the place, what should be the focus, and so on. Well, there
are a lot of very able people around here who think very hard about our nature
and mission, and we really didn't want a designer who was going to try to
impose his views on us. Some graphic designers have a slightly Napoleonic
view of what their roles are or should be. Other designers we saw had a very
distinct house style, which, impressive as it might be, made us feel like we
would be absorbed into that style, and that didn't seem to be a particularly
attractive option. What was really attractive about Peter was that he had a
terrific sense of the dynamics of the institution, what happens here, what
our goals are. He let us know that he wanted to find a design style for us that
mirrored the goals and ambitions of the institution itself.

*Peter told me that in his first meeting with you he advised against what he called
a "rubber stamp" logo.*

MCCAUGHEY: Absolutely.

Were you originally looking for a logo?

MCCAUGHEY: No. I'm deeply opposed to logos. More time and tears are spent debating what logos should be like than they're ever worth. The idea that we would spend our lifetimes worrying about a damned logo seemed to be the most unprofitable place to start. But recently Peter designed a wonderful mark for our 150th anniversary, which we can stamp on letterheads and paste on the back of envelopes and so on. It's a convincing image of the Atheneum, and it has emerged from our continuing and deepening relationship.

One of the things that's so impressive about all the work the museum has produced—the annual reports, capital campaign brochure, invitations, newsletter—is the quality; a consistently higher quality than one usually associates with nonprofit organizations on small budgets. How do you keep up the quality?

MCCAUGHEY: If you get a great designer like Peter Good you also try to live up to his expectations. He keeps the institute's expectations high as to what the graphic design should be like. We've got an annual budget of just over five million; we're not rich but not starving. It was quite a conscious decision—and now one which is part of the basic culture of the institution—that our graphic communications should be of high quality and maintain our image in the surrounding community upon whom we depend critically for financial help. Peter Good has helped us enormously from time to time by knowing people in the trade who can donate paper and so forth. But at other times we pay. He gives us a very favorable rate, but we've learned to pay for quality.

When you say you've learned to pay, was there some resistance to that in the beginning?

MCCAUGHEY: Not exactly resistance, but it certainly caused some general adjustments around here. And not all good design is necessarily expensive.

Can we talk a bit about how specific projects are handled? Let's say an event is coming up for which you need graphics and you have a briefing or discussion with Peter. What kind of presentation do you like to see?

MCCAUGHEY: It's a much closer relationship than that. We might say to him, we've got this idea, now show us what it should look like.

Is his working relationship primarily with you, or are there other people on the museum staff that he works with?

MCCAUGHEY: He deals mainly with the director of public information, because that's where much of the graphic work is channeled. And you know what happens occasionally in even the best-run places: one too many people talks to the designer, who gets a bit confused, and then we all have a session where we try to sort out what's really happening.

Do you work with his staff? In other words, do you see this relationship as two organizations working together, or is it more like two individuals?

MCCAUGHEY: It's closer to two individuals, but in respect to Peter's staff he's obviously much in demand and we have to trust his shop. On the larger, more important productions—the catalog, the annual report, the capital campaign document—Peter and I have a very close connection. He has a tremendous instinctive feeling for the visual arts. I mean his wife is an artist and he is a close friend of Sol and Carol LeWitt, and so forth. He has a tremendous sense about the Atheneum, that it is a collection of the most diverse art collected over 150 years. It's sort of a pocket battleship of a museum.

Pocket battleship?

MCCAUGHEY: You've seen that for the size of the museum, and for the size of the city, it has a collection of astonishingly high quality. The best pictures of Hartford are equal to the best pictures of Boston and so on.

But if your newsletter hadn't been chosen for the Communication Arts Annual, *I would never have heard of the Atheneum. That would have been my loss, but it would have been a shame. Everyone driving to Boston or northern New England from New York or points south has to go through Hartford. As far as I know, very few people on the way to Vermont say, "Let's stop at the Atheneum and see the art." Why is that?*

MCCAUGHEY: Usually because there are no signs on the highway. There is one now, thank God, a sign that says Wadsworth Atheneum.

Do people know what it is?

MCCAUGHEY: Some do and some don't. In some circles the museum has tremendous, tremendous fame. Yet you and I know that there are people who don't want to stop off and look at museums on their way. I wish more did.

Well, there's a fine small museum at Williams College in Williamstown, Massachusetts —the Clark Institute. And even though it's off the beaten track, people visiting the Berkshires will bike, hike, trek to get there. I'm bringing this up because some designers have found that museums can be very keen on things like the shopping bag—which people see after they're already there. But when it comes to actually bringing people in by putting up attention-getting billboards or bus posters or advertising in the newspaper weekend section, they're very hesitant to do that. They might see it as somehow inappropriate.

MCCAUGHEY: It's both an untruthful and irritating myth that museums think they're in some kind of ivory tower and the world will just flock in. No good museums think that any more, and we expend an enormous amount of energy turning the walls outward to get people to come in. It's just that one has to apply the resources of the museum to its priorities. It's difficult to get and hang onto those pockets of dollars. You know what the rates are like to advertise, and they're very, very heavy indeed. The problem is that Hartford isn't yet a tourist destination, but we're working on some ideas, like a nineteenth-century theme with our Hudson River School and the Mark Twain Museum and some of the other public buildings here.

What are your plans for the future in terms of graphics?

MCCAUGHEY: Our five buildings were sort of banged together over the last 125 years, and as you've seen, the museum is the most glorious maze that gives you long wonderful vistas and eternal multiple choice. But one doesn't know which way to go because there is so much to see and look at. Now, I love this idea of the maze, but we also do have to take pity on the visitor who needs a sense of how the place works. . . .

A signage program.

MCCAUGHEY: Exactly, and I still have a great undone bit of business to raise a lot of funds for it and get a really good graphics system running through the building, so, when people turn up at the front desk, they're able to find their way to the Barbizon School without having to search the whole museum to find it.

If you were addressing a gathering of other museum directors who were looking to improve their own institution's graphic identity and publications, what is the key thing you would say to them?

MCCAUGHEY: I'd say that you really have to find a designer who can embrace the artistic goals and ambitions of your museum, and the capacity to translate them without stereotyping and without making everything exactly uniform. Your graphic communications must reflect the genuinely diverse life of the museum. Obviously one doesn't want an invitation to a great important event like the opening of our Ralph Earl exhibition to look like something that promotes your summer children's program.

Now let's say you were addressing a group of graphic designers who were interested in working for museums. What would you say to them?

MCCAUGHEY: I'd say: the first job you have to do is to talk to people in the museum and become familiar with the style of the museum or the style it wishes to have. You have to think hard about what these people want to achieve, what this curator wants to do with this exhibition, and so forth, and then ask yourself, how can I make that idea really speak in a catalog, in a flyer, in a poster, and so on. Peter Good is an absolute object lesson to people in his field, to young graphic designers, and that's because of his tremendous ability to listen and to understand other people's ambitions.

LATER, I SPOKE WITH PETER GOOD.

Patrick McCaughey characterized the process that was used to select your firm as a "beauty contest." How do you feel about that? What was the selection process like for you?

GOOD: I'd rather that they'd used a term that was more professional than "beauty contest," but the selection process was handled very professionally. I made a presentation to a committee, expressed my philosophy of design, showed about ten projects, and spoke about what I thought was important to the museum. I emphasized that I had grown up in Hartford and had always loved the museum. My first experiences of the applied visual world were there; it was there that I saw my first Picasso, my first Caravaggio, my first Egyptian mummy. And I tried to make three specific points: One, the museum presents a unique identity problem because it doesn't have a singular specialty. It's like a mini-Metropolitan: there's a major twentieth-century collection with terrific experimental stuff, as well as Renaissance art and collections of almost every other period. The identity must express this wide breadth. Two, the identity should evolve over time from a lot of materials rather than be a rubber-stamp "logo." Three, the name Wadsworth Atheneum is distinctive and different and should be kept.

Did they ask if you thought the name should be changed?

GOOD: At several meetings people on the committee brought it up. Some people wanted to call it the Wadsworth. Some simply the Atheneum.

Tell me about the committee. Have you been required to satisfy a committee all along? That can be tough.

GOOD: The committee consisted of seven or eight people: Patrick and his assistant, two outside consultants, the president of the board of trustees, and several other people. Although the committee was very involved in selecting the designer, it hasn't gotten involved with approving designs. Patrick and a few others are the only people who do that, and since the beginning there's been very few changes to our work. In one instance Patrick requested an alternative for a cover design he felt did not accurately represent the exhibition. He was right. In terms of committees, the only people I have difficulty with are those who consider themselves "marketing experts." I usually find them too focus-group driven. Focus-group results should be one element a designer can consider, but not the driving force. In designing a T-shirt, for example, you can get caught up in issues like "which T-shirt will sell" rather than "which T-shirt will make a great image." Because of thinking like that, there are a lot of mediocre T-shirts around. I also have difficulties with those who ask for work on spec: "Just show us how you might approach this. . . ." I was worried that this might happen in this case.

Did it?

GOOD: Fortunately, no. Before my presentation I called Patrick to let him know that speculative work is against my policy, and he said that it wasn't necessary to prove or show them what I would do if I were hired. He said he just wanted to hear my general ideas. That made me want to work for him. But I did some sketches for my own benefit, to clarify my ideas before coming in to speak.

Did your presentation include examples of work for other museums?

GOOD: No.

You've got to give any prospective client credit for not insisting that they see something exactly like what they're looking for in a designer's portfolio.

GOOD: I've lost projects because of that kind of myopic thinking. A client should be able to have confidence in you as a generalist. My firm does a wide range of work; the only thing we don't do is retail advertising. Someone looking at our portfolio could say, "This is a well-rounded firm that could move over a wide range of design problems." We were able to demonstrate our history of work in the arts, though, such as corporate posters for exhibitions at the Atheneum sponsored by United Technologies. One project I was very proud of at the time—and still am—was "The American Experience," sponsored by Aetna. We do all the graphics, posters, mailers, and national ads, and this project demonstrates the application of a look or system to all kinds of visual materials. We were also able to show a range of pragmatic solutions, the organization of complex information.

Let's return for a moment to your second point, that you thought a logo would have been wrong for the Atheneum. Why?

GOOD: The two symmetrical letterforms WA offer infinite possibilities, and it would have been easy to come up with something that looked marvelous. But I think it would have been irresponsible. A symbol would sway the perception of the museum, which goes from Rubens to Rauschenberg. Should the logo look contemporary? Should it be Gothic or classical? At the meeting I expressed my feeling that the museum should have a more open approach to identity.

Did they make it clear to you at the outset that they weren't looking for a logo?

GOOD: No, but they stressed the importance of continuity of design. It's usually the opposite: people insist that they want a logo, something they think will make everything neat and simple.

You use a fairly wide range of typefaces.

GOOD: Yes, but I've established certain guidelines. The typography is Garamond, Sabon, and Bodoni. I like Bodoni because it reflects the fine balance between the classic and the modern. It has limitations, however, when used for large amounts of small text. While there is typographic consistency—sometimes it's hard to point to because I violate certain rules when appropriate.

How do you keep up the quality on a museum budget?

GOOD: We keep up the quality by hard work. We do things over and over. We're very, very fussy. Our office has that dedication, and once you establish a certain level you can't fall back. Doing it within the budget is a constant battle. Sometimes we don't even cover our expenses. We work all the time to get corporate sponsors, paper companies, and printers to donate services.

I'm impressed by the quality of the art and photography. Designers always cringe at getting that box of old photos when they begin a project for a nonprofit organization.

GOOD: We do all the illustrations here, and the photos are supplied by the client. The art is picked up from resource books, or we'll do line drawings, sketches, mezzotints, silhouettes, anything to save a photo. We work at finding the right balance between text and art. You'll notice that depending upon who donates it, the paper stock for the newsletter changes from issue to issue.

Yet it is a four-color newsletter.

GOOD: That is a luxury.

Paintings never look very good reproduced in black and white.

GOOD: No, and we might lose the budget for four-color. But Patrick always manages to find the funds somewhere. To keep costs down where we can, all the invitations are one or two colors. There are several reasons why all this effort is worthwhile. One is Patrick. He is brilliant. And he and I have a common goal: to make people in and outside Connecticut aware of this exceptional museum. There are still people in Connecticut who don't know about it. Yet it has an incredible legacy—look at the timeline in the case statement—the Atheneum was the first American museum to install a Picasso exhibition, the first to buy a Mondrian and a Dali.

Building public awareness is a slow process, isn't it?

GOOD: It is, especially when you're limited by funds. When it comes down to whether you'll run an ad or fix the leaking skylights, you fix the skylights.

Many designers say that they would rather do a great design for nothing than do a bad design for a lot of money.

GOOD: When someone trusts you and gives you that opportunity, you'll work harder. You accept the challenge to do the best possible work for them—and yourself. On the other hand, if your work is scrutinized by a board of trustees, if you feel there are multiple agendas to please, you lose interest, because that kind of critical overview inhibits intuitive solutions.

More and more designers are positioning themselves as marketing and communications consultants in addition to visual communicators. Patrick made it clear to me that he rejected designers who wanted to advise the museum about what it should be or how it should promote itself. How do you think he would react if you recommended an ad campaign or a way to get publicity in tourist guidebooks so that more people would know about the Atheneum?

GOOD: I think he would be open to it, but that would depend on how it were presented. If someone comes in and says to a scholar, which Patrick is, "This is the way you should do things," it might be viewed as insulting. Having that kind of attitude is a mistake a lot of designers make. You have to remember that trustees and curators know their subject matter a lot better than you do. But if someone comes in and says, "I have an idea I'd like to discuss with you, how do you feel about this?" it would probably be well received. For example, the commemorative poster I did for the 150th anniversary was entirely my concept, and it was accepted enthusiastically. I welcome collaboration.

Your work is elegant, clear, and classic; the type is usually printed in black ink on white paper, and it reads from left to right, top to bottom, all of which is somewhat unusual today. Tell me about your approach to style.

GOOD: I like to think I have no style. Style is created when a problem is solved. To me, there is enchantment in expressing ideas in a simple way. The art and the glory of the institution should be the stars, not my way of working with type and color. The Mapplethorpe invitation, for example, is simple elegance. If I did anything that said, "This was done by a trendy designer," it would be self-serving. I get my satisfaction from doing something that gets people to come to the museum, for example, a calendar that's clear and informational.

How is it running a design business in semi-rural Chester, Connecticut? Were you ever interested in coming to New York?

GOOD: I worked in New York at Chermayeff & Geismar for a while, and Applebaum & Curtis. I loved Manhattan but I didn't like living there. I wanted the convenience of small-town life. It wasn't easy starting a business in a place that no one knows. And it was in the pre-fax, even pre-FedEx days, so my client base was much more limited then.

And things have changed. How?

GOOD: Over the years we've branched out. Our work — particularly posters, which are a special love of mine — has been reproduced in periodicals, exhibited in international competitions and invitationals. We have worked for clients in France and Japan. The way communication is today, one can easily work for a company for years and never visit its offices. For us, it's opened a much larger world.

INDEX

BOOKS FROM ALLWORTH PRESS

Business and Legal Forms for Graphic Designers, Third Edition by Tad Crawford and Eva Doman Bruck (paperback, 8½ × 11, 208 pages, includes CD-ROM, $29.95)

The Education of a Design Entrepreneur edited by Steven Heller (paperback, 6¾ × 9⅞, 288 pages, $21.95)

Inside the Business of Graphic Design by Catharine Fishel (paperback, 6 × 9, 288 pages, $19.95)

AIGA Professional Business Practices in Graphic Design edited by Tad Crawford (paperback, 6¾ × 10, 320 pages, $24.95)

The Graphic Designer's Guide to Pricing, Estimating, and Budgeting, Revised Edition by Theo Stephan Williams (paperback, 6¾ × 9⅞, 208 pages, $19.95)

Careers By Design: A Business Guide for Graphic Designers, Third Edition by Roz Goldfarb (paperback, 6 × 9, 232 pages, $19.95)

Starting Your Career As a Freelance Illustrator or Graphic Designer, Revised Edition by Michael Fleishman (paperback, 6 × 9, 272 pages, $19.95)

Digital Design Business Practices by Liane Sebastian (paperback 6¾ × 10, 384 pages, $29.95)

Licensing Art and Design, Revised Edition by Caryn R. Leland (paperback, 6 × 9, 128 pages, $16.95)

Selling Graphic Design, Second Edition by Don Sparkman (paperback, 6 × 9, 256 pages, $19.95)

Emotional Branding: The New Paradigm for Connecting Brands to People by Marc Gobé (hardcover, 6¼ × 9¼, 352 pages, $24.95)

Citizen Brand: 10 Commandments for Transforming Brands in a Consumer Democracy by Marc Gobé (hardcover, 5¾ × 8¾, 288 pages, $24.95)